A New German Public Sector?
Reform, Adaptation and Stability

A New German Public Sector?
Reform, Adaptation and Stability

Edited by
ARTHUR BENZ
University of Halle-Wittenberg

and

KLAUS H. GOETZ
London School of Economics and Political Science

Dartmouth

Aldershot • Brookfield USA • Singapore • Sydney

Published by
Dartmouth Publishing Company Limited
Gower House
Croft Road
Aldershot
Hants GU11 3HR
England

Dartmouth Publishing Company
Old Post Road
Brookfield
Vermont 05036
USA

British Library Cataloguing in Publication Data
A new German public sector? : reform, adaptation and
   stability. – (Association for the Study of German Politics)
   1.Political planning – Germany   2.Germany – Politics and
   government – 1945–1990   3.Germany – Politics and government
   – 1990–
   I.Benz, Arthur   II.Goetz, Klaus H.   III.Association for the
   Study of German Politics
   350'.000943

Library of Congress Cataloging-in-Publication Data
A new German public sector? : reform, adaptation and stability /
   edited by Arthur Benz and Klaus H. Goetz.
        p.   cm. – (Association for the study of German politics)
     Revision of papers presented at a workshop held at the European
   Institute of the London School of Economics and Political Science.
     Includes bibliographical references and index.
     ISBN 1-85521-710-4
     1. Germany–Politics and government–1990- –Congresses.
   2. Privatization–Germany–Congresses.   I. Benz, Arthur.
   II. Goetz, Klaus H.   III. Series: Association for the study of
   German politics (Series)
   JN3971.A58N46   1996
   338.943–dc20   96-14976
                                                                       CIP

ISBN 1 85521 710 4

Typeset by Manton Typesetters, 5–7 Eastfield Road, Louth, Lincolnshire LN11 7AJ, UK.
Printed and bound in Great Britain by
Biddles Ltd, Guildford and King's Lynn

Contents

Series Foreword

The Association for the Study of German Politics (ASGP) was established to encourage teaching and research in the politics and society of the German-speaking countries. Since its formation in 1974, the ASGP has brought together academics from a variety of disciplines – politics, languages, history, economics and other social sciences – who, along with others with practical and personal interests, are concerned with contemporary developments in these countries. Through its conferences, research seminars, and its journal *German Politics*, the ASGP has proved itself to be an invaluable forum for discussion and research. This series represents a significant extension of ASGP activities. The Association believes that its wide range of expertise will ensure that the series will be of value to teachers, students, and those involved in policy and research, providing them with readily accessible material on current issues.

Preface

This book seeks to provide an assessment of major developments in the German public sector over the last decade. It examines the impact of international administrative trends – including privatization, the New Public Management, decentralization and Europeanization – and discusses the administrative consequences of unification.

With two exceptions, earlier versions of the papers collected in this volume were presented at a workshop on 'German Public Sector Reform in Light of the British Experience', held at the European Institute, London School of Economics and Political Science. All papers were subsequently extensively revised and updated for publication. The editors would like to thank the contributors for their willingness to try to meet our editorial demands and their patience in waiting for their work to appear in print.

The London meeting was made possible by a generous grant from the Anglo-German Foundation for the Study of Industrial Society, whose support we gratefully acknowledge. We would also like to thank the Association for the Study of German Politics for supporting the publication of this volume. Klaus H. Goetz wishes to express his gratitude to the Nuffield Foundation for a grant that enabled him to carry out research in Germany.

ARTHUR BENZ
KLAUS H. GOETZ

List of Contributors

Arthur Benz, Professor, Institute for Political Science, University of Halle-Wittenberg.

Roland Czada, Professor, Policy Analysis and Administrative Science, University of Hagen.

Hans-Ulrich Derlien, Professor, Chair for Administrative Science, University of Bamberg.

Dietrich Fürst, Professor, Institute for Territorial Planning, University of Hanover.

Klaus H. Goetz, Dr., Department of Government, London School of Economics and Political Science.

Dirk Lehmkuhl, Dr., European University Institute, Florence.

Susanne K. Schmidt, Dr., Max Planck Institute for Societal Research, Cologne.

Hellmut Wollmann, Professor, Institute for Political Science, Humboldt University, Berlin.

1   The German Public Sector: National Priorities and the International Reform Agenda

Arthur Benz and Klaus H. Goetz

Public-sector traditions under Attack: Germany and the International Reform Agenda

The academic literature on public-sector development in Western Europe is dominated by the idiom of fundamental challenges, profound change, large-scale reform and even 'administrative revolutions'. As a recent comparative survey remarked, it 'would appear (...) that Western Europe has truly entered "the age of administrative reform" after years of sporadic, pragmatic and limited change' (Wright, 1994b: 104). This reshaping of the public sector seems to extend to all its defining features, including its legal bases, organizational structures, processes, instruments, personnel, tasks and, perhaps most decisively, the nature of the relations between the public and the private sectors.

Amongst the forces driving the transformation of the public sector, four in particular have attracted wide interest.

1   *Privatization*   Understood here as the transfer of public assets, in particular public enterprises, into private ownership, privatization has become an increasingly central part of attempts at 'rolling back the frontiers of the state' in a growing number of West European countries (see, for example, Vickers and Wright, 1989; Wright, 1994a). Whilst in the UK, which was the European trendsetter in privatization, the potential for the denationalization of state-owned enterprises appears to have been largely exhausted, large-scale privatization programmes are being pur-

sued in other European countries, such as France and Italy, with traditionally extensive public industrial ownership.

2 *New Public Management* Change around the New Public Management
(NPM) agenda has been a major feature of public-sector development in
a number of West European countries. According to Hood, the core
components of NPM include 'hands on professional management' in the
public sector; explicit standards and measures of performance; a greater
emphasis on output controls; a shift to disaggregation of units and greater
competition in the public sector; a stress on private-sector styles of
management; and an emphasis on greater discipline and parsimony in
resource use (Hood, 1991: 4–5). Although there remain 'sharply varying
levels of implementation across countries' (Dunleavy, 1994: 43), the
transformative effects of NPM-related change are often said to constitute one of the most powerful forces of public-sector reorganization.

3 *Decentralization* The strengthening of subcentral governments through
decentralization, regionalization and federalization was one of the key
themes in the analysis of West European politics and government during
the 1980s, with most accounts stressing the growing strength of local,
regional and 'meso-level' governments (see, for example, Rhodes and
Wright, 1987). Viewed from the perspective of the mid-1990s, some of
the more ambitious claims for the problem-solving potential of decentralization policies put forward during the 1980s appear discredited; but
their transformative impact on public-sector organization and the continued attraction of decentralization initiatives are clearly evident (Hesse,
1991; Sharpe, 1993).

4 *Europeanization* Europeanization is increasingly considered to be one
of the principal features of change in European public administrations
(Jones, 1993). For the most part, Europeanization is synonymous with
'Communitarization' and as such refers to the impact of the economic
and political imperatives arising out of EU membership on national
governmental–administrative structures, policy-making procedures and
instruments, public personnel and the substance of public policies. The
discussion of public-sector Europeanization is still largely reliant on
unsystematic and non-comparative evidence; but there seems to emerge
a growing consensus that 'To an extent which is not fully appreciated,
the EU is slowly redefining existing political arrangements, altering
traditional policy networks, triggering institutional change, reshaping
the opportunity structures of member states and their major interests'
(Müller and Wright, 1994: 6).

Taking these international trends as a point of departure for the analysis of
German public-sector development, several questions arise:

- To what extent and in what form has Germany shared in the agenda of administrative development focused on privatization, NPM precepts, strengthened subcentral government and Europeanization?
- Have there been other trends that have rivalled their importance? In other words, has there been an alternative agenda which, while perhaps more diffuse, might nevertheless have had a major transformative effect?
- What are the key parameters which help explain the specific course of public-sector development in Germany? In this connection, particular attention needs to be paid to Germany's state tradition, the doctrine of the rule of law, the welfare state orientation and the federal system.
- Has the combined impact of international trends and national preoccupations led to a reshaping of the public sector and, if so, how can this change best be described in substantive terms?

These issues have to be considered in the context of the momentous change in the history of the German state marked by unification. Unification and its political, economic and social consequences partly alter the parameters which shape public-sector development. Perhaps more importantly, however, unification may in itself be a major driving force of administrative transformation that is associated with quantitative and qualitative changes whose overall importance may surpass the implications of the international reform agenda. What is of interest here is not just the relative significance of international concerns, on the one hand, and specifically German challenges, on the other, but also the manner in which they have interacted. In particular, it is important to examine whether unification has tended to lessen or reinforce the impact of the international reform trends on the German public sector.

The following seeks to address some of these questions. It starts by reviewing German public-sector development during the 1980s and up to unification. The aim here is to assess, first, the extent to which Germany was affected by international administrative trends and, second, the importance of more specifically German concerns. The chapter then discusses the administrative implications of unification. The demise of the German Democratic Republic and the integration of five new Länder and East Berlin into the West German political–institutional order have not only created a whole host of new problems, but have also been followed by some new departures in public-sector development. To a certain extent, this could be described as a process of 'catching up' with international trends, and it might seem that in the aftermath of unification some of the 'reform blockages' so often alluded to during the 1980s have been removed. This leads to the question of whether future large-scale change is indeed likely. In addressing this question, it is useful to recall, first, key institutional and political parameters of administrative development in Germany that help to explain the course and outcome of past reform and modernization initiatives. Second, one needs to ask whether these parameters have themselves been subject to major change in recent years. The overall direction of change that we observe can, in substantive terms, be described as a gradual move away from the 'public bureaucracy state'.

The German Public Sector during the 1980s: Stagnation or Modernization?

To many observers, public-sector development in Germany during the 1980s was characterized by a large, unbridgeable gap between the need for fundamental change, on the one hand, and very limited reform capacities, on the other. Fritz W. Scharpf, for example, strongly argued in favour of institutional reforms that would go beyond limited adjustments, stressing the need for 'explicit political decisions that will abolish, reorganize, or re-establish public institutions' (Scharpf, 1987/88: 106). Carl Böhret pointed out that flexible adaptation alone was inadequate for dealing with the challenges faced by public administration and underlined the need for reforms aimed at 'fundamental, relatively permanent improvements in structures and processes [which] are guided by political decisions and have a broad impact' (Böhret, 1982: 134; our translation). In a similar vein, Thomas Ellwein, discussing organizational problems in ministerial departments, called for urgent comprehensive reforms, of which, however, he saw very little prospect (Ellwein, 1979). In this respect, all three authors, together with most other writers on the subject, were in agreement: large-scale reforms were necessary, but limited innovation capacities made it unlikely that they would be attempted and even more improbable that they could be successful. The main impeding factors cited included the interdepartmental and intergovernmental dispersion of relevant political, legal and financial powers, responsibilities and resources; the difficulties of achieving cross-party consensus in a governmental system where coalition government and a strong representation of the national opposition parties in Länder governments are the norm; and the pervasive institutionalized influence of affected interests and reform addressees in the decision-making process.

It was against the background of such gloomy assessments of the likelihood of comprehensive reform that some academic analysts began to stress the virtues of permanent administrative 'modernization' which would be at the core of a continuous institutional (or administrative) policy (Hesse and Benz, 1987/88). Such a policy, it was argued, would recognize that the complexity of societal conditions and the corresponding complexity of the administrative system have further increased the manifold practical and legal difficulties which have always existed in the case of reforms. As a result, the chances of success for large-scale, complex reforms are today considerably reduced. In the future, it will, therefore, be more important than ever to make sure – by means of continuous small-scale improvements, i.e. continuous 'organizational development', or 'permanent reform' – that large-scale reforms remain as far as possible unnecessary. (Brohm, 1988: 22; our translation)

From this perspective, the real challenge of administrative development was to ensure 'the permanent flexibility of institutional frameworks' (Hesse and Benz, 1987/88: 399):

a realistic institutional policy endeavours to create the conditions for the continuous 'procedural' adaptation and transformation of governmental organization (…) Procedural adaptation does not primarily refer to the reform of organizational structures but points to changed manners of action and behaviour, which have a particular influence on the actual degree of flexibility. (Ibid.: 400)

Thus German public-sector organization appeared more susceptible to change than an emphasis on reform would have suggested. The reformability of public institutions might be questionable, but, it was argued, there was clear evidence of gradual adaptation or modernization, notably in procedural organization and in the capacity of public-sector institutions to absorb new tasks successfully.

Focusing on the international mega-trends of privatization, NPM-related change, decentralization and Europeanization, there is certainly little indication of large-scale change through concerted reform initiatives. Efforts to 'roll back the state' through privatization remained on a relatively modest scale. The boldest steps were taken at the Federal level, where, between 1980 and 1990, the number of industrial assets in which the Federation held a stake fell from 899 to 411. The main enterprises from which the Federation withdrew included VEBA, VIAG, Volkswagen and Salzgitter. As a result, the total personnel employed by commercial enterprises in which the Federation or one of its 'special funds' held a majority stake fell from 270 000 in 1982 to 153 000 in 1991 (note that this figure excludes the staff employed directly by the post, telecommunications and postbank services and the public railways). By contrast, at the Länder and local levels, the wholesale or partial disposal of publicly owned enterprises hardly progressed at all, although some states, such as Lower Saxony, gave it somewhat higher priority (König, 1988). The fact that German policy makers did not push ahead with privatization can partly be explained by the lack of a strong anti-etatist ideology amongst the major political parties; but it should also be remembered that the public enterprise sector in Germany in the early 1980s was considerably smaller and less costly than in the UK, France or Italy. For this reason alone, denationalization was less likely to form a core element of public-sector change.

Turning to NPM, Germany appeared even more immune to international administrative trends. At no time during the 1980s was the public administration paradigm seriously called into question by the doctrines of public management; in fact, NPM did not even feature in academic discussions. Accordingly, there were no determined moves towards central tenets of NPM, such as managerialism, the definition of performance indicators and monitoring, service quality initiatives, more decentralized personnel management operating with selective incentives, the creation of internal markets characterized by purchaser–provider splits, or contractorization and public tendering. The absence of change was perhaps most notable in the civil service, which continued to be governed by a highly complex legal framework affording minimal scope for flexible personnel policy. Accordingly, even very modest proposals, such as the introduction of some elements of performance-related pay for civil servants, met with strong and successful opposition.

Against this background, it is not surprising that some analysts now call the 1980s the 'lost decade' of administrative development. However, whilst there was evidently no profound reorganization of the public sector along NPM lines, it may be argued that the German public sector already displayed certain NPM characteristics. Institutional disaggregation, for example, which in the UK is most commonly associated with the creation of Next Steps agencies, was unlikely to be a central concern of policy makers in Federal and Länder governments, since German public administration has traditionally known a large number of non-ministerial Federal and state offices which operate at some distance from the comparatively small ministerial departments (Becker, 1978). In the late 1980s, their total number at the Federal level reached almost 100. In addition, there were more than 20 institutions of indirect Federal administration (such as the Federal Labour Office) and a significant number of private law institutions which fulfilled important administrative tasks for the Federation.

If Germany could be characterized as a laggard in privatization and public management, its decentralization record is rather more ambiguous. In view of Germany's federal constitutional arrangements and the strong legal protection afforded to local self-government, it is not surprising that intergovernmental relations have traditionally attracted a great deal of attention amongst public-sector analysts. In fact, much of the most influential conceptual and theoretical writing on the German public sector during the last two decades has relied heavily on empirical examples drawn from the field of intergovernmental relations, with sometimes problematic consequences. This applies, in particular, to Fritz W. Scharpf's analysis of policy-interlocking (*Politikverflechtung*) from the 1970s (Scharpf *et al.*, 1976) and the more recent writings of Hesse and Benz on institutional policy and public-sector modernization (Hesse and Benz, 1987/88; 1990). As a result, there has been a tendency to treat what are specific features of public policy making in the intergovernmental system as characteristic properties of the public sector generally.

As regards the development of intergovernmental relations during the 1980s, it is possible to identify at least three distinct points of view (see Goetz, 1992: 54–70): the policy-interlocking perspective, which stressed the growing importance of joint Federal–Länder policy making, giving rise to 'the pathologies of public policy associated with joint decisions' (Scharpf, 1988: 265); a centralization argument, according to which the German federal system was characterized by the steady accretion of policy making powers at the Federal level, notably the power to legislate, and the concomitant erosion of state government discretion (see, for example, Ossenbühl, 1989); and what might be called a 'regional resilience' perspective, which underlined not only the considerable, and growing, policy making resources at the disposal of subcentral governments, but also the scope for the independent formulation and implementation of subcentral public policies. Thus it was argued that Länder-level activities had become more important, in particular in the area of industrial policy and economic promotion:

> In the context of policies coping with changes in industrial structures, regionalized strategies have gained in importance. They allow for flexible and differentiated solutions to problems, which are adjusted to the genuine situations and demands of the local industry and require close cooperation among public and private institutions. With such de facto decentralization, industrial policy is made more innovative and more precisely tailored to specific problems. (Benz, 1989: 212)

In retrospect, this assessment still holds true, though some observers rather overestimated the potential of subcentral policy making. What increased during the 1980s was, perhaps, less the scope for regional policy makers to develop and implement independent initiatives than their determination to make use of the hitherto neglected potential for subcentral policy making. Certainly change in the intergovernmental system was piecemeal rather than comprehensive and centred on procedural and policy adaptations rather than major structural innovations.

As regards, finally, the Europeanization of the German public sector, both the ambiguity of the concept and a lack of systematic inquiry into its practical implications make an assessment difficult. Europeanization is often invoked as a major driving force behind the changes in politics, government and policy which the (West) European countries are undergoing; at the same time, the concept is frequently used to characterize the substance of these changes. In current usage, Europeanization as a cause of change in national governance refers principally to the process of European integration in the framework of the European Union; but the opening of Central and Eastern Europe has widened this agenda. Concerning Europeanization as an effect, it can be understood in different ways: sometimes Europeanization merely stands for the adaptive reactions in the European states to political and economic integration; sometimes it implies convergence, a process which progressively reduces the differences between the political–institutional systems of European countries; and sometimes it suggests a decline in the importance of national arrangements as powers are moving 'upwards' to the European Union.

So far, however, there have been few systematic attempts at studying the empirical reality of Europeanization of German institutional arrangements (Bulmer, 1986; Bulmer and Paterson, 1987; Héritier *et al.*, 1994: Hesse and Goetz, 1992). The most manifest examples of structural, procedural and policy adaptations during the 1980s and early 1990s were found in the federal order and intergovernmental relations (Goetz, 1995b). Here the Länder have sought to strengthen their direct access to decision making in Brussels and, in particular, their influence on the Federation's EU-related policy making. To this end, the Länder have, *inter alia*,

- opened their own liaison offices in Brussels;
- urged the Federation to advocate the creation of the Committee of the Regions at the EU level;
- built up EU policy making capacities in the offices of the Länder Minister–Presidents to enable them to play a proactive role in EU affairs;
- set up a 'European Chamber' in the Bundesrat designed to facilitate the effective use of their participatory rights in EU-related policy making. These rights were considerably strengthened through the new Article 23 of the Basic Law ('Article on European Union') and the 'Law on the co-operation between the Federation and the Länder relating to matters of the European Union' of March 1993; and
- established a conference of the Länder Ministers of European Affairs to improve inter-Länder coordination.

Adaptations such as these represent very visible signs of Europeanization, but they have largely followed existing patterns of public-sector organization. They have reaffirmed, and perhaps even reinforced, pre-existing features of the federal system and, in fact, the German governmental–administrative system more generally. Europeanization has not, therefore, been equivalent to the systemic transformation of German public administration.

To a large extent, this also holds true for the impact of European administrative law on German administrative law, which has received growing attention in recent years (Rengeling, 1994; Zuleeg, 1994). Thus it would appear that, although Community law is reshaping the legal bases of German public administration, the changes provoked by integration can largely be accommodated without challenging the 'deep structure' of national administrative law. Some authors, however, also identify instances where Community law leads to 'fundamental structural change in the administrative law orders of the member states' (Schmidt-Aßmann, 1993: 932; our translation), including, for example, the principle that administrative action is to be founded on clearly identifiable legal bases or the functions of judicial review of administrative actions. However, the actual implications of this finding for the operation of administrative institutions have so far scarcely been explored.

To summarize, the 1980s were not a decade of far-reaching public-sector change in Germany in terms of the international reform agenda of privatization, NPM-induced reorganization, decentralization and Europeanization. Certainly the language of 'administrative revolutions' would have been inappropriate in the German context. Instead continuity and stability were the hallmarks of public-sector development. This said, it scarcely needs stressing that to view German administrative development solely through the lens of international trends is to gain only a partial picture, and other potential forces of administrative transformation should not be ignored. Those which were most widely discussed during the 1980s included informatization and its impact on the organization of public administration (Reinermann *et al.*, 1988) and 'ecological modernization', that is, the growing recognition of the need to integrate environmental concerns into mainstream policy making (Henke and Fürst, 1987/88). Again, however, there is no strong evidence to suggest that they resulted in systemic changes in administrative practice.

Overall, then, it is difficult to avoid the impression that, compared to the radical transformation in the administrative systems in some other Western industrialized countries (see, for example, OECD, 1990), Germany was a backwater of administrative development. The traditional defining features of German public bureaucracy survived very much intact, at a time when other countries embarked on large-scale reform experiments. The question is now whether unification and its aftermath have significantly altered this picture.

Unification as a Sea Change?

The demise of the Communist regime in the GDR in 1989 created a host of new and unexpected challenges for West German government and public administration. As a result of unification, the effects of political, economic and institutional transformation in the East spilled over to the Federal Republic, and many observers anticipated profound changes in the Western political and governmental system (Lehmbruch, 1990). There were certainly good reasons to expect such a development. On the one hand, the need for a hugely costly restructuring of the East German economy, the social dislocation caused by economic and political transformation and the challenge of a complete reconstruction of the institutional framework of government and administration confronted the Western institutions with new tasks for which they had not been designed. On the other, the shock of unification was regarded by many as a unique window of opportunity for a comprehensive reform of the Western public sector that should finally address long-standing performance deficits and, at the same time, take account of the new requirements of the unified country.

In the mid-1990s, the debate on the transformative effects of unification is, not surprisingly, still not settled. Some observers talk of the emergence of a 'Third Republic' (Czada, 1994) whose institutional arrangements differ decisively from the old Federal Republic, a perspective which is well captured in the title of an edited collection on post-unification German politics, *From Bundesrepublik to Deutschland* (Huelshoff *et al.*, 1993). Others argue that the central features of the West German political process, such as cooperative federalism, cooperative opposition and neo-corporatism have survived intact. In fact, 'Far from the political system of the old Federal Republic having been transformed by unification, its principal distinguishing traits appear rather to have been reinforced' (Sally and Webber, 1994: 39). Unification has thus resulted in 'the second coming of the Bonn republic' (Webber, 1995).

As far as the public sector is concerned, stability and continuity seem indeed to have prevailed. The uncertainty created by the rapidly unfolding events of 1989 at first resulted in political muddling through with a heavy reliance on informal institutional arrangements that, at times, went beyond legal limits; this was followed by a limited reorganization of existing institutions in the West where the case for change was unanswerable (Czada, 1994: 259–161). As a consequence, the German public sector seems to have been stabilized by minor adjustments rather than far-reaching reforms. And, similar to developments before 1989, the federalized nature of the institutional system again plays a decisive role in explaining this outcome. A look at some of the central components of Germany's political–governmental system may help to substantiate this point. As regards the constitutional order of the political system, relatively little change has taken place. The revision of the Basic Law, which was initiated in 1991 by the establishment of the Joint Bundesrat–Bundestag Commission on the Constitution, ended in October 1994, when a package of constitutional reform legislation came into force (Goetz and Cullen, 1995). Although the detailed amendments were numerous, their overall significance was limited, with the exception of the amendments adopted in connection with the ratification of the Maastricht Treaty in December 1992 (Ress, 1995). In particular, the Federal and Länder governments could not agree on decisive changes in intergovernmental relations or an extensive overhaul of the intergovernmental fiscal system, despite widespread calls for radical change with a view to strengthening the financial autonomy of the Länder (Benz, 1995).

Turning to the Federal administration, basic ministerial structures have largely been maintained, and proposals for the creation of a Ministry for 'Aufbau Ost' (Reconstruction East), which would have coordinated Federal policy for the new Länder, were quickly brushed aside. Inevitably, the planned move of the Federal government to Berlin will be accompanied by some reorganization, especially where the political and administrative sections of ministerial departments are to be separated between Berlin and Bonn. The solution envisaged at present, which means that some ministries are fully transferred to Berlin, while others will lead a permanently split existence, is in large part the result of a political compromise between the Federal government and the government of North Rhine–Westphalia, in which the desire to lessen the impact of the move to Berlin on the Bonn economy played a much greater role than principles of effective administrative organization.

At the Länder level, too, established administrative arrangements and routines seem to have been largely preserved. At least during the first five years of unification, the rising problems generated by East–West migration and, more critically, the fiscal stress following massive public resource transfers to the new Länder did not trigger major reform projects. The Western Länder governments at first tried to avoid the financial burdens of unification by making financial assistance to the East the exclusive responsibility of the Federal government. At the same time, they played a major role in the process of transferring Western institutional arrangements to the Eastern Länder (Goetz, 1993; 1996a), notably through the formation of West–East 'partnership agreements' and the secondment of Länder public servants who were charged with establishing a functioning public administration in the East along traditional West German lines (Derlien, 1993; König, 1993). It was this inter-Länder cooperation which proved decisive in establishing Western models of administrative organization in the East, thus restricting the scope for institutional innovation in the new Länder.

At the local level, a similar picture of continuity in the West and institutional reconstruction on the basis of Western blueprints in the East would seem to emerge. In response to East–West migration within Germany and growing numbers of *Aussiedler* (immigrants of German extraction) from Eastern Europe, Western local governments found themselves under intense pressure to provide housing and a sufficient infrastructure for a rising population. Faced with often severe financial problems and the need to act swiftly and decisively, innovative institutional experiments initially tended to be eschewed in favour of crisis management, although in some Länder efforts to improve local government organization, notably by bolstering the executive powers of the popularly elected mayor, gathered strength. In the new Länder, Western blueprints for local government organization have, in some cases, been adapted to specific circumstances (Naßmacher *et al.*, 1994; Wollmann in the present volume), something which can also be observed in relation to territorial reorganization and the organization of the regional (or intermediate) level (Fürst in the present volume). Moreover, there is evidence that policy making in the newly established institutions is to some extent shaped by an administrative culture which differs from that in the West (Seibel, 1993). None of this, however, amounts to a major new departure in local government organization.

At the same time, the degree of institutional continuity with the 'old' Federal Republic can be overstressed, and there are growing signs that Germany is beginning to share much more vigorously in the international reform agenda, notably as regards NPM-related innovations, than was the case during the 1980s. Unquestionably, during the past few years, the climate of the political and academic discussion on the public sector has changed decisively and, for the first time in the history of the Federal Republic, the public bureaucracy paradigm has come under sustained intellectual attack, with key arguments borrowed from the Anglo-Saxon experience. Dissenting voices appear, for the moment at least, somewhat marginalized (Heuer, 1995; König, 1995). More importantly, a growing number of local governments have begun to embark on reform projects which might, in the longer term, lead to substantial changes in Germany's public sector. The new trend is marked by a growing interest in privatization and NPM, leading to experiments with functional decentralization, budgetary reform and new controlling concepts that constitute the main elements of a 'quality and success-oriented public management' which is now widely advocated (Banner, 1994; Budäus, 1994; Naschold, 1993; Reichard, 1994). Amongst the trendsetters in this respect have been the cities of Duisburg, Cologne, Offenbach, Hanover and Nuremberg, and more than 100 local authorities have since followed suit. Länder governments are increasingly fostering such 'modernization' policies at the local level by providing financial incentives and by adapting the legal framework in which local government operates.

At the levels of the Federation and the Länder, core administrations have so far been largely unaffected by NPM. There is, however, no lack of NPM-inspired comprehensive reform proposals for the Federal administration (for example, Jann, 1994; Clasen *et al*., 1995) and there is also growing willingness amongst political decision makers to examine such recommendations. At the Länder level, the relatively narrow emphasis on debureaucratization which characterized most political initiatives during the 1980s (Wilkes, 1989) is progressively broadened. This reveals an important shift in the established consensus of what the public sector should do and how it should be organized and may, eventually, give rise to the emergence of a new 'design archetype' (Miller and Friesen, 1984) replacing the public bureaucracy paradigm.

While these modernization efforts aim primarily at reorganizing the internal structures of government and administration, territorial decentralization, in particular in the form of regionalization, continues to gain in importance. It is promoted, on the one hand, by a movement from below, as local governments realize the need for cooperation amongst subcentral actors if urgent tasks of economic development, planning and infrastructural provision are to be effectively fulfilled. On the other hand, decentralization is supported by efforts to increase the efficiency and effectiveness of large public institutions. A notable example of this trend is the transfer of the responsibility for local public transport from the Federal railways to the Länder and local governments as part of the transformation of the public railways into a listed company under private law (see Lehmkuhl in the present volume).

Another, perhaps even more significant initiative was the liquidation of the Treuhandanstalt and the creation of a number of deconcentrated successor institutions at the end of 1994. The Treuhand, a huge bureaucracy responsible for the transformation of the socialist economy into a market economy, stood for a centralist legacy (Seibel, 1994; Czada in the present volume). Even before its dissolution, the governments of the new Länder sought to gain influence on its policy making to protect their regional economic interests, and some formal agreements were concluded between Länder governments and the Treuhand. Now the role of the Länder in regional economic policy is strengthened, whereas the power of the Treuhand successor institutions is reduced. In sum, in contrast to what many feared at the beginning of the 1990s, unification and the accession of the new Länder do not seem to have strengthened the position of the Federation in the long term (Goetz, 1995a; 1996a).

The impact of unification on the German public sector is in part reinforced, but also in part restricted, by the simultaneous process of European integration. The overall consequences of the Europeanization of national public administration require much further investigation, but the process of functional and territorial differentiation of administrative structures can be analyzed as a reaction to the evolution of the Single Market and the European Union and a consequence of unification. This holds true, in particular, for deregulation and privatization in transport and communication services. Moreover, European regional policy supports cooperative forms of policy making at the regional level and thus challenges the existing joint regional policy of the Federal and Länder governments.

In sum, current political and academic debate on the public sector and important new departures may turn out to mark the beginning of a process of profound redirection, although it is too early to talk of a reorientation in which 'Prevailing ideas and values have lost their legitimacy and become discredited. In their place, an alternative interpretative scheme emerges carrying with it a different pattern of structural arrangements' (Hinings and Greenwood, 1988: 21–32). Certainly functional and territorial decentralization, privatization of public services, efficiency and public management, and Europeanization have become popular slogans and 'public management' has begun to challenge the ascendency of the idiom of *öffentliche Verwaltung* (public administration) in political and academic discourse. However, it is not yet clear how much of these new ideas will, in the end, be translated into concrete action and what their long-term effects will be. In fact, given Germany's record of administrative reform discussions that fail to be followed by decisive reform action, it is not unlikely that they will end in an 'aborted or unresolved excursion' of institutional development (Hinings and Greenwood, 1988: 35). What will be of critical importance in this respect are the state and political traditions which act as parameters within which public-sector development takes place. We can only expect major new departures in the way in which the German public sector develops if it can be shown that these parameters are themselves subject to redefinition.

State and Political Traditions as Parameters of Public-sector Development

State and political traditions establish the key parameters for public-sector development. Although they do not necessarily determine the outcome of reform and modernization initiatives, they constitute the framework in which these emerge and are carried through and, thus, strongly affect the direction of developments. At the same time, state and political traditions influence the evaluation of institutions and their performance; in other words, they represent important normative points of reference in political and academic discourse on the public sector and they demarcate the space within which politically acceptable ideas about the form and substance of administrative policy are likely to develop.

From a comparative point of view, Germany represents the continental tradition of a state-centred society (Dyson, 1980). With a focus on the structures and functions of the state, four basic defining elements can be distinguished: statism combined with the principle of the rule of law (the idea of the *Rechtsstaat*), federalism, a welfare state orientation, and, closely linked to the latter, a particular organizational pattern of linking state, society and market. Statism stands as a convenient shorthand for the traditional predominance of the state in the process of economic and societal development, with the state acting as the central agent in political modernization. This does not imply that reform policies necessarily emerge 'from above'. Whilst an enlightened Prussian state bureaucracy introduced the first steps in the development of the modern state in Germany (Kosellek, 1976), the practice of institutional policy in the Federal Republic is far removed from an authoritative model. But it is undoubtedly public administration itself which has been the decisive driving force behind institutional reforms, and it also serves as a key transmitter of societal demands into politics. However, although the state remains a crucial actor, its power and potential to implement policy have, since the Second World War, been fundamentally altered by at least two institutional factors – the *Rechtsstaat* principle and the federal principle – both of which contributed to the emergence of the 'semi-sovereign state' (Katzenstein, 1987). Both principles have, of course, played a central role in the historical development of German statehood, but their postwar impact has been markedly different from that in previous periods.

The first institutional factor modifying statism has been the strong legalistic orientation of politics and administration in the Federal Republic. The concept of the *Rechtsstaat* was central to German political thinking even before the achievement of German unity in the 1870s (Böckenförde, 1991), but its chief tenets – the supremacy of law, full state liability for illegal public actions, comprehensive rights of appeal against administrative acts (see Johnson, 1981: 15) – were only fully and effectively realized in the Federal Republic. More importantly, it was only in postwar Germany that the *Rechtsstaat* idea became infused with a natural rights content. Accordingly, 'we find that the Basic Law of the Federal Republic opens with a long catalogue of human rights, setting out what might be described as the ethical content of the Rechtsstaat' (Johnson, 1981: 16). It is consistent with this orientation that formal rules and regulations governing public action and their stability and predictability are highly valued. It also implies an inherent conservatism in institutional matters, since institutional change tends to require the need to go through formal procedures, a process which encourages participation and open confrontation of conflicting interests and thus works against swift, single-handed institutional reorganization. Moreover, the highly developed public law system associated with the *Rechtsstaat* means a reduced scope for public-sector reforms which aim at deregulation or output-oriented guidance and control mechanisms. In practice, this structural conservatism is, however, moderated by a good deal of pragmatism and informal flexibility, which exists alongside the legalistic tradition. The rule of law has to be reconciled with the conditions of an efficient administration, and the potential tension between the two is usually resolved through informal routines (Ellwein, 1990; Ellwein and Hesse, 1994: 17–18), which can be found in political institutions (Schulze-Fielitz, 1984) and in public administration (Bohne, 1981; Dreier, 1994).

The second structural feature of the German state which reduces its internal sovereignty is its federal organization and the fragmented nature of the state apparatus. Again the consequences for public-sector change are ambivalent. In an organizationally differentiated structure, it is difficult to implement 'reforms from above', and this is even more the case where, as in the German federal system, there exist strong interlinkages of policy making between the central (Federal) and subcentral (Länder) levels (Scharpf *et al.*, 1976). As Fritz W. Scharpf has demonstrated, such a structurally and procedurally interlocked system is not favourable to institutional reforms, and this is one of the key factors which helps to explain why the Federal and Länder governments followed an incrementalist institutional policy during the 1970s and 1980s, while other Western governments reacted to new challenges with ambitious reform projects (Hesse and Benz, 1990; Lehmbruch *et al.*, 1988). Such incremental institutional adaptation was made possible by shifting the focus of policy making between levels of government, by using redundancies of the federal structure and by altering policy networks. To provide an example for the first mode of adaptation, we can refer to social policy. Here problem solving by regulation draws the Federal government in, while a service-oriented approach leads to decentralization. The second mode can be illustrated by pointing out that Federal responsibility for labour market policy does not prevent the Länder and local governments from carrying out their own measures to deal with specific regional and local situations. The third mode can be studied in regional policy, where the bureaucratic network of Federal and Länder administrations is confronted by the emergence of regional networks of public and private actors.

Beyond such inherent flexibility, the decentralized structure of the federal system has also provided opportunities for partial reorganizations at the lower levels of government. Accordingly, many impulses for innovation in the public sector have come from the regional and local administrations responsible for implementing the law and for providing public services to citizens. Horizontal and vertical intergovernmental linkages impede comprehensive reforms, but, at the same time, they facilitate the diffusion of ideas about, and experiences with, organizational innovations that emerge from regional or local policy making. However, at the subcentral level, too, large-scale change typically requires a lead from above and is, in fact, often closely restrained by the centrally set legal framework. Civil service legislation, which is, in effect, almost completely controlled by the Federation, provides a good example of this.

While the *Rechtsstaat* and federal principles constitute the essential formal parameters for policy making and public-sector change, the market economy and the welfare state establish substantial norms which delineate functions and responsibilities of the state. At first sight, the two principles are, of course, in conflict. The acceptance of a market economy limits state intervention, whereas a welfare state requires very broadly defined interventionary powers on the part of the state to cope with the deficiencies of the market. It is because of these extensive state powers associated with the welfare state paradigm that it tends to lead to the expansion of the public sector which, in turn, threatens to drive out the market-based private sector. In the case of Germany, this seeming contradiction is to some extent resolved by the pattern of interaction between the public and the private sectors. The two are very closely linked in cooperative structures which encompass all levels of government and extend to most sectors of the economy. These patterns of a 'negotiated order' manifest themselves in a wide range of intermediary organizations that partly assume public functions and partly represent private economic interests. They include paragovernmental organizations such as chambers of commerce and industry; public and private banks which play an important role in industrial policy; employers' associations; trade unions; and non-profit organizations active in social service provision (*Wohlfahrtsverbände*). As a consequence, the assumption of welfare state functions, rather than resulting in an ever-growing state bureaucracy, has led to an increasing differentiation in organizational arrangements and a blurring of state–society boundaries. Moreover, problems created by the market have not necessarily been addressed through hierarchical state regulation, but are often dealt with through public–private cooperation or by non-governmental organizations.

These complex arrangements between state and market economy, based on neo-corporatist linkages and intermediary organizations, allow the co-existence of market ideals such as free enterprise, individualism and subsidiarity, with a positive evaluation of the welfare state. Both constitute stable normative bases of state activity and, thus, make any reduction of state responsibilities difficult. There are two main factors underpinning this stability. First, an alternative normative framework to the welfare state would require the consent of a multitude of public, semi-public and private institutions, something which is – at least in the short term – impossible to achieve. Second, any major change in the institutional setting of the German welfare system or far-reaching shifts in the interplay and division of functions between state and market would jeopardize the very existence of powerful organizations that are able to mobilize resistance in the political process. As a consequence, the pattern of state–society relations is fairly resistant to a major reorientation guided by market ideologies. But this does not mean that the German public sector is ossified and inflexible. On the contrary, the differentiated structures and linkages provide for ample opportunities to adjust interorganizational strategies if necessary. Moreover, the intermediary sector works as a buffer against immediate problem pressure on the state and serves as a receptive warning system for crisis tendencies both in the economy and in society.

It is, then, this combination of structural inertia and procedural flexibility which explains why the German public sector develops through incremental change rather than radical reforms. The roots of this type of development can be traced back to a specific idea of the state, political traditions and basic institutional parameters, most of which precede the Federal Republic. What remains to be answered, however, is whether these parameters might not themselves be subject to fundamental challenges that could open new options for administrative development. In this connection, the impact of German unification and European integration deserves particular attention.

If we turn, first, to the implications of unification, its effect on the normative and structural parameters of public policy making and institutional change has been limited. In fact, the argument could be made that it has tended to strengthen state and political traditions – notably statism, the adherence to the welfare state and the interlocking between state and market – rather than call them into question. Wolfgang Seibel, for example, maintains that East Germany, even under the Communist regime, adhered to an East European political culture in which the state represents the driving force of modernization (Seibel, 1993: 27). In addition, the experience of East German citizens with social welfare institutions of the former GDR has led them to expect corresponding provisions in the Federal Republic, an expectation which the (West) German government has sought to meet with huge financial transfers. As far as the federal principle is concerned, unification has, according to most observers, supported federalism as an organizational paradigm for the German state, despite the emergence of a 'divided federalism' characterized by more centralization in the Eastern and more decentralization in the Western part of Germany (Benz, 1993). Similarly, the basic norm of a state under the rule of law has not been weakened, notwithstanding evidence of highly informal and, in part, illegal practices during the first phase of institutional transfer (Czada, 1994; Lehmbruch, 1991). Finally, the importance of paragovernmental institutions located between state and market in German governance has been underlined by the experience of the Treuhandanstalt which carried out the massive privatization programme in the new Länder (Czada in the present volume).

One should not ignore counter-tendencies that might undermine the stability of the normative bases of the German public sector. Growing fiscal pressure, caused by the cost of rebuilding the East German economy and administration, forces the government into cuts in social service provisions and encourages the privatization of public utilities and services. At the Länder and local levels, the adoption of NPM concepts is stimulated by rising budget deficits. To a certain extent, such policies reflect a new view of the public sector that stresses efficiency, marketized relations between public service providers and consumers, and a retreat of the state to 'core functions' such as enabling private activities, moderating and regulating conflicting interests, and social control. However, these ideas do not completely replace the old normative framework of the social market economy and the welfare state, to say nothing of the principles of federalism and the rule of law, which the new concepts of the public sector would seem to bolster rather than call into question. On the whole, changes in the norms and traditions guiding public policy making have, so far, been only moderate and incremental, and new ideas have been implemented in a pragmatic fashion.

In contrast, European integration may have a much more profound impact on the German public sector. It is associated with strong pressures to extending the market sector by reducing public service provision, limiting state regulation and public subsidies and by exposing traditional public monopolies to competitive forces. Many observers have also feared that federalism may be challenged, while others have pointed out the regionalist tendencies in the European Union. Representatives of the trade unions see the German welfare system as exposed to severe challenges in view of the open competition with countries that offer social provisions on a much lower level than Germany. Up to now, the process is marked by conflicting traditions and ideas which are far from emerging into a dominant pattern. Europeanization appears to reinforce tendencies associated with unification: the substantial norms of public policy making connected to the specific German combination of market economy and welfare state seem to face a greater challenge than the principles of the rule of law and federalism. This may change in the future, if the process of 'positive integration' advances. So far, divergent national traditions of the member states still predominate in the policy making of the European Union. Therefore, referring to basic institutional parameters of the public sector, we can expect that individual member states will have ample scope to follow their own way. This holds particularly true for leading countries in the EU, such as Germany.

This said, as European integration continues apace, German public institutions increasingly acquire a dual character, that is both German and European (Goetz, 1996b). Its orientation towards integration is a congenital, constitutive, rather than a contingent feature of the German state and so is the predominance of political over economic considerations. There is growing evidence that, over time, the political preference for European integration has become part of the institutional logic of the German state, providing a fundamental value which informs institutional behaviour. Europeanization thus goes increasingly beyond the need for adjustment of national institutions to progressive integration and congruence in German and EU institutional practice; more fundamentally, it implies a generalized institutional orientation towards integration. In other words, the European project has ceased to be an external influence on the development of the German state and public administration, and has, instead, become part of their rationale. Institutionally, this is reflected in the emergence of what has been called the European 'fused federal state' (Wessels, 1992), as the latest stage in the development of European statehood.

The Public Bureaucracy State in Decline

What are we to make of the public-sector trends outlined so far? Certainly, there is no single overriding force reshaping the public sector, and there is no unambiguous direction in which it is moving. Administrative change in Germany is not inspired by a broad reform design that encompasses different parts of the public sector, extends to different levels and has a reasonably coherent set of reform objectives. Instead, a range of external adaptive pressures have an impact on the public sector and combine with political motivations, bureaucratic politics and a legal–administrative inheritance to produce a highly variegated patchwork of adaptations and permutations. But it seems clear that the combined effect of the trends outlined above is a move away from the 'public bureaucracy state' (see Dunleavy and Hood, 1993). There are at least three closely interacting strands to this process. First, there is *the progressive blurring of the public–private distinction*. German public-sector change has not principally been a matter of moving the boundaries between state, society and market ('rolling back the state') but has blurred previously reasonably clear-cut distinctions. Internal reorganization along business lines means that public-sector institutions increasingly take on characteristics traditionally associated exclusively or primarily with the private sector. The current NPM wave at the local level provides an example. Perhaps more importantly, one finds a rapidly growing reliance on paragovernment and hybrid organizations, indirect administrations, and administrative institutions established under private law. NPM, unification, ecological modernization and decentralization have all contributed to 'organizational privatization' and they have extended private law institutions into areas involving the exercise of sovereign state powers (Erbguth and Stoosmann, 1993). In the majority of cases, this type of privatization relies on tried and tested institutional models. To borrow an image of Hood, the species populating the German zoo of parapublic institutions have remained fairly unchanged, but the animals are becoming ever more numerous and stronger and they are increasingly found outside their traditional enclosures.

Second, there is *the de-hierarchization of state–private relations*. During the last decade or so, non-hierarchical and cooperative forms of interaction between state and private actors have come to the fore, indicating a gradual move away from state action conceived principally as the exercise of sovereign powers. In the German literature this development is often referred to as the growth of the cooperative and negotiating state. Authoritative action through the implementation of formal rules has never been the sole mode of public action (see Benz in the present volume); but it would appear that administration through negotiations, understandings, arrangements, informal agreements and private law treaties is gaining in importance (Burmeister, 1993; Hoffmann-Riem and Lamb, 1994; Krebs, 1993).

The third strand is *the redefinition of the role of generalized rules*. Both the blurring of the public–private distinction, notably through administration by private-law entities, and the rise of the cooperative state imply a change in the status of generalized rules in the form of administrative law. In some respects this change may be described as a downgrading of general rules. Thus the setting up of private-law entities is often explicitly justified by reference to the restrictions which administration under public law is said to impose. However, for the most part, generalized rules are complemented rather than replaced by novel types of regulations. The growing practice of public authorities entering into contracts with private actors provides a good example. As a result, administration does not become less rule-bound, but the nature of the rules is changing, as are the means of enforcement. Germany is still a long way away from the 'contractual state' discussed by some British writers. In public interinstitutional relations, they seem still of marginal importance, and in the relations between public and private actors, they do not (yet?) constitute a dominant feature. However, contract-type arrangements are likely to gain steadily in significance.

All three developments just outlined relate to patterns of external and internal interaction. In fact, it is perhaps such interactive patterns which provide the key to analyzing the public administration of the future. This observation relates in particular to contextualization, interadministrative relations and public–private cooperation.

As regards the contextualization of the German administrative system within the European legal, political and administrative framework, it is becoming increasingly impossible to understand the workings of German public administration without constant and systematic reference to its embeddedness in the European order. The scope and content of administrative action, the national institutional setting, administrative procedures and personnel policy are influenced by European integration to an extent where it is becoming increasingly problematic to conceptualize integration as an external force affecting domestically defined administrative arrangements. Already the interactive ties between the national administrative system and its European environment are of such a variety and intensity that they constitute a decisive new element in Germany's administrative history.

Then there are interadministrative relations in the national setting. Its high degree of functional and organizational differentiation has long been recognized as one of the central characteristics of the German administrative system, along with the complex machinery for interinstitutional and, here in particular, intergovernmental coordination and cooperation to which it has given rise. Organizational privatization and the creation of internal markets (still very much in its infant stages) further add to differentiation and pose new coordination and cooperation challenges between public and parapublic institutions. Over time they can be expected to engender novel patterns of interinstitutional supervision, guidance, steering and control.

Finally, the growing reliance on negotiation in public policy making, even in the implementation of regulatory legislation, is part of a wider restructuring of public–private interactions. It involves the replacement of hierarchy by cooperative arrangements, whose importance in many policy areas (environmental policy, regional policy, labour market policy and so on) is evidence of the limitations of an administrative policy making style which relies primarily on authority (sovereignty) for the realization of political objectives.

References

Banner, G. (1994) 'Steuerung kommunalen Handelns', in R. Roth and H. Wollmann (eds), *Kommunalpolitik*, Opladen: Leske & Budrich, 350–61.
Becker, B. (1978) 'Zentrale nichtministerielle Organisationseinheiten der unmittelbaren Bundesverwaltung', *Verwaltungsarchiv*, **69**, 149–202.
Benz, A. (1989) 'Intergovernmental Relations in the 1980s: Recent Trends and Developments', *Publius: Journal of Federalism*, **19**, 203–20.

Benz, A. (1993) 'Reformbedarf und Reformchancen des kooperativen Föderalismus nach der Vereinigung Deutschlands', in W. Seibel, A. Benz and H. Mäding (eds), *Verwaltungsreform und Verwaltungspolitik im Prozeß der deutschen Einigung*, Baden-Baden: Nomos Verlagsgesellschaft, 454–73.

Benz, A. (1995) 'Verfassungspolitik im Bundesstaat', in K. Bentele, R. Schettkat and B. Reissert (eds), *Die Reformfähigkeit von Industriegesellschaften*, Frankfurt/New York: Campus, 145–63.

Böckenförde, E.W. (1991) 'The Origin and Development of the Concept of the *Rechtsstaat*', in *State, Society and Liberty: Studies in Political Theory and Constitutional Law*, Oxford: Berg.

Bohne, E. (1981) *Der informale Rechtsstaat*, Berlin: Duncker & Humblot.

Böhret, C. (1982) 'Reform und Anpassungsflexibilität der öffentlichen Verwaltung', in J.J. Hesse (ed.), *Politikwissenschaft und Verwaltungswissenschaft* (PVS-Sonderheft 13), Opladen: Westdeutscher Verlag, 134–50.

Brohm, W. (1988) 'Funktionsbedingungen für Verwaltungsreformen', *Die Verwaltung*, **21**, 1–22.

Budäus, D. (1994) *Public Management. Konzepte und Verfahren zur Modernisierung öffentlicher Verwaltungen*, Berlin: Ed. Sigma.

Bulmer, S. (1986) *The Domestic Structure of European Community Policy-Making in West Germany*, New York/London: Garland.

Bulmer, S. (1989) 'Unity, Diversity and Stability: the "Efficient Secrets" behind West German Public Policy?', in S. Bulmer (ed.), *The Changing Agenda of West German Public Policy*, Aldershot: Dartmouth, 13–39.

Bulmer, S. and W. Paterson (1987) *The Federal Republic of Germany and the European Community*, London: Allen & Unwin.

Burmeister, J. (1993) 'Verträge und Absprachen zwischen der Verwaltung und Privaten', *Veröffentlichungen der Vereinigung der Deutschen Staatsrechtslehrer*, **52**, 181–247.

Clasen, R. *et al.* (1995) *"Effizienz und Verantwortlichkeit". Reformempfehlungen für eine effiziente, aufgabengerechte und bürgernahe Verwaltung*, manuscript, Berlin.

Czada, R. (1994) 'Schleichwege in die "Dritte Republik". Politik der Vereinigung und politischer Wandel in Deutschland', *Politische Vierteljahresschrift*, **35**, 245–70.

Derlien, H.-U. (1993) 'German Unification and Bureaucratic Transformation', *International Political Science Review*, **14**, 319–34.

Dreier, H. (1994) 'Informal Administrative Actions', *Jahrbuch zur Staats- und Verwaltungswissenschaft*, **7**, 159–93.

Dunleavy, P. (1994) 'The Globalization of Public Services Production: Can Government be "Best in World"?', *Public Policy and Administration*, **9**, 36–64.

Dunleavy, P. and C. Hood (1993) *From Old Public Administration to New Public Management*, London: LSE Public Policy Paper no. 4.

Dyson, K. (1980) *The State Tradition in Europe*, Oxford: Robertson.

Ellwein, Th. (1979) 'Organisationsprobleme in Ministerien', *Die Betriebswirtschaft*, **39**, 73–87.

Ellwein, Th. (1990) 'Über Verwaltungskunst oder: Grenzen der Verwaltungsführung und der Verwaltungswissenschaft', *Staatswissenschaften und Staatspraxis*, **1**, 89–104.

Ellwein, T. and J.J. Hesse (1994) *Der überforderte Staat*, Baden-Baden: Nomos Verlagsgesellschaft.

Erbguth, W. and F. Stoosmann (1993) 'Erfüllung öffentlicher Aufgaben durch private Rechtssubjekte? Zu den Kriterien bei der Wahl der Rechtsform', *Die Öffentliche Verwaltung*, **46**, 799–809.

Goetz, K.H. (1992) *Intergovernmental Relations and State Government Discretion*, Baden-Baden: Nomos Verlagsgesellschaft.

Goetz, K.H. (1993) 'Rebuilding Public Administration in the New German Länder: Transfer and Differentiation', *West European Politics*, **16**, 447–69.

Goetz, K.H. (1995a) 'Kooperation und Verflechtung im Bundesstaat. Zur Leistungsfähigkeit verhandlungsbasierter Politik', in R. Voigt (ed.), *Der kooperative Staat*, Baden-Baden: Nomos Verlagsgesellschaft, 145–66.

Goetz, K.H. (1995b) 'National Governance and European Integration: Intergovernmental Relations in Germany', *Journal of Common Market Studies*, **33**, 91–116.

Goetz, K.H. (1996a) 'Administrative Reconstruction in the New Länder: The Federal Dimension', in C. Jeffery (ed.), *German Federalism in the 1990s*, London: Leicester University Press, forthcoming.

Goetz, K.H. (1996b) 'Integration Policy in a Europeanized State: Germany and the Intergovernmental Conference', *Journal of European Public Policy*, **3**, 23–44.

Goetz, K.H. and P.J. Cullen (eds) (1995) *Constitutional Policy in Unified Germany*, London: Frank Cass.

Henke, K.-D. and D. Fürst (1987/88) 'Between Desire and Reality: Ecological Renewal of the Industrialized State', *Yearbook on Government and Public Administration*, **1**, 531–50.

Héritier, A. *et al.* (1994) *Die Veränderung von Staatlichkeit in Europa*, Opladen: Leske & Budrich.

Hesse, J.J. (ed.) (1991) *Local Government and Urban Affairs in International Perspective*, Baden-Baden: Nomos Verlagsgesellschaft.

Hesse, J.J. and A. Benz (1987/88) 'Institutional Policy: An International Comparison', *Yearbook on Government and Public Administration*, **1**, 377–403.

Hesse, J.J. and A. Benz (1990) *Die Modernisierung der Staatsorganisation*, Baden-Baden: Nomos Verlagsgesellschaft.

Hesse, J.J. and K.H. Goetz (1992) 'Early Administrative Adjustment to the European Communities: The Case of the Federal Republic of Germany', *Yearbook of European Administrative History*, **4**, 181–205.

Heuer, E. (1995) 'Privatwirtschaftliche Wege und Modelle zu einem modernen (anderen?) Staat', *Die Öffentliche Verwaltung*, **48**, 85–95.

Hinings, Ch. R. and R. Greenwood (1988) *The Dynamics of Strategic Change*, Oxford: Blackwell.

Hoffmann-Riem, W. and I. Lamb (1994) 'Negotiation and Mediation in the Public Sector – the German Experience', *Public Administration*, **72**, 309–26.

Hood, C. (1991) 'A Public Management for All Seasons?', *Public Administration*, **69**, 3–19.

Huelshoff, M.G. *et al.* (eds) (1993) *From Bundesrepublik to Deutschland: German Politics after Unification*, Ann Arbor: University of Michigan Press.

Jann, W. (1994) *Moderner Staat und effiziente Verwaltung. Zur Reform des öffentlichen Sektors in Deutschland*, Bonn: Friedrich Ebert Stiftung.

Johnson, N. (1981) *State and Government in the Federal Republic of Germany: The Executive at Work*, 2nd edn, Oxford: Pergamon.

Jones, G. (1993) *International Trends in Public Administration*, London: LSE Public Policy Group Paper no. 7.

Katzenstein, P. (1987) *Politics and Policy in West Germany: The Growth of a Semi-sovereign State*, Philadelphia: Temple University Press.

König, K. (1988) 'Developments in Privatization in the Federal Republic of Germany', *International Review of Administrative Sciences*, **54**, 517–51.

König, K. (1993) 'Bureaucratic Integration by Elite Transfer: The Case of the Former GDR', *Governance*, **6**, 386–96.

König, K. (1995) '"Neue" Verwaltung oder Verwaltungsmodernisierung: Verwaltungspolitik in den 90er Jahren', *Die Öffentliche Verwaltung*, **48**, 349–58.

Kosellek, R. (1967) *Preußen zwischen Reform und Revolution. Allgemeines Landrecht, Verwaltung und soziale Bewegung*, Stuttgart: Kohlhammer.

Krebs, W. (1993) 'Verträge und Absprachen zwischen der Verwaltung und Privaten', *Veröffentlichungen der Vereinigung der Deutschen Staatsrechtslehrer*, **52**, 248–84.

Lehmbruch, G. (1990) 'Die improvisierte Vereinigung: Die dritte deutsche Republik', *Leviathan*, **18**, 462–86.

Lehmbruch, G. (1991) 'Die deutsche Vereinigung: Strukturen und Strategien', *Politische Vierteljahresschrift*, **32**, 585–604.

Lehmbruch, G. *et al.* (1988) 'Institutionelle Bedingungen ordnungspolitischen Strategiewechsels im internationalen Vergleich', in M.G. Schmidt (ed.), *Staatstätigkeit* (PVS-Sonderheft 19), Opladen: Westdeutscher Verlag, 251–83.

Miller, D. and P.H. Friesen (1984) *Organizations – A Quantum View*, New York: Prentice Hall.

Müller, W.C. and V. Wright (1994) 'Reshaping the State in Western Europe: The Limits to Retreat', *West European Politics*, **17**, 1–11.

Naschold, F. (1993) *Modernisierung des Staates. Zur Ordnungs- und Innovationspolitik des öffentlichen Sektors*, Berlin: Ed. Sigma.

Naßmacher, H. *et al.* (eds) (1994) *Politische Strukturen im Umbruch*, Berlin: Akademie Verlag.

OECD (1990) *Public Sector Management Developments: Survey 1990*, Paris: OECD.

Ossenbühl, F. (1989) 'Föderalismus nach 40 Jahren Grundgesetz', *Deutsches Verwaltungsblatt*, **104**, 1230–37.

Reichard, C. (1994) *Umdenken im Rathaus. Neue Steuerungsmodelle in der deutschen Kommunalverwaltung*, Berlin: Ed. Sigma.

Reinermann, H. *et al.* (eds) (1988) *Neue Informationstechnik – neue Verwaltungsstrukturen*, Heidelberg: Decker & Müller.

Rengeling, H.W. (1994) 'Deutsches und europäisches Verwaltungsrecht – wechselseitige Einwirkungen', *Veröffentlichungen der Vereinigung der Deutschen Staatsrechtslehrer*, **53**, 202–39.

Ress, G. (1995) 'The Constitution and the Maastricht Treaty: Between Co-operation and Conflict', in K.H. Goetz and P.J. Cullen (eds), *Constitutional Policy in Unified Germany*, London: Frank Cass, 47–74.

Rhodes, R.A.W. and V. Wright (eds) (1987) *Tensions in the Territorial Politics of Western Europe*, London: Frank Cass.

Sally, R. and D. Webber (1994) 'The German Solidarity Pact: A Case Study in the Politics of the Unified Germany', *German Politics*, 3, 239–78.

Scharpf, F.W. (1987/88) 'The Limits of Institutional Reform', *Yearbook on Government and Public Administration,* 1, 99–130.

Scharpf, F.W. (1988) 'The Joint-Decision Trap: Lessons from German Federalism and European Integration', *Public Administration*, 66, 239–78.

Scharpf, F.W., B. Reissert and F. Schnabel (1976) *Politikverflechtung: Theorie und Empirie des kooperativen Föderalismus in der Bundesrepublik*, Kronberg/Ts.: Scriptor.

Schmidt-Aßmann, E. (1993) 'Deutsches und Europäisches Verwaltungsrecht', *Deutsches Verwaltungsblatt*, 108, 924–36.

Schulze-Fielitz, H. (1984) *Der informale Verfassungsstaat*, Berlin: Duncker & Humblot.

Seibel, W. (1993) 'Verwaltungsintegration im vereinten Deutschland. Ein Problemaufriß für die Verwaltungswissenschaft', in W. Seibel, A. Benz and H. Mäding (eds), *Verwaltungsreform und Verwaltungspolitik im Prozeß der deutschen Einigung*, Baden-Baden: Nomos Verlagsgesellschaft, 15–29.

Seibel, W. (1994) 'Das zentralistische Erbe. Die institutionelle Entwicklung der Treuhandanstalt und die Nachhaltigkeit ihrer Auswirkungen auf die bundesdeutschen Verfassungsstrukturen', *Aus Parlament und Zeitgeschichte*, B 33/34, 3–13.

Sharpe, L.J. (ed.) (1993) *The Rise of Meso Government in Europe*, London: Sage.

Vickers, J. and V. Wright (eds) (1989) *The Politics of Privatisation in Western Europe*, London: Frank Cass.

Webber, D. (1995) *The Second Coming of the Bonn Republic*, Birmingham: Institute for German Studies, Discussion Papers in German Studies no. IGS95/1.

Wessels, W. (1992) 'Staat und (westeuropäische) Integration. Die Fusionsthese', in M. Kriele (ed.), *Die Integration Europas* (PVS-Sonderheft no. 23), Opladen: Westdeutscher Verlag, 26–61.

Wilkes, Christopher (1989) 'Institutionalisierung der Entbürokratisierung. Zur Fortsetzung der Rechtsvereinfachung in Bund und Ländern', *Die Verwaltung*, 22, 333–51.

Wright, V. (ed.) (1994a) *Privatization in Western Europe: Pressures, Problems and Paradoxes*, London: Pinter.

Wright, V. (1994b) 'Reshaping the State: The Implications for Public Administration', *West European Politics*, 17, 102–37.

Zuleeg, M. (1994) 'Deutsches und europäisches Verwaltungsrecht – wechselseitige Einwirkungen', *Veröffentlichungen der Vereinigung der Deutschen Staatsrechtslehrer*, 53, 154–201.

2 Patterns of Postwar Administrative Development in Germany

Hans-Ulrich Derlien

Introduction

Three periods of administrative development in the Federal Republic can be roughly distinguished: modernization from 1964 to the mid-1970s, consolidation in the 1980s and reforms subsequent to unification. However, there is considerable overlap between the first two periods. On the one hand, modernization was continued, albeit at a slower pace, in the 1980s, and reforms in the Federal machinery of government during the early 1970s were later partly replicated in the Länder. On the other hand, retrenchment, debureaucratization and privatization were not inventions of the conservative–liberal government led by Chancellor Kohl since 1982, but had precursors in some Länder dating back to the mid-1970s. Between 1982 and 1990, however, the Federal government's determination to promote the partial withdrawal of the state from society grew and, in this respect, the Germans followed the international trend. The innovations of the previous phases in organization, budgeting, personnel policy and analytical techniques were not abandoned. What changed were primarily the substantive policy programmes, including the activities of public enterprises, while the structures of the administrative system, budgeting, decision making and managing remained more or less unchanged during the consolidation period of the 1980s.

Unification heralded an administrative revolution for the East Germans. West Germany exported its institutions and personnel to create equivalent institutions in the Eastern part of the country. This process did not just involve the Federal government, but was a joint operation that included all levels of government and public administration. The evolving decentralized system in the new Länder drew on lessons learnt from past experience in the old Länder and allowed for some variation of Western models. In Bonn, financial crisis management became predominant and relied on established budgetary techniques, though previously relatively infrequently used devices were now employed more often, including, for example, supplementary budgets, of which there were five in 1991 alone, the creation of special funds outside the main budget and consolidation laws.

It may then be argued that administrative reform has been a continuous process that reached peaks in the period 1965–73 and again after 1990. The intervening years constituted a less innovative period of consolidation, reinforced by the change of government in 1982. It is, however, important to stress that administrative policy was principally prompted by substantive policy changes rather than by explicit structural reform programmes aiming at the traditional features of the machinery of the state. This said, international managerial concepts have entered the German debate in recent years and are being taken up, albeit, until now, primarily at the local government level. It is arguable that 'old wine in new bottles' is concealed by the metaphorical postmodernist language of those who advocate current austerity concepts. Therefore one main purpose of this chapter is to recall earlier reform or modernization initiatives which seem to have been partly forgotten by practitioners and academic commentators.

The remainder of this chapter is divided into four sections. We first recall various modernization attempts made during the first period of reform, whose central concerns partly resurfaced after 1990. Dominant concerns during the consolidation phase are then examined, under the heading of 'economizing and debureaucratization'. The following section discusses the export of administrative structures and personnel to the new Länder since 1990, with a particular focus on elements that had featured in the West German reform discussions during the preceding two decades. The transformation process in Eastern Germany invited a new look at West German administrative practice and helped the assessment of the institutional condition of the state. Finally, we return, in part, to the 1980s and ask whether it is possible to identify a German equivalent to 'Thatcherism', in an attempt to adopt a second, more international perspective, in which the new German managerialism appears, partly at least, as a product of semantic change. A brief conclusion summarizes the main arguments emerging from the discussion.

Modernizing the Machinery of Government

Administrative reforms between the mid-1960s and the mid-1970s were ultimately aimed at modernizing the machinery of government at all levels. Their primary objective was to increase the effectiveness of internal administrative operations. In many key functional respects, the administrative machinery had remained unchanged since 1949 and in many ways rested on structures inherited from the Weimar Republic. Some of the reforms attempted during this phase were successful, others proved abortive. Moreover, there were spillovers between Federal and Länder governments and belated learning occurred when concepts from the 1970s were rediscovered and reapplied elsewhere a decade later.

Territorial Local Government Reform

In 1964, the German Association of Lawyers suggested that larger units of local government should be formed to promote more professional administration and better services in rural areas, more comprehensive area planning in urban areas and better revenue flows for cities which provided the infrastructure for people living in increasingly more prosperous surrounding villages. Territorial reform was a matter for the individual Länder, which pursued no common policy. Between 1965 and the conclusion of territorial reform in Bavaria in 1978, the number of local governments was reduced from 24 000 to 8500, partly in the face of massive resistance by local notables (Thieme and Prillwitz, 1981). While the Social Democrat-governed states of North Rhine–Westphalia and Hesse carried through radical reforms by creating large unitary local governments, others, in particular the South German Länder, favoured voluntary associations with a smaller minimum size. County boundaries were adjusted and regional administrations occasionally abandoned, but the process of transferring former Länder functions to the local level, that is functional reform, proved cumbersome and not altogether successful. Dissatisfaction was widespread, because the larger local authorities did not receive greater autonomy from the Länder through increased substantive competences. The experience of territorial and related functional reforms should prove helpful later in the transformation of public administration in the new Länder.

Redrawing Länder Boundaries

Another reform issue that was to experience a renaissance in the 1990s, albeit one of a short-lived nature, involved proposals to change Länder boundaries and to achieve some amalgamations. The Federal government set up the Ernst Commission in 1969 to consider territorial reforms of the Länder. Boundaries established after the Second World War had already been adjusted by the merger of Württemberg and Baden in 1951 and the incorporation of the Saarland in 1956. The central criteria which were to inform decisions on territorial amalgamation were economic structures, adequate financial revenues and cultural homogeneity. Reform suggestions included, for example, the creation of a large North German state, incorporating Lower Saxony, Schleswig-Holstein and the city states of Hamburg and Bremen. Together with joint Federal–Länder programmes for regional development since 1969, the idea to restructure the Länder seemed logical and consistent with the rationale of the first comprehensive development plans that were produced in Hesse and North Rhine–Westphalia. They were respectively governed by Social Democrat and Social-Liberal administrations that had a major influence on the planning approach adopted in Bonn. However, the discussions ultimately proved abortive, since the smaller Länder, including the Social Democrat strongholds of Hamburg and Bremen, resisted any change. Not surprisingly, the topic of redrawing Länder boundaries resurfaced in 1990, when the Unification Treaty was negotiated.

Budgetary Reform

During the first half of the 1960s, it was widely felt that the 1922 budgetary code and the overall system of public finances were in urgent need of updating, in particular to allow for Keynesian economic policy. Reform proposals were produced in 1964 by the Troeger Commission. Modernizing the Federal budgetary system and public-sector financial management as a whole required changes to the Federal Constitution. These became possible when, in the wake of the economic crisis of 1965/6, a grand coalition of Christian and Social Democrats was formed in Bonn. As a result, between 1967 and 1969 a number of constitutional amendments were passed which partly altered the system of public finance and budgeting. These amendments provided a constitutional basis for economic intervention policy; a common framework to coordinate budgetary policy and medium-range financial planning encompassing all levels of government; the so-called joint tasks, that is, joint Federal–Länder programmes for structural policies in the fields of higher education and research, agriculture and regional development; and for Federal legislative powers to set civil service pay.

Reforming the Machinery of Government

During the late 1960s, in the light of the above reforms and innovative policy initiatives such as the 1969 labour market and vocational training laws, the machinery of the Federal government was increasingly seen to be suffering from 'disorganization stress' (Schatz, 1973). An interdepartmental reform group was set up in 1968 in the Federal Ministry of the Interior, which, in Germany, has traditionally been the classic department responsible for administrative organization and the public service. The reform group's emphasis was on improving internal governmental decision making and meta-policy making in general and not, as some critical observers suggested, the comprehensive planning of the economy and society (Derlien, 1978). Interdepartmental coordination and cooperation, including the Federal Chancellery, were to be improved, and a planning division was set up in the Chancellery to facilitate comprehensive coordination and to counteract departmental particularism. Through a number of special reports, the reform group dealt with division of responsibilities between ministries (1969), including the question of whether to create a Ministry for European Community Affairs (1972). While the latter was never created and the Federal government to this date relies on a complicated committee system to coordinate interactions with Brussels (Derlien, 1991b), the incoming Social–Liberal government of Chancellor Brandt effected a number of changes in the departmental structure. In addition, the number of junior ministers (parliamentary state secretary, a position first created in 1967) progressively increased. Their purpose was to reduce the workload of cabinet ministers, especially with regard to parliamentary relations.

A procedural integration of planning and budgeting, however, as an operation involving the government as a whole, was never achieved, not least because, by 1969, the Planning-Programming-Budgeting System PPBS was considered to have failed in the USA. Nevertheless, with the help of McKinsey consultants, the task force introduced a PPBS-type system in the Agriculture Ministry, where it was sold as a management system. With the advent of the Kohl government in October 1982, some internal rearrangements took place in the Chancellery and the ministries. These changes essentially concerned the procedures established in 1970 to improve planning and coordination. However, it was the labels rather than the substance that changed. Sections responsible for prognoses, cost–benefit analyses or evaluation were maintained, while the divisions to which they belonged changed their titles from 'planning' to 'principal matters'. Thus policy science instruments proved to be politically neutral (Derlien, 1985). In 1987, even technology assessment was institutionalized, but as a parliamentary rather than a governmental function.

Efforts to improve administrative planning in the 1970s were partly mirrored at the level of the Länder, and coordination in state chancelleries, that is the Minister–President's Offices, improved (König, 1976; Siedentopf, 1976). These concepts were revived in 1985, when the Minister–President of Baden–Württemberg appointed an expert commission to devise a new management structure for the Land government. Apart from the idea of computerizing the government and concentrating all Land ministries in one building (a suggestion which, predictably, was never implemented), academic experts were called in to advise on three issues which had already occupied the Federal reform group during 1968–72. First, there was the problem of the interdepartmental distribution of competences and, second, the question of control spans within the ministries. In respect of both issues, analysts were able to capitalize on the expertise gained some 15 years earlier (Mayntz and Scharpf, 1975) and they produced concepts which were no longer current at the Länder level (Derlien, 1988). Third, the civil service reform issue of 1973 of introducing fixed-term appointments for top administrators was re-examined (Siedentopf, 1985), but, as in the 1970s, this remained controversial for legal reasons. Reform commissions with a more or less comprehensive remit were also set up in a number of other Länder in the mid-to-late 1980s (Hauschild, 1991; Seibel, 1992) and the continuity of reform efforts at the Länder level is probably best documented by the establishment of a think-tank (*Denkfabrik*) in the office of the Minister–President of Schleswig-Holstein in 1988. This stock of knowledge and expertise could be easily drawn upon when it came to establishing ministerial bureaucracies in the new Länder (König, 1993).

Civil Service Reform

Minor adaptations to Federal and Länder civil service codes are frequent, for instance concerning the grading system with a view to making certain posts more attractive on the labour market. There have also, on occasions, been more far-reaching changes, for example the opening of higher civil service careers to economists and social scientists in the early 1970s. An attempt to launch a fully-fledged reform of the civil service was made between 1969 and 1973, when a reform commission developed proposals to abolish the traditional separation of status groups in the public service (labourers, employees and civil servants) and to improve vertical mobility. These reform recommendations followed the imperatives of effectiveness and individual development in the public service. The abolition of the status distinctions and the creation of a unified public service had been plans advocated by Social Democrats and trade unions since the nineteenth century. However, conflicts between the trade unions representing the three status groups and the political parties with which they were aligned prevented the necessary changes to the Federal Constitution, and the three status groups were maintained.

Nonetheless, the civil service reform commission had at least produced a thorough evaluation of the status quo, backed by social science research and drawing on international comparisons. Not only were certain elements of its report widely discussed (for example, the suggestion to appoint top administrators on a fixed-term basis) but some of those recommendations that did not require constitutional change were, in fact, adopted after 1973. They included, *inter alia*, improved performance appraisal and a reassessment of the balance between salary grade and job requirements. The approach to performance pay was to try to secure adequate remuneration and promotion to better paid jobs for those who performed well; by contrast, the idea of performance-related bonuses for top administrators was rejected. It is important to note that the extent to which these reforms were implemented depended on the willingness of individual Federal departments and the Länder, since, despite the 1969 centralization of salary legislation, both had preserved their considerable autonomy in personnel policy. A fully-fledged civil service ministry or interdepartmental personnel commissions are alien to the German system and, without a focal point for promoting administrative change, the reform movement generated in the late 1960s and early 1970s finally ran out of steam around 1978 (Siedentopf, 1979).

However, civil service training was considerably broadened at all levels of government. Grades below university-trained higher civil service personnel had to pass special courses in internal training colleges at Federal and Länder levels before their appointment. Also the higher civil servants of all ranks could participate in continuous training courses at the Federal Civil Service Academy, which was created in 1969 in line with the British Civil Service Training College. For non-lawyers, participation in such courses was obligatory. Alternatively, they could attend leadership training courses at the Graduate School of Administrative Sciences in Speyer, where management models were, at that time, under discussion (Böhret and Junkers, 1976).

Two reforms in civil service policy in the 1980s are worth highlighting. First, implementing some of the proposals of the Bulling commission of 1985, Baden–Württemberg, in 1986, opened its own academy to train an elite reservoir for the higher civil service. Modelled on the Ecole Nationale d'Administration, the courses incorporated both postings abroad and stages in private industry. The Speyer Graduate School, whose costs are borne by all the Länder and the Federal government, sought to match this 'island of excellence' in 1991 by launching a special training programme for high-fliers from four Länder. The majority of the Länder, however, declined to take part, arguing that the early distinction between elite and rank-and-file officials was problematic.

Finally, it should be noted that, since 1987, equal opportunity policies for women in the public service have been endorsed in Bonn and elsewhere, with special measures to compensate for disadvantages, particularly in higher civil service careers. The forerunners in this respect have been the Länder and local government, where commissioners for equal opportunities or gender issues have been installed in almost all major offices.

Increasing Legitimacy

Democratization was regarded as the correlate of modernization by the Brandt government and represented a response to the 1968 student movement that had pressed for, among other things, more participation in university affairs. Unfortunately, while the Civil Service Reform Commission was working hard to show the participatory component of its reform suggestions, the Federal Chancellor and the Länder Minister–Presidents decided, in 1972, to enforce the principle of loyalty to the Constitution through mandatory checks into the background of civil service applicants. This was naturally a controversial issue in civil service policy that lasted until the mid-1980s (Braunthal, 1990).

Another dimension of modernization that silently shaped public administration was computerization. Loyalty screening was considerably simplified by the use of computers in the Federal Constitutional Protection Agency. However, there was a general demand that the use and dissemination of personal data should be protected, leading to legislation at both Länder and Federal levels. One institutional result was the introduction of data protection commissioners by 1978. The office of the Federal Data Protection Commissioner even became institutionalized in Parliament in 1993, after the President of the Federal Audit Office had been elected by Parliament already since 1985.

Finally, it is worth mentioning that, as a response to the citizen initiative movement, new forms of popular participation, particularly in local development planning, became increasingly widespread during the 1970s. More generally, under the banner of *Bürgernähe* (proximity to the citizen), many local authorities sought to improve the interactions between local administrative offices and citizens/clients.

Economizing and Debureaucratization

Owing to the problems of consensus building in the political system and the financial burdens of additional reform programmes, but also in response to the growing awareness of the energy crisis and 'the limits of growth', the speed of domestic policy reforms slowed down from around 1974 when, following Willy Brandt's resignation, Chancellor Schmidt took office. At the time, many observers felt that the political–administrative system had become overly complicated and that programmatic and structural reforms were progressively undermining governability, societal system performance and political legitimacy. The steering capacity of the political system was widely perceived to have reached its limits, and many feared that the state was blocking itself by making decision making procedures ever more complex, particularly in the field of intergovernmental relations (Hochschule Speyer, 1975; Scharpf *et al.*, 1976). Thus, as early as 1975, there were calls for decentralization, greater fiscal autonomy of the Länder from the Federal government and, in particular, changes to the joint Federal–Länder planning system. In addition, concern shifted from launching new reform legislation to the effective implementation of reform programmes (Mayntz *et al.*, 1978). There was also a growing interest in simulating programme performance (Böhret and Hugger, 1979), which added to the repertoire of policy analysis tools available to decision makers in Bonn and the Länder capitals.

With a view to subsequent developments in the 1980s, it is worth pointing out that curbing public expenditure and the reassessment of public tasks had been under way, at the local level, since about 1974 (Dieckmann, 1977; Mäding, 1978); moreover, the debate over the privatization of public tasks and enterprises had begun quite some time before the advent of the conservative Kohl government in 1982. Last, but not least, the 'flood of regulations' and bureaucratization were the subject of vocal complaints (Geissler, 1978; Lohmar, 1978) and simplification was widely demanded. After Chancellor Schmidt had publicly joked that he was unable to decipher his own water bill, the Federal Ministry of the Interior, in 1980, convened a scientific hearing on debureaucratization in the broadest sense, including what later came to be discussed as deregulation and privatization. In 1983, a Federal commission was appointed to scrutinize Federal internal administrative rules. At the Länder level, numerous commissions with a remit to 'simplify public administration and administrative regulation' (*Rechts- und Verwaltungsvereinfachung*) were set up from late 1970s and had mostly completed their work by 1985. Amongst other things, they recommended the abolition of thousands of dated (internal) rules (Ellwein, 1989) and stricter criteria by which to assess the necessity and style of any new regulations to be adopted. In some Länder, rules are now to expire automatically, in line with the concept of 'sunset' legislation. Although the main purpose of these administrative reform and modernization commissions was to increase efficiency in order to speed up governmental–administrative decision making and to facilitate private investment, one important side-effect was the delegation of more decisions to the local government level – a trend that had already started a decade earlier under the heading of functional reform (Seibel, 1992: 20f).

Reunification: Export of the Tried and Tested and Innovation

Reunification brought reforms to East Germany on a scale that made West German administrative reforms appear insignificant by comparison. By joining the Federal Republic of Germany, and through the restructuring of its economy, the former German Democratic Republic accepted basic West German national institutions and abolished its own central government institutions. Blueprints of functioning West German institutions were readily available to fill the institutional vacuum at the Länder level and to reorganize existing structures, notably at the level of local government (Derlien, 1993). In many instances, problems which had been more or less solved in the West now appeared on the agenda in the East and, in most cases, Western solutions were adopted to solve them, although, in principle, there existed considerable opportunities for institutional experimentation within the overall parameters established by the Unification Treaty and the Federal Republic's constitutional and institutional order.

In the opinion of many experts, differences in the size and economic strength amongst both Western and Eastern Länder constituted a major problem, both with respect to the distribution of powers in the federal system and in view of the Länder's future function as regional units in the European Union. Thus the decision to reintroduce the five Eastern Länder more or less on the basis of their original 1947 boundaries seemed to aggravate already existing disparities and imbalances in the federal system. The attempt of the Federal Ministry of the Interior to allow for a redrawing of the new Länder boundaries in the Unification Treaty failed, as a result of resistance from the small Western Länder which felt that their own existence might be called into question (Scharpf, 1991: 151ff). The sole exception is the merger of Berlin and Brandenburg, which has been agreed to by the parliaments of both Länder, but still awaits approval in popular referenda.

Western experience also played a major role in the restructuring of local government (see Wollmann in the present volume). Judged by West German standards, most of the existing 7500 local government units were considered far too small, and reform legislation in the new Länder drew heavily on the Western history of territorial local government reform, as far as both substantive institutional choices and reform procedures were concerned.

The internal structure of local authorities in Germany varies considerably, as this is an area of legislation dealt with by the individual Länder. The East Germans, in early 1990, adopted their own local government charter for the entire GDR, which in a fairly eclectic manner sought to combine what the East German parliament considered were the strong points of the various Western models. In view of approaching unification, Eastern decision makers had consulted Western experts and proposed a local government charter that would obviate the need for dramatic changes when, following unification, the new Länder adopted their individual local government charters. By 1994, the 1990 charter had been replaced in all of the new Länder, and the new Länder charters, on the whole, closely resemble what is customary in the Western Länder. As in former West Germany, there has been a clear tendency to move towards the South German model, in which the popularly elected mayor simultaneously holds the positions of local chief executive and council chairman (Derlien, 1994).

Structural conservatism can be observed in the way the vacuum at the top of the Länder administrations was filled. Together with the import of personnel from the West, the West–East Länder partnerships resulted in a process of institutional transfer which more or less copied the structure of the ministerial bureaucracy in the provincial capitals of the Western partner states. In October 1990, the pressure to set up bureaucracies for the newly elected governments that could immediately provide imported experts with a familiar working environment ruled out major reform considerations. Only the Minister–President of Saxony, a Western import himself, announced – in the then fashionable jargon – that he wanted a 'lean administration'.

As to the civil service, reunification initially served to highlight many unresolved problems, since the uniform East German state service had to be transformed into the traditional West German personnel system. However, as has been argued elsewhere (Derlien, 1991a), the complete deviation from the classical West European civil service model in the East, in particular the politicized incompetence of the Eastern state functionaries, in fact underlined many of the positive qualities of the traditional German civil service. This positive assessment was further reinforced by the great technical skill which the Federal ministerial bureaucracy showed in the drafting of the Unification Treaty and also by the thousands of officials from all levels of government who served in East Germany to assist the process of reconstruction (Derlien, 1993). The partial move of the Federal bureaucracy to Berlin towards the end of the century will constitute more of a shake-up than a reform. Some ministries will stay in Bonn, some will be split, while others will move in their entirety (Derlien, 1995). Moreover, the relocation of many Federal agencies to the Eastern Länder, but also the transfer of existing agencies in the Berlin area to Bonn, could be viewed as a reform, although not necessarily of a structural type.

Turning to intergovernmental fiscal relations, the Unification Treaty stipulated that the East German Länder were exempt from the revenue sharing between Federation and Länder and also the redistribution mechanism between poorer and wealthier Länder until the end of 1994. Without this exemption, even the poor Western Länder would have immediately become paymasters in the system of fiscal equalization. In 1993, this system was reformed to accommodate the Eastern Länder. Under this agreement, the bulk of costs falls onto the Federal budget, which has already been heavily burdened by transfer payments to the East. The problem of horizontal, inter-Länder revenue distribution was solved by increased vertical Federal–Länder redistribution in the so-called 'Federal Consolidation Programme'. A comprehensive revision of the status quo, which the Länder had consistently criticized since the 1970s, was not achieved, since all sides wanted to avoid a conflict and the Federal government felt under pressure to accept a compromise before the exemption status for the Eastern Länder expired.

Finally, the budgetary response to managing the costs of unification has been an innovation of doubtful character. After 1990, several special funds, outside the regular Federal budget, were created which, in 1994, were amalgamated in a 'legacy-burden' fund of some DM500bn. Previously, there had been funds for special purposes (not debts), such as the successor of the Marshall Plan fund or the budget of the Federal railways. Technically, the use of special funds is thus a traditional budgetary solution, as are the giant cutback operations for the years to come to which the Länder agreed as the price for the Federal Consolidation Programme. The 'semantic management' at least, has been innovative, but the 1969 budgetary system has not been altered.

A German 'Thatcherism'?

In 1982, the incoming government of Chancellor Kohl, facing an economic crisis, took up earlier reform impulses and incorporated them into the governmental programme. Although the Federal government promoted the reforms on a larger scale than its predecessor, parallels to 'financial management initiatives', Next Steps and deregulation in the UK were largely superficial and rhetorical, although, admittedly, there were some philosophical affinities. The substance of 'withdrawing the state from society' was different in that the constitutional principle of the welfare state (*Sozialstaat*) set limits. Moreover, the Federal government could only take initiatives in its own area of jurisdiction and was not in a position to impose administrative reform objectives on the Länder and local governments which, however, to some extent independently pursued a similar agenda.

One chief objective of public-sector reform was the reduction of public deficits. In 1983, Federal expenditures were cut and budget reallocations took place. Attempts to curb subsidies were not very successful and they fell only slightly, from 1.7 per cent of GDP in 1980 to 1.5 per cent in 1986 (König, 1988: 25). Also the extent of reductions in public personnel remained limited. Despite a temporary halt to recruitment imposed by the new government, the number of Federal staff only declined by 10 000 between 1980 and 1983 (König, 1988: 20). In addition, the Federal government started to sell shares in corporations with a Federal stake. By 1987 and 1988, respectively, the remaining Federal shares in VEBA (a public enterprise since Prussian times and one of the largest energy producers) and Volkswagen had been sold (König, 1988: 58). It could, however, be argued that this policy was simply the completion of a process started in the 1960s, when the Federal government had sold its majority shareholdings in both corporations. Overall, privatization remained limited. Between 1982 and 1989, the number of corporations under Federal control declined only slightly, from 84 to 77 in 1989, and increased again to 82 in 1991. There was, however, a more vigorous disposal of indirect holdings, which went down from 958 in 1982 to 381 in 1991. The total revenue from privatization between 1984 and 1989 amounted to a mere DM9bn, compared to a UK privatization income of DM100bn between 1979 and 1987 (Seibel, 1992: 5f). The constraints on the Federal government in influencing the public sector in this respect become apparent when one looks at the Länder's reaction to Federal privatizations. Thus, unlike the Federation, Lower Saxony did not sell its Volkswagen shares, and Bavaria actually bought VIAG shares that had been sold by the Federal government (Seibel, 1992: 7) and also objected to the sale of more Lufthansa shares. Unlike the situation in the UK and France, there was no large-scale nationalization of industries after the Second World War, and what was being privatized had in the main been in public ownership before the war. The Länder have been extremely reluctant to dispose of these assets, which they tend to see as important instruments for regional and employment policy. Accordingly, much of what has happened under the label of privatization at Länder and local levels has merely involved a transformation from public to private law status, as in the cases of gas and water supply or local transport.

During the 1980s, contracting out was limited, though it did not constitute a novelty. Many local authorities during the 1970s had already started to have building cleaning, the maintenance of public parks and construction planning performed by private enterprises, and competitive tendering has been an established practice for decades. On another level, deregulation has taken place most significantly in the telecommunications sector and has been driven by technological change and EC policy (see Schmidt in the present volume). The most spectacular instance of public-sector change was the division, in 1987, of the Federal post and telecommunications services into three separate enterprises, which was followed, in 1994, by their full corporatization. It is expected that this development will eventually lead to the substantive privatization of at least the telecommunications and post banking services. As in the case of the Federal railways (see Lehmkuhl in the present volume), corporatization required a change in the Federal Constitution.

It would be superficial to take the international similarity in rhetoric as a basis for comparing reform projects. Of course there have always been cross-fertilizations: PPBS had an impact on financial planning in many countries, including Germany, and the British Fulton Commission left its traces in Bonn. In general, however, many tasks that have been privatized in Britain were never a public responsibility in Germany or were left to the 'third sector' (Seibel, 1992), decentralized to public self-governing bodies (for example pensions and health insurance) or are a matter for the Länder (prisons) and local government (water supply). The functional problems connected with Next Steps, such as the delegation of authority or the decentralization of budgetary responsibility while preserving ministerial accountability, however, certainly have their equivalents in the German context, although, until recently, they have not been broadly discussed.

Finally, privatization has been taking place in Eastern Germany on an unprecedented scale, at the same time as public tasks have again increased and Federal deficits have sky-rocketed. Although the Federal privatization agency, the Treuhandanstalt (see Czada in the present volume), was a creation of the GDR and had to cope with an unparalleled task, the organizational solution of the public law status for the agency under the supervision of the Federal Ministry of Finance was highly bureaucratic compared to the institutional set-up in Poland or the Czech Republic.

Conclusion

Looking back over the past few decades, the public sector in postwar Germany has experienced two major reform peaks: the decade from 1965 to 1975 and the period since reunification. However, this is not to say that no reform measures were undertaken before the mid-1960s or between the mid-1970s and the late 1980s. On the contrary, we have tried to show that reforms and adjustments have been a constant feature of the German public sector throughout the postwar decades. In the first major reform period this was a positive movement, which paralleled developments abroad, particularly in the UK (civil service and local government reforms, ministerial bureaucracy) and the USA (planning, budgeting and evaluation). It was on these modernizing developments that reforms in the new Länder could later draw. The imperative to contain public expenditures and to cut back budgets is, by contrast, a negative impetus enforced by adverse economic and financial circumstances. It was a permanent feature of the period from the mid-

1970s to the mid-1980s, reinforced by the political rhetoric of the time, and has become even more visible as a consequence of the heavy financial burdens that unification has entailed. In particular, local government has appeared to be more innovative in responding to scarcity, owing to the vulnerability of its revenue base and the ever-increasing financial burdens imposed by Federal cutbacks. Thus, it is small wonder that local government was the first to jump on the new managerialist bandwagon, stressing the service function of local government in rhetoric (Banner, 1991) and reinforcing cost accounting and the controller concept in practice.

At the time they occur, reforms are often praised as thorough and perceived as ground-breaking by participants and academic observers. In the German case, however, they appear to produce a patchwork limited to individual levels of government in the federal framework, or even to a few of the Länder; they are often confined to one functional aspect of the machinery of government, or concerned with a specific policy area only. At the same time, as has been argued in detail elsewhere (Derlien, 1996), from approximately 1965 to 1975, and since 1990, this disjointed incrementalism and piecemeal engineering have taken on features of a more encompassing reform movement. Yet, as a consequence of Germany's particular type of fragmented government, including federalism and the predominance of co-alition governments, and the strong influence of the *Sozialstaat* tradition, there has never been a coherent reform philosophy or comprehensive central reform programme which would have embraced all levels and sectors of governance (unlike the situation in the UK and some other Commonwealth states in the 1980s). It is precisely because there never existed a comprehensive reform philosophy and an effective overall reform impetus that the number of individual administrative reforms of the last 30 years that come to mind is large. Admittedly, the new managerialism that is sweeping the Northern hemisphere has been gaining ground in Germany too, in particular at the local level. But it is doubtful that such a practitioners' philosophy (see Hood and Jackson, 1994), full of ambiguity and metaphors as it is, will be able to provide an effective unifying reform concept.

Of course the picture drawn above is to a certain extent the result of an analytical device, in that an attempt has been made to distinguish polity aspects from the policy dimension, which is often not done in discussions of public-sector reforms in the 1980s (Derlien, 1992) when, admittedly, structural and substantive aspects tended to be combined. This shortcoming, in turn, may have contributed to the concept of the 'public sector' being applied more frequently in scientific discourse than used to be the case in the 1970s. Moreover, a parallel to the renaissance of the state concept is evident. In both cases the functional or policy dimension of public affairs is addressed. The focus of analysis is then more on the macrosociological relationship of the public sector to the economy and society than on internal administrative reforms that try to address a given stock of public tasks. To a certain degree, reasoning about 'the public sector' tends to lack conceptual detachment from the object under investigation which, in fact, is continually changing. For empirical and analytical purposes a differentiation between structural (polity) and functional (policy) aspects should be made to restore some historical and intellectual perspectives to previous reforms. Thus it is maintained that, in Germany, we have experienced a case of some new wine in fundamentally old bottles, although they have occasionally been polished.

References

Banner, G. (1991) 'Von der Behörde zum Dienstleistungsunternehmen', *Verwaltungsführung, Organisation, Personal*, **13**, 6–11.

Böhret, C. and W. Hugger (1979) 'Bessere Gesetze durch Test der Entwürfe?', *Zeitschrift für Parlamentsfragen*, **10**, 245–59.

Böhret, C. and M.-T. Junkers (1976) *Führungskonzepte für die öffentliche Verwaltung*, Stuttgart: Kohlhammer.

Braunthal, G. (1990) *Political Loyalty and the Public Service in West Germany. The 1972 Decree against Radicals and its Consequences*, Amherst: The University of Massachusetts Press.

Derlien, H.-U. (1978) 'Ursachen und Erfolg von Strukturreformen im Bereich der Bundesregierung unter besonderer Berücksichtigung der wissenschaftlichen Beratung', in C. Böhret (ed.), *Verwaltungsreformen und politische Wissenschaft*, Baden-Baden: Nomos Verlagsgesellschaft.

Derlien, H.-U. (ed.) (1985) *Programmforschung unter den Bedingungen einer Konsolidierungspolitik*, Munich: Gesellschaft für Programmforschung.

Derlien, H.-U. (1988) *Innere Struktur der Landesministerien in Baden–Württemberg*, Baden-Baden: Nomos Verlagsgesellschaft.

Derlien, H.-U. (1991a) 'Historical Legacy and Recent Developments of the German Higher Civil Service', *International Review of Administrative Sciences*, **57**, 385–401.

Derlien, H.-U. (1991b) 'The Horizontal and Vertical Coordination of German EC Policy', *Hallinnon Tutkimus* (Finland), 3–10.

Derlien, H.-U. (1992) 'Observations on the State of Comparative Administration Research in Europe – More Comparable than Comparative', *Governance*, **5**, 279–311.

Derlien, H.-U. (1993) 'German Unification and Bureaucratic Transformation', *International Political Science Review*, **14**, 319–34.

Derlien, H.-U. (1994) 'Kommunalverfassung zwischen Reform und Revolution', in O.W. Gabriel (ed.), *Kommunalpolitik*, Munich: Minerva.

Derlien, H.-U. (1995) 'Regierung und Verwaltung in der räumlichen Zweiteilung', in W. Süß (ed.), *Hauptstadt Berlin*, Vol.2, Berlin: Arno Spitz.

Derlien, H.-U. (1996) 'Germany: The Intelligence of Bureaucracy in a Decentralized Polity', in Olsen J. and Peters G. (eds), *Lessons from Experience*, Oslo: Scandinavian University Press.

Dieckmann, R. (1977) *Aufgabenkritik in einer Großstadtverwaltung*, Berlin: Duncker & Humblot.

Ellwein, T. (1989) *Verwaltung und Verwaltungsvorschriften, Notwendigkeit und Chance der Vorschriftenvereinfachung*, Opladen: Westdeutscher Verlag.

Geissler, H. (ed.) (1978) *Verwaltete Bürger – Gesellschaft in Fesseln. Bürokratisierung und ihre Folgen für Staat, Wirtschaft und Gesellschaft*, Frankfurt: Ullstein.

Hauschild, C. (1991) 'Die Modernisierung des öffentlichen Dienstes im internationalen Vergleich', *Verwaltungsarchiv*, **82**, 81–109.

Hochschule Speyer (ed.) (1975) *Politikverflechtung zwischen Bund, Ländern und Gemeinden*, Berlin: Duncker & Humblot.

Hood, C. and M. Jackson (1994) 'Keys for Locks in Administrative Argument', *Administration and Society*, **25**, 467–88.

König, K. (ed.) (1976) *Koordination und integrierte Planung in den Staatskanzleien*, Berlin: Duncker & Humblot.

König, K. (1988) *Kritik öffentlicher Aufgaben*, Speyer: Hochschule für Verwaltungswissenschaften, Forschungsbericht 72.

König, K. (1993) *Staatskanzleien. Funktionen und Organisation*, Opladen: Leske und Budrich.

Lohmar, U. (1978) *Staatsbürokratie. Das hoheitliche Gewerbe*, Munich: Goldmann.

Mäding, E. (1978) 'Aufgabenkritik', in Konrad Adenauer Stiftung (ed.), *Reform kommunaler Aufgaben*, Bonn: Eichholz.

Mayntz, R. and F.W. Scharpf (1975) *Policymaking in the German Federal Executive*, Amsterdam: Elsevier.

Mayntz, R. *et al.* (1978) *Vollzugsprobleme der Umweltpolitik*, Stuttgart: Kohlhammer.

Scharpf, F.W. (1991) 'Entwicklungslinien des bundesdeutschen Föderalismus', in B. Blanke and H. Wollmann (eds), *Die alte Bundesrepublik. Kontinuität und Wandel*, Opladen: Westdeutscher Verlag.

Scharpf, F.W. *et al.* (1976) *Politikverflechtung: Theorie und Empire des kooperativen Föderalismus in der Bundesrepublik*, Kronberg: Athenäum.

Schatz, H. (1973) 'Auf der Suche nach neuen Problemlösungsstrategien: Die Entwicklung der politischen Planung auf Bundesebene', in R. Mayntz and F.W. Scharpf (eds), *Planungsorganisation*, Munich: Pieper.

Seibel, W. (1992) *Task Reform: Privatization, Deregulation, Debureaucratization, Third Sector Development*, Konstanz: unpublished research report.

Siedentopf, H. (ed.) (1976) *Regierungspolitik und Koordination*, Berlin: Duncker & Humblot.

Siedentopf, H. (1979) 'Abschied von der Dienstrechtsreform?', *Die Verwaltung*, **12**, 457–78.

Siedentopf, H. (1985) 'Führungsfunktionen auf Zeit in der staatlichen Verwaltung', *Die Öffentliche Verwaltung*, **38**, 1033–42.

Thieme, W. and G. Prillwitz (1981) *Durchführung und Ergebnisse der kommunalen Gebietsreform*, Baden-Baden: Nomos Verlagsgesellschaft.

3   Privatizing the Federal Postal and Telecommunications Services[1]

Susanne K. Schmidt

Introduction

Efforts to accommodate international change in the national legal framework for telecommunications have been central to the reform of the German Federal Administration for Posts and Telecommunications. Traditional comprehensive monopolies have been difficult to sustain in the face of rapid technical and economic change. The necessary introduction of market forces has required a comprehensive organizational reform of administrative structures. In Germany, the first reform of the Deutsche Bundespost (DBP), aimed at partial liberalization, came into force in 1989. Only three years later, in 1992, political pressure for further reform intensified, aimed at corporatization and, ultimately, privatization in terms of organization and service provision. This shift was to be accompanied by a reduction in the scope for political control. These efforts culminated in the adoption of a second reform package in 1994.

As a consequence of the international telecommunications network, national policies in the telecommunications sector are subject to international pressures to an unusually large extent. Relatively simple technical options, such as the possibility of routing telecommunications traffic through the low-cost networks of other countries, exert significant pressure on national policy makers to take action. The creation of favourable domestic conditions for cheap and technologically advanced telecommunications in some countries necessarily affects the status quo in others, as they participate in an international network. Moreover, if growth forecasts are to be believed, the telecommunications sector is soon to enjoy an economic importance equal to that of the automobile industry. Together with the high rate of technical and market change, national policy reactions become all the more important. Telecommunications policy thus provides a striking example of the growing international interdependence or embeddedness of domestic policies as a consequence of international trade and economic linkages, with the resultant constraints on national sovereignty (Kohler-Koch, 1991; Scharpf, 1993; Hollingsworth and Streeck, 1994).

The activities of the Commission of the European Communities in the area of telecommunications policy, commencing with the publication of the Green Paper in 1987, added to the external pressure for national reform. By redefining the existing state administrations as public enterprises, the Commission has successfully assumed political responsibility for the sector (Schneider and Werle, 1990). The policy pursued by the EC has at least in part been codetermined by German politicians, so that the distinction between external and domestic influences is blurred. Certainly, national reform of the telecommunications sector is not exclusively a reaction to external developments. The initiation of reform was also promoted by the domestic ideological shift towards neo-liberalism in the 1980s and a corresponding desire 'to roll back the state' (Lehmbruch *et al.*, 1988).

Seen from a comparative perspective, it is not so much the fact that reforms have occurred that merits comment, but the manner in which the implications of international interdependence have permeated the national policy making process. In sum, owing to the character of the international network, telecommunications may be particularly well suited to analysis of the way pressures resulting from the international environment are translated into national administrative reforms (Goetz, 1993). The German case is also an interesting example in its own right, as the German conditions for policy making, with the ever-present dangers of 'joint-decision traps' (Scharpf, 1988), are generally considered unfavourable for sweeping organizational and policy change.

The Institutionalized Stability of the Bundespost

The single most important determinant of posts and telecommunications policy has been its inclusion in Article 87 of the Basic Law. In its original version, Article 87 defined posts and telecommunications as one of the few direct Federal administrations, different from the predominant constitutional pattern which favours administration by the Länder. This provision meant that posts and telecommunications were part of the public service administration (*Leistungsverwaltung*); state provision in this sector was, thus, constitutionally determined, with an emphasis on political rather than economic objectives. In addition, according to Article 73 of the Basic Law, posts and telecommunications were to be subject to exclusive Federal legislation. However, according to Article 80 II, ordinances specifying conditions and tariffs for the use of posts and telecommunications required the consent of the Bundesrat, which meant that the federal principle was not bypassed altogether. Since amendments to the Basic Law require a two-thirds majority in both the Bundestag and the Bundesrat, Article 87 for a long time provided a decisive source of stability, ruling out both corporatization and privatization (Plagemann and Bachmann, 1987).

For much of the history of the Federal Republic, posts and telecommunications have been administered by a separate ministerial department, the Federal Ministry for Posts and Telecommunications (BMPT), which combined – until the reform of 1989 – the exercise of sovereign state powers (*hoheitliche Aufgaben*), political supervision, regulatory authority and operational responsibility. The Bundespost was constituted as a public authority subordinate to the BMPT, and was organized hierarchically and territorially into 21 regional authorities (*Oberpostdirektionen*), each responsible for the post offices in its area (Meckel and Kronthaler, 1967). The Länder did not share administrative responsibility. As a result, the Federal government formally enjoyed a comparatively high degree of autonomy in telecommunications decision making, in contrast to most other domestic policy domains in which joint Federal–Länder policy making is common.

In addition to constitutional safeguards, the Bundespost's position was also strengthened by the fact that it operated under the institution of a special fund (*Sondervermögen*), which made the DBP independent of annual Federal budget resolutions. This provision dated back to the 1920s, as did other major legal provisions affecting the Bundespost, which likewise remained largely unaltered until the 1989 reform. These provisions concerned, for instance, the DBP's extensive monopoly rights and the establishment of the Postal Administration Council. The latter, reconstituted in 1953, was a corporatist body comprising representatives of the Länder, trade unions, manufacturers, users and peak industry associations, and enjoyed consultation and control rights covering most aspects of the Bundespost's operations. Other relevant actors in the field were the main equipment suppliers, which entertained close informal relations with the Bundespost for network construction and maintenance, as the DBP did not possess its own manufacturing facilities. Another pivotal actor in its own right was the postal workers' union (*Deutsche Postgewerkschaft* – DPG) which represented about 75 per cent of the Bundespost's staff.

By international standards, the Bundespost enjoyed a high degree of autonomy and continuity.[2] This position was supported by a relatively good performance record and a positive public image. However, pressures to change the status quo intensified from the early 1970s onwards. The Free Democratic Party (FDP), the Federal Economics Ministry, the Monopoly Commission and various private-sector interests were all arguing for greater private-sector participation in telecommunications, primarily to prevent the Bundespost from extending its monopoly rights in parallel with the new technical possibilities that opened up through the growing convergence with computing. When the Christian Democratic–Liberal (CDU/CSU–FDP) coalition took office in 1982, postal and telecommunications reform had a relatively low priority on the agenda of the incoming government. In 1985, an expert commission, the so-called *Witte Kommission*, was set up, which comprised members from the different political parties, the trade unions, users' and peak industry associations. Its remit was to study the possibilities for the reform of telecommunications; other activities of the DBP were not included in the commission's brief. The mandate of the *Witte Kommission* was also explicitly confined to examining changes within the limits circumscribed by Article 87 of the Basic Law. Despite the considerable formal policy autonomy of the Federal government, which at the time could also count on a majority in the Bundesrat, the government's approach was consensus-oriented. The setting up of expert commissions is a typical feature of German policy making in 'the search for a rationalist consensus' (Dyson, 1982) and also an effective means of deferring decisions.

The strength of legal, institutional and political factors underlying the status quo (see Webber, 1986) made it imperative to search for a solid basis for reform if any significant change was to be achieved. The failed attempt in the early 1970s to reform the Bundespost (Werle, 1990: 154–60) had demonstrated its capacity to resist change. Any reform initiative was bound to be highly voter-sensitive. The strongly unionized workforce could not be ignored, so that a reform effort was likely to rely on a neo-corporatist policy making approach (Czada, 1988). Moreover, the ideological basis for reform in the Federal coalition government was ambiguous. Neo-liberal ideologies, in general, were much less strongly endorsed in Germany than in the UK and the USA (Lehmbruch *et al.*, 1988). The CDU/CSU, in particular, also embraced many traditional conservative values and, most importantly, needed to take account of the divergent interests of the Länder in which it governed. Amongst the Länder, concerns for infrastructural provision at least partly overshadowed the interest in reform. This was especially true for the CSU, the CDU's Bavarian sister-party.

It is not necessary here to detail all the steps leading up to the 1989 reform package, but it may be useful to give a brief indication of the major positions taken. These positions did not sufficiently converge to produce a universally shared reform model in the preparation of the 1989 reform, and the differences again gained importance during the second reform process.

Schneider and Werle (1991: 125–6) distinguish four main groups in the policy network. The first group consisted of the Social Democrats (SPD), the Greens and the trade unions, which either considered the reform too far-reaching or opposed it entirely, arguing that liberalization would occur at the expense of the general public and DBP staff. Second, there were the strong proponents of reform, including the FDP, large users and peak business associations, which saw the 1989 reform as a first step towards comprehensive liberalization and eventual privatization. The third group was made up of what could be called 'stipulators', including the Länder, which agreed on the need for reform in principle, but demanded specific modifications. Finally, there were those broadly in favour of reform, including the CDU/CSU, the Bundespost itself, the EC Commission and the large manufacturers.

On the basis of this constellation, the reform debate had ideological overtones and drew on the general set of arguments on deregulation and privatization which were then prevalent in the Federal Republic (see Vogelsang, 1988). Concerns about the demise of the welfare state, endangered public responsibility and infrastructural duties were often directly linked to the provisions of Article 87 of the Basic Law, which constituted an effective obstacle to primarily profit-oriented supply. These arguments were contrasted with the principle of subsidiarity of state action which, so the proponents of reform suggested, needed to be reaffirmed in the face of changed technical and economic circumstances. Finally, those broadly in favour of reform saw it as a viable compromise between the extension of private-sector activity and the recognition of public responsibilities.

The 1989 Reform

The final 1989 reform package, contained in the Postal Constitution Act (*Poststrukturgesetz*),[3] came into force on 1 July 1989 and combined a new approach to the regulation of telecommunications with a fundamental reorganization of the Bundespost. In telecommunications, the principle of *Ordnungspolitik* changed from the general monopoly of the DBP to competition and private-sector market provision; where the DBP would continue to enjoy a monopoly, this would be regarded as the exception to the rule. Nevertheless, by international comparison, the reform outcome was moderate, with continued monopoly rights for the stationary network and the telephony service as compensation for the DBP's obligation to meet public-service obligations and infrastructural requirements. All other services and the entire terminal equipment market were now open to competitors. With the exception of the possibility of stipulating certain services which the

DBP would be legally required to provide, the 1989 reform was in line with the liberalization measures proposed in the EC Commission's Green Paper on telecommunications (CEC, 1987).

The organizational restructuring of the DBP provided the basis for limited liberalization, while it recognized the constraints imposed by the Bundespost's status as a Federal administration. In line with EC policy, the regulatory authority, the BMPT, was separated from the operational side, the DBP. It was hoped that this would enable the DBP to operate more like a private company, despite its continuing status as an administrative body. As a second fundamental change, the operation of the DBP was split into three separate branches: postal services, telecommunications and banking. This should permit more independent management and the control of financial transactions and cross-subsidies between the three branches. Each branch was to have its own supervisory board and management board, with the latter acting as the legal representative of the enterprise and being responsible for its operation according to market principles. Thus, although telecommunications had been the focus of the reform, both the postal service and banking also received a new organizational structure. The parallel restructuring offered the potential to reduce administrative inflexibilities that had hampered the competitiveness of the DBP in some areas, including private parcel deliveries, and caused financial losses. Also the organizational separation of the three enterprises opened the possibility of freeing the telecommunications branch from the burden of cross-subsidizing other loss-making activities.

The implementation of these key provisions of the 1989 administrative reform was by no means straightforward, as the structure of an enterprise within the formal status of an administrative authority was not a clear-cut legal construct (Königshofen, 1992). The enterprises were given a partially autonomous status to be able to act independently in commercial matters, while the unity of the Bundespost was safeguarded and the ultimate responsibility of the BMPT as the formal head of the Federal postal and telecommunications administration was retained. The position of the BMPT was particularly ambiguous. Regulatory responsibilities and sovereign rights in telecommunications, including, for example, type approval, licensing, international representation and standardization, were only part of the ministry's task. Added to this was the overall legal and political responsibility of the minister for the operation of the enterprises. Finally, the BMPT was accountable as the owner, representing the Federal Republic's interests in DBP Telekom as a profitable company, a point which only began to be critically discussed after the reform had been enacted (Broß, 1992: 52).

Figure 3.1 summarizes the organizational model following the 1989 reform. Apart from the BMPT, other ministries that had traditionally been involved in posts and telecommunications continued to play a role. The finance minister had a claim to a levy of 10 per cent on turnover until the end of 1993, after which the levy was to be progressively reduced, to bring it in line with ordinary business taxation by 1996. Quite late in the reform process, two additional bodies were added to the already complex administrative structure in an attempt to broaden the political and social consensus on the reform. The first of these was the common board of directors of the DBP, which was set up to meet the SPD's demands and counter the persistent opposition of the postal union. Its task was to assume responsibility for specific issues affecting industrial relations and staff matters (Grande, 1989: 227, 235). Second, an Infrastructure Council was established, comprising members of the Bundestag and the Bundesrat. This was to compensate the Länder for their loss of influence as a result of the abolition of the former Postal Administration Council. The Infrastructure Council should participate in BMPT decisions with infrastructural implications, for instance the setting of monopoly tariffs and the stipulation of mandatory services.

Although it was not a direct response to new supranational requirements, the outcome of the German reform process was, in substance and effect, an adaptation to the EC Commission's policy that had taken shape since the

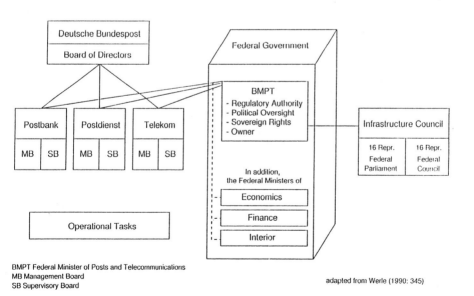

BMPT Federal Minister of Posts and Telecommunications
MB Management Board
SB Supervisory Board

adapted from Werle (1990: 345)

Figure 3.1

mid-1980s. Its details reflected the need to reconcile supranational pressures with domestic institutional conditions and interest constellations. The complicated organizational structure which resulted from the domestic compromise meant that it was difficult to predict how effective the reform would turn out to be. But it was clear that under the remaining restrictions of a Federal administration the Bundespost enterprises could not operate as flexibly as private corporations.

Unification and Accumulating Pressures for Reform[4]

Parallel to the implementation of the new organizational structures, events in East Germany began to unfold that radically challenged the status quo. Before the new management of Telekom assumed control on 1 January 1990, discussions had already begun on the modernization of the East German network. After the Berlin Wall came down in November 1989, the lack of adequate inter-German connections and the unsatisfactory technical state of the eastern network proved a major bottleneck for the exploitation of new business opportunities. Many parts of the eastern network dated from the inter-war period. Coupled with the poor technical state was a low penetration rate and a large backlog of orders for telephone connections.

The scale of the new responsibilities for Telekom soon became apparent. By May 1990, the East German ministry had been reorganized along the lines of its western counterpart, so that the two administrations could merge in October 1990, on the day after unification took effect. It was on this basis that Telekom presented its infrastructural investment programme, 'Telekom 2000', involving capital expenditure of some DM55bn, with which the eastern network was to be upgraded to western standards by 1997 (Ricke, 1991).[5] Thus obligations were imposed on Telekom that were very different from those that had motivated the 1989 reform. While the 1989 measures had aimed to introduce more market forces into telecommunications to prepare Telekom to compete with private providers in innovative market segments, unification meant that basic infrastructure investment now became the dominant task.[6] Investment in eastern modernization was not, however, solely politically motivated; it also corresponded to the operational interests of Telekom since it promised future profits. Inactivity would have jeopardized the new post-1989 status quo, and foreign competitors, for instance AT&T, were only too ready to become involved in the modernization of the eastern network.

As the parameters of Telekom's operation were now drastically altered, the fragile consensus which had made possible the 1989 reform began to become unstable. The postal union argued that the heavy infrastructural burden was reason enough to rethink the 1989 liberalization measures so as not to undermine the strength of Telekom. The minister for posts and telecommunications was later cited as saying that, in view of the new situation created by unification, the 1989 reform bill would probably not have been passed if it had come six months later (CWI, 1993a). By contrast, those in favour of more far-reaching liberalization responded by criticizing Telekom for delays in network modernization, while business associations and large users soon demanded the right to private network build-up. In April 1991, the Monopoly Commission issued a special statement in which it argued for the partial privatization of networks (Monopolkommission, 1991).

There were further repercussions of unification that prompted new reform considerations. In flagrant disregard of the stated intentions of the 1989 reform act to free telecommunications operations from daily political interference, the Federal finance minister announced in early 1991 that he would be raising the levy on the DBP by an additional DM5bn per annum for the years 1991 to 1994. This was a strong assault, announced without prior consultation of the BMPT, and it coincided with a rapid decrease in Telekom's equity ratio below the required 33 per cent to 27 per cent in 1991, and 24 per cent in 1992. This development would require Telekom to seek additional capital from the finance minister. In view of the existing levy on turnover of 10 per cent, which was higher than normal business taxes, and the infrastructural commitments in the new Länder, where Telekom did not receive the Federal investment subsidies to which private enterprise was entitled, the finance minister's request was clearly unacceptable to Telekom. In subsequent talks between the BMPT and the finance minister, the extra levy was considerably reduced, not least because a possible rise in telephone tariffs shortly before an important election in Rhineland–Palatinate was judged to be politically too sensitive. Nevertheless, in the eyes of Telekom, which up to then had not actively pressed for a change in its organizational status, the finance minister's request demonstrated that only full corporatization would afford an effective safeguard against political interference. Furthermore, both the SPD and the postal union became increasingly concerned that further reform might be necessary to secure the long-term future of the DBP (Bock, 1992) and they began to consider possible changes to Article 87 of the Basic Law.

Finally, key aspects of the organizational framework created in 1989 were proving unsatisfactory. A conflict in 1991 over the tariffs for leased lines to be paid by Mannesmann, the private digital mobile network operator, highlighted the ambiguous role of the BMPT and underlined the complicated demarcation of authority in general. First, the BMPT was responsible for arbitrating in the conflict between Telekom and Mannesmann as the independent regulator. Second, the minister represented the ownership interests and was, therefore, required to support the vital interests of Telekom. As the responsible minister, he had to promote the overall political aims of the Federal government, and here the tariffs were relevant in demonstrating the continued support for liberalization. At the same time, outside the field of telecommunications, the relationship between the postal services and the banking service was emerging as a major problem. The main bone of contention were the payments the bank had to make to the postal service for the joint use of office space. The postal service and the bank for a long time failed to reach agreement on the level of the charges, which raised infrastructural concerns, as the dense network of post offices was operating at a loss. In 1992, the BMPT had to intervene to force a settlement. In its aftermath, the banking branch developed a plan under which it would concentrate its services in the major post offices, a clear signal of its intention to withdraw support in the longer term.

Three domestic factors thus combined to put a second reform on the political agenda: the infrastructural burdens created by unification; the attempt to exploit telecommunications profits to support the Federal budget; and problems in the implementation of the 1989 reform framework.[7] In particular, Telekom's declining equity ratio created effective pressure for change, more than any general debate on the advantages and disadvantages of public versus private-sector responsibility for infrastructure investment could have done. Reform was no longer merely seen to promote private-sector opportunities, but became necessary as a defensive measure to protect the long-term viability of Telekom. Reform pressure was further increased by the conflict between the postal and the banking services, which threatened the viability of the dense network of post offices and highlighted the possible employment effects of rationalization.

These domestic pressures on the status quo had a major influence on the national policy process. Especially during the initiation stages of the second reform package, domestic considerations clearly overshadowed the more important, but less immediately apparent, changing international context of the German telecommunications regime. In the EC, liberalization measures progressed and led to the adoption of a resolution of the Council of Ministers to liberalize voice telephony by 1998 (Council, 1993). Without monopoly profits from the telephone business, the pursuit of public policy objectives through public provisions would lose its financial basis. In addition, corporate activities have become rapidly internationalized, replacing the former clearly segmented structure of exclusively nationally oriented post, telephone and telegraph administrations (PTTs). The disadvantages public administrations faced in international competition were exemplified when the US carrier MCI chose British Telecom as its European partner, despite earlier negotiations with Telekom and France Télécom. In addition to general administrative inflexibilities, Telekom had its financial resources largely tied to infrastructure investment, a fact which further widened the gap between itself and private operators. Moreover, within the legal framework of a Federal administration, international activities of a purely commercial kind were problematic, especially if they were not exclusively managed by a subsidiary under private law.[8] Telekom was, therefore, forced to concentrate on infrastructure development activities.

The foreseeable end of monopoly profits to compensate for public policy obligations, the administrative constraints associated with public law industrial relations, lower productivity, a low equity ratio and restrictions on international activities all pointed to the growing vulnerability of Telekom. German politicians increasingly feared that, without reform, Telekom would gradually decline to the level of an operator of only regional significance. Moreover, German manufacturing industry hoped that increasing international activities on the part of the German operator would improve its access to foreign markets. This added industrial policy interests in support of reform – in sharp contrast to the UK experience, where equipment manufacturers were among the losers from privatization.

The Second Reform: Actors and Procedures

As was argued above, the new reform discussions on the Bundespost were determined by a combination of domestic and international factors. Of crucial importance was the growing perception that a reform was needed to secure the long-term future of the DBP. Increasingly, key actors came to believe that only corporatization and, eventually, privatization could secure sufficient organizational flexibility and capital to make Telekom internationally competitive. It was against this background that the process of amending the Basic Law was ventured into. This initiative could only succeed if a cross-party two-thirds majority in favour of reform could be secured in both the Bundestag and the Bundesrat.

The necessity of a constitutional amendment meant that the legislative reform process changed. Whereas the 1989 reform act required, above all, the coordination of the responsible ministries and their respective interest-group clienteles (Mayntz and Scharpf, 1975), a constitutional amendment puts a premium on consensus amongst the main parliamentary parties. In addition, the Länder assume greater importance, because they have a decisive influence on the outcome of any amending legislation through their representation in the Bundesrat. Thus the Länder moved from a previously fairly marginal role in posts and telecommunications policy making to centre stage. Arguably, the special circumstances of reform policy making which required a constitutional amendment implied both specific opportunities and new constraints, since the circle of relevant policy actors was significantly altered. In particular, compared to the 1989 reform, the different procedures and decision rules of a constitutional amendment added veto power, but reduced the number of veto players.

After earlier sporadic talks between the Federal government and the opposition, and a period during which the CDU/CSU and the SPD internally defined their views on the necessary reform measures, a commission for inter-party negotiations between the Federal coalition and the SPD was set up in the summer of 1992. To prepare the ground for the necessary changes in the DBP's constitutional status, the commission was charged with achieving consensus on the entire reform package, including both constitutional legislation and the raft of ordinary legislation by which it would need to be accompanied. It was initially hoped that the reform measures could be finalized by the following year.

Although they agreed on the need for reform, the political parties held very different views regarding the degree to which posts and telecommunications should remain committed to public policy objectives. These differences found their initial expression in the preferred organizational designs that were to replace the administrative model. The coalition favoured the transformation of the three enterprises into joint-stock companies. By contrast, the SPD wanted to give the three Bundespost branches the status of statutory bodies under public law (*Anstalten des öffentlichen Rechts*), an institutional status which is used, for example, for public savings banks and the banks of the Länder. In contrast to a joint-stock company, which prohibits direct political control to safeguard the interests of the shareholders, a statutory body would have made it easier to reconcile general public policy objectives and infrastructural obligations with private market activities (Püttner, 1985: 61). Public policy objectives could be formally determined, while some of the constraints under which a public administration operates would be removed, including restrictions on employment and international activities. Private capital could also be raised through participating certificates without voting rights.

From the start of the reform discussions, the SPD was under strong pressure from the postal union (*Deutsche Postgewerkschaft* – DPG), from which only parts of the party were prepared to distance themselves. The DPG enjoyed the advantages of a powerful trade union and it resolutely opposed the transformation of DBP enterprises into joint-stock companies and subsequent privatization. However, it did acknowledge the need for reform and had already agreed with the SPD on the creation of statutory bodies under public law as the goal of the inter-party negotiations. Having to contend with the vocal and persistent opposition of the DPG, the Social

Democrats lacked a uniform position throughout the inter-party discussions. While the SPD was committed to accommodating the wishes of the trade unions, some Social Democrats repeatedly spoke out in support of the creation of joint-stock companies (see, for example, Börnsen, 1992). Against this background, an inter-party agreement appeared imminent on a number of occasions, but the SPD's close relationship with the trade union made it a demanding and vacillating negotiator, ready to follow up every agreement with a list of contentious points. The future of infrastructure obligations, industrial relations and the details of organizational transformation as well as the precise privatization procedure were all issues to be raised. Moreover, the SPD's close cooperation with the Federal government on several other legislative reforms, including health reform, nursing insurance and political asylum, meant that the party felt under growing pressure to demonstrate a more distinct profile, as numerous elections loomed in 1994.

For its part, the ruling coalition started the negotiations with a less detailed position, which was mainly focused on its chief aim of transforming the three DBP branches into joint-stock companies so that posts and telecommunications would eventually become a normal private sector economic activity, governed by the relevant general legislation. The negotiation position of the CDU/CSU was, however, complicated by the resignation, at the end of 1992, of its long-standing minister for posts and telecommunications, Christian Schwarz-Schilling. Although the immediate trigger of Schwarz-Schilling's resignation was his disenchantment with the government's attitude towards the war in the former Yugoslavia, it was widely thought that his decision was also influenced by what he perceived as a lack of support from the Chancellor for the new reform attempt. His successor, Wolfgang Bötsch, from the CSU, was seen as less knowledgeable in the field of posts and telecommunications. As for the FDP, it maintained a low profile during the inter-party negotiations and only occasionally underlined its demand that organizational change be accompanied by rapid liberalization. However, it failed to put any weight behind this demand, and was effectively sidelined during the inter-party talks between the two main parliamentary parties. Overall, amongst the negotiating parties, the SPD was in a relatively strong position. During the inter-party discussions, its link with the postal union provided the latter with the most consistent veto position of any external interest group. This threatened the success of the inter-party talks and the reform until the very end. Other major constraints on the negotiations should not be overlooked, however. In particular, because capital shortages played such an important role as a reform catalyst, any compromise regarding telecommunications activities had to be attractive to private capital. Consequently, the financial markets imposed an independent restriction on political preferences.[9]

To understand the course of the negotiations, it is also useful to consider the 'default condition' (Ostrom, 1986), that is the consequences of non-agreement. The default condition is particularly interesting here since, as was argued earlier, the reform process was to a considerable extent a defensive measure. The status quo was under significant external international pressure, combined with domestic difficulties, notably the declining equity ratio. The more time elapsed, the more the financial situation worsened and international commercial opportunities decreased, a fact which added an element of urgency to the negotiations. This was made explicit by Minister Schwarz-Schilling at the end of 1992: without reform, Telekom would have to raise more than DM10bn between the years 1995 and 2000 to be able to service its debts, which were estimated at DM100bn (CWI, 1993b), and cut investment by DM7.5bn, with possibly disastrous consequences for the German economy (FAZ, 1992). Seen from this angle, the promoters of joint-stock companies had an incentive to accede to SPD and trade union demands in order to expedite the privatization process. Yet the default condition did not exclusively favour one side. The SPD and the DPG were under pressure, too, because of the discretionary scope in the existing legal framework. First, there were the significant statutory possibilities of the BMPT, which allowed the minister to license private operators of posts and telecommunications. Second, as early as 1992, Telekom had announced that it would soon have to regroup its competitive and profitable operations into private law subsidiaries, in order to evade many of the public law restrictions under which it operated. The establishment of such subsidiaries would require a decision by the supervisory council and the authorization of the BMPT. Although far from optimal compared to a 'real' reform, this option gave Telekom some independence from the political process. As far as the DPG was concerned, any further fragmentation of the Bundespost could only weaken its influence, since it would cease to be the unchallenged partner in pay negotiations. As for the SPD, any regrouping of the expanding and profitable activities implied that, in central areas of infrastructural concern, the SPD's political influence would be limited, regardless of the outcome of the reform talks.

The Negotiations on Privatization

During the summer of 1992, the transformation of the three enterprises into joint-stock companies emerged as the most likely reform compromise, in line with the coalition proposal. As a concession to the SPD, there was also to be a public law statutory body which would act as a holding organization for the three companies, but in a way this merely shifted the conflict, since the controversy surrounding the design of the holding organization and its competences mirrored the concern for continued public-sector involvement which had initially led the SPD to argue for the statutory status as public law bodies of the three enterprises. Consequently, the conflict over the future organizational structure of Telekom occupied a considerable amount of time.

A compromise on the general degree of public-sector responsibilities and political involvement was not all that was required, as the change in status from a Federal administration to the private sector entailed considerable difficulties. For instance, at the time of this first inter-party rapprochement, the following issues were raised by the SPD: the precise authority of the holding organization; the means to improve cooperation between postal service and banking which could not simply be merged (owing to EC directives); the protection of the rights of staff; the contentious issue of staff codetermination; and difficult questions regarding retrospective pension contributions. Moreover, the precise procedure for privatization had still to be agreed. In particular, the SPD wanted the proceeds from the sell-off to be used to improve Telekom's equity ratio instead of allowing them go to the Federal budget.

While details of privatization and organizational restructuring were at the centre of the inter-party negotiations, the future shape of telecommunications regulation had a low profile. For a long time, the question of how long a privatized Telekom would continue to enjoy monopoly rights remained unresolved. The BMPT argued that liberalization of all market segments would be a necessary consequence of privatization (Broß, 1992: 60); by contrast, the SPD regarded organizational and regulatory reform as two separate issues, and favoured the continuation of Telekom's monopoly to secure a financial basis to meet its infrastructural obligations.

At the end of 1992, benchmark positions were agreed between the parties, which built on the earlier compromise and included the changing of the three enterprises into joint-stock companies under the roof of a statutory public law body for property administration. Also the extension of monopoly rights for at least five years was included in the terms. Nevertheless, one of the SPD delegates on the inter-party committee withdrew from these negotiated positions and insisted again on the creation of statutory bodies under public law for each of the three enterprises. The chances for reform increased significantly when the economics ministers of the Länder endorsed the benchmark positions. This was important not only with a view to the necessary two-thirds majority in the Bundesrat, but also because it was the Länder that were most interested in the continued infrastructural obligations which were of such concern to the SPD. To add steel to the SPD's somewhat unsteady support of the benchmarks, Schwarz-Schilling, in one of his last acts as minister, repeated his threat to approve the establishment of a private law operating company for international activities, in which not only parts of Telekom but also private German companies could participate, 'to the detriment of Telekom and its employees' (FAZ, 1992b). The minister planned to prepare a proposal early in 1993, to be implemented by the end of the year, should the SPD not stick by the benchmark positions. The SPD repeatedly tried to counter with the threat that it would not cooperate in the reform if the status quo was changed before the inter-party negotiations were concluded, but this warning had only a limited effect. Telekom regrouped certain activities, for instance all of its mobile telephony operations, where its administrative status hampered competitiveness with the private digital mobile-network operators.

Thus the chances for reform kept rising and falling, a reflection of the changeable position of the SPD and the determined opposition of the postal union, which continued to hold out against joint-stock companies. Disagreement in the SPD was exemplified when two SPD-governed Länder re-emphasized their support for a quick reform, in the hope that both the new Federal minister and the postal union would be more flexible, with the latter giving up its opposition to a private law organization (FAZ, 1993). At the same time, some members of the parliamentary group repeatedly stressed their support for the trade union's position.

At the end of January 1993, Wolfgang Bötsch was appointed as new Federal minister for posts and telecommunications and, in the inter-party negotiating commission, two delegates from the SPD, who had taken conflicting positions, were replaced. A new inter-party agreement was reached in May 1993, and it appeared that, compared to his predecessor, the new minister was more conciliatory in his approach, intent on securing the overall reform design while being flexible on specific issues. But whereas the coalition's parliamentary parties endorsed the agreement in June 1993, the SPD parliamentary group merely agreed to take notice of the compromise, even though the agreement accommodated many of the SPD's concerns. At the same time, the inter-party agreement was also criticized in the opposite camp. Both the Chamber of German Industry and Commerce and the Federation of German Industry rejected the compromise on the grounds that it would not be marketable on the stock exchange, since it left in place too many opportunities for political control and interference.

Following the agreement reached in the summer of 1993, a further crisis was precipitated when a draft reform law proposal was leaked from the BMPT, which seemed to solve the hitherto largely ignored liberalization issue in a strictly market-oriented fashion that went far beyond anything agreed during the inter-party negotiations. In order not to endanger the political reform compromise, Minister Bötsch distanced himself from the proposal by arguing that it did not have his approval; this was taken as an indication that he had at least partly lost his grip on his ministry. The position of the SPD also remained precarious and led to repeated postponements of a vote by the parliamentary party on the inter-party agreement. By the end of 1993, the questions of whether privatization revenue could be used for an equity ratio improvement and of who would pay the pensions of Bundespost civil servants (an amount now estimated to total approximately DM100bn), were still unsolved. Bötsch had to take some blame for the slow pace of the reform process (HB, 1993) and, by now, the coming year's spate of elections at the Federal and Länder levels was further increasing the pressure for reform.

In January 1994, the previously neglected issue concerning the scope of liberalization threatened to derail the reform for a second time, as the FDP insisted that the telephone monopoly be ended by December 1997, a measure which the SPD seriously opposed. However, a compromise was achieved whereby the relevant parts of the law would only remain in force until that date, so that a final decision was effectively postponed. By the beginning of February, once the negotiating political parties had agreed in principle to the framework, the draft laws could finally be submitted to Parliament for a first reading (BT-Drucksache 12/6717; 12/6718). The draft bills still left many issues unresolved, including the equity ratio improvement and the open pension entitlements. As far as the latter were concerned, a decision had to be taken on who would eventually pay the non-contributory pensions of the civil servants who would remain employed in the three joint-stock companies. The total civil servant pension entitlements that had accrued before corporatization were estimated at DM60bn for the postal service, DM36bn for Telekom and DM4bn for the postal bank; this compared to a total capitalization of DM10bn, DM40bn and DM4bn, respectively (FAZ, 1994a). Moreover, the postal union continued to oppose corporatization, and the difficulties for the SPD in voting against the wishes of the trade union shortly before the next general elections persisted. Consequently, the SPD continued to raise demands, while the Länder also pushed for more rights.

In May 1994, while the numerous open points were gradually settled under severe time constraints, the postal union organized a strike to force the start of negotiations for a collective agreement on the future pay scale and social benefits for the 670 000 Bundespost staff and the status of the work councils following corporatization. The SPD made the settlement of the agreement a precondition for its parliamentary approval, which left the adoption of a final reform package uncertain and strengthened the bargaining power of the trade union. As a strong opponent of corporatization and privatization, the postal union only stood to gain from a strike that could ultimately jeopardize the whole reform. The union's determination was enhanced by the uncertainty which it faced in regard to its own long-term future. After corporatization, the three companies might sooner or later choose another trade union as a negotiation partner, a development which the DPG would not be able to prevent.[10] Even though negotiations started, the DPG continued the strike in order to keep up the pressure. After 30 days of strikes, an agreement was signed which secured the existing pay scale and social entitlements for the following two years, and guaranteed certain specific benefits, such as subsidized housing, on a long-term basis.

The reluctance of the SPD to take a stand against the trade union thus succeeded in extracting important concessions, despite the continued assertions of the employers and the BMPT that they would not agree to 'a reform at all costs' and despite the possibilities of achieving important changes on the basis of the existing legal framework as part of the default condition. The duration of the negotiations and the desirability of an altered constitutional status, coupled with the need for a two-thirds majority, favoured the SPD and the DPG as veto position holders. Other interest groups, by contrast, had no noticeable impact on the reform. Owing to the difficult details of the organizational reform, market issues never became the focus of attention. Instead, as argued above, their conflictual potential was successfully circumvented with the agreement to limit the validity of the relevant parts of the bill to three years, which would, at least initially, retain the status quo. This solution can be seen as an effective decoupling and sequencing of conflictual reform issues (Simon, 1990). The final bill was adopted by both the Bundestag and the Bundesrat at the last possible date before Parliament went into recess for the summer vacation. The reform package secured organizational change and the necessary constitutional amendments, but effectively postponed liberalization and regulatory issues until a later, third reform attempt.

The New Organizational Model

The final reform bill consisted of the Basic Law amendments, several new laws and numerous amendments to existing ordinary legislation (BT-Drucksache 12/8060; 12/8101). Building on the separation of the three enterprises that was achieved in 1989, each enterprise was to be transformed into a joint-stock company at the beginning of 1995. Telekom was to be the first to be partly privatized through the issuing of new shares on the stock exchange. The profits would be used to improve its equity ratio. The Federation would not trade its shares on the official stock exchange for five years, in order not to interfere with the raising of new share capital. With respect to the postal services, the Länder achieved a constitutional guarantee that, if the Federation planned to give up its majority of shares, this could only be done on the basis of legislation requiring Bundesrat consent; no such measure could be adopted until the year 2000. The reform package also created a public law holding organization which is, however, not meant to interfere with the commercial activities of the three joint-stock companies, and serves primarily as a holding organization for the Federal shares. In addition, it has some coordination and social responsibilities, but its most important function is to act as the negotiation partner for the collective pay and conditions agreements of the three companies.

As far as liberalization and regulatory issues are concerned, the relevant laws will only stay in force until the end of 1997, in accordance with EU policies. The contentious question of liberalization was set aside and no changes were included in the reform package. However, the minister of posts and telecommunications, who retains responsibility for regulation, still possesses the right to license private companies to provide postal and telecommunications services. A new regulatory council replaced the infrastructure council, and through their representation in the regulatory council the Länder could increase their influence on policy making. In addition to their previous rights, the Länder now participate in licensing decisions, in the administration of frequencies and numbering, and in advising the minister on the employment of high-level employees for regulatory matters. The Federal government can, however, overrule their opinion. The Basic Law amendments also included an infrastructural provision to ensure that a sufficient level of postal and telecommunications services would be maintained throughout the country. The details were to be regulated through a Federal law requiring the consent of the Bundesrat.

The issue of pensions was the most pressing aspect of the generally difficult question of how to adjust the existing civil service employment, which included almost half of the Bundespost staff, that is about 300 000 civil servants, to a private law context. As a constitutional amendment formed the basis of the reform, Parliament had considerable freedom to act.[11] Nevertheless, finding a workable solution was not easy. The solution chosen was to bestow the authority of instruction of personnel (*Dienstherrenbefugnis*) on the joint-stock companies, while the Federation would retain overall administrative supervision (*Dienstherrenaufsicht*). All long-term entitlements of civil servants were to be guaranteed. They may, if they choose, volunteer to accept employee status, which is likewise possible for a limited period only. The public law holding organization has been given some rights of arbitration in personnel matters. As for pensions, it was decided that each enterprise would establish a special support fund (which would also cover some liabilities on health insurance), so that these liabilities need not appear on the balance sheets of the companies. Until 1999, each company bears sole responsibility for such payments. After that date, 33 per cent of the salaries of their active civil servants before tax have to be contributed to the funds, the Federation being responsible for the additional claims. In essence, the Federation will cover 60 per cent of the obligations, to be funded from the profit of the sale of shares. This means that the companies themselves are burdened with total claims which are likely to reach approximately DM40bn (FAZ, 1994b).

In sum, the reform bill included a range of specific measures designed to address the difficulties of transforming an administration into joint-stock companies, while simultaneously adapting a national market sector to international pressures. Owing to the serious time constraints on the negotiations, it was not clear at the time of the adoption of the reform package to what extent all details had been satisfactorily covered. The many contingencies make it difficult to assess the overall appropriateness of the reform as a response to national and international pressures. Certain issues, for instance the cooperation between postal services and banking, are set to remain problematic, as is the question of their long-term future in the absence of cross-subsidies from the telecommunications branch. Similarly, it remains to be seen to what extent flexibility in personnel policy has really increased, as industrial relations will continue to be heavily influenced by the former administrative status of the DBP for a long time. Also the impact of the civil service pensions' obligations on the new companies will only become clear over time; certainly, this adds a burden which their private competitors do not have to shoulder.

Conclusion

The 1989 reform constituted an attempt to separate the main operational activities of the Bundespost on an organizational basis, while leaving intact the overall framework established by Article 87 of the Basic Law. The 1989 reform incorporated both political–administrative and economic issues in a relatively complicated organizational structure. In view of the overall organization of the DBP as a Federal administration, which was, as such, not dedicated to the private market but to public activities, many compromises had to be made, resulting in an institutional structure of operational activities that was situated somewhere between the traditional public service obligation and liberalized market activities.

The unexpectedly rapid development of international trade and service competition, together with the infrastructural repercussions of unification, exposed the newly reformed institutional framework to extreme and contradictory requirements that it was not designed to cope with. Thus further pressure for change quickly built up. The financial consequences of unification undermined the operational basis of Telekom and, by implication, of the Bundespost as a whole. In contrast to the first reform, where the form and the extent of the response to technical–economic and international regime changes were at stake, by the early 1990s the status quo had been undermined. This made further reform vital if the long-term viability of the DBP was to be secured.

As a necessary defensive measure, and under the default condition of a rapid deterioration of the status quo, the second reform could secure enough support to make a constitutional amendment possible. Since a change of Article 87 was the only means to regain controlled stability, compared to the alternative of an increasingly fragmented organizational structure, the major pillar upholding the previous institutional stability of the Bundespost became the subject of political negotiation. The need to secure qualified majorities in both the Bundestag and the Bundesrat made agreement between the parliamentary parties imperative. This formal consensus obligation had implications for the decision making procedure and negotiations were restricted to a special inter-party commission. Despite the large qualified majority required and the related veto power accorded to the SPD and the Länder, this change in relevant actors, compared to the 1989 reform, created new opportunities for consensus. As for external actors, only the postal union had a strong bargaining position. Its influence derived from the constraints of a legislative period that was coming to a close, the union's close links with the SPD and its absolute opposition to key elements of the reform. In contrast, other societal actors that supported a constitutional amendment, including the industrial interest groups, were not in a position to press their demands in a way that could have endangered the compromise reached.

The successful restriction of external veto positions was combined with a partial separation of complex reform issues. The contentious aspects of future liberalization and regulation, which were not closely bound up with the necessary constitutional change, were largely ignored and later formally set aside by the imposition of a time restriction on the validity of the relevant laws. Thus, after the unexpectedly rapid obsolescence of the first reform model, the second reform already, in part, anticipated its successor.

For the next reform, the extent to which the incremental reform steps have shifted the interests of the different actors towards a greater degree of liberalization will be crucial. For instance, equipment manufacturers have become interested in increasing the international activities of Telekom as a possible means of gaining access to foreign markets. Accordingly, they may regard an end of the network monopoly as an opportunity to sell more equipment to other network operators. Domestic liberalization may also become a more salient political issue if it is indeed a necessary precondition for Telekom's activities in other liberalized markets.

The reform of posts and telecommunications in Germany is, thus, an incremental and path-dependent process (Werle, 1994). International pressures did not confront a domestic *tabula rasa* that gave way to all external requirements. While Germany's intricate institutional structure offers many advantages (Streeck, 1993), these do not include a high degree of flexibility and responsiveness to outside pressures. For the second postal reform, it was primarily the unexpected event of unification that translated international pressures into a form that corresponded to the domestic policy making process. And while Germany may be ill-equipped to produce an ideal legal framework to steer politically the national response to the international technological race in telecommunications, the significant scope of de facto adjustments must not be underestimated. In fact, even without reform, there were still possibilities for adaptation which reflected the considerable autonomy of Federal policy making in the area of posts and telecommunications. For example, Telekom was able to make a significant investment commitment to the US carrier Sprint despite Article 87 and its status of a public administration – to say nothing of regrouping its mobile services in a private subsidiary which allowed it to catch up with, and even overtake, its competitor, Mannesmann. Likewise, the importance of the powers of the BMPT in awarding licences must not be underestimated, as was shown by the decision to allow RWE, Deutsche Bank and Mannesmann to merge their corporate networks, which may signal the beginning of a second national network operator.

Despite repeated deadlock in inter-party negotiations, the German telecommunications sector has thus adapted continuously to international pressures. This adaptation took place even though the international context tended to be ignored in the domestic reform discussions, which were dominated by national considerations and financial constraints. The fact that privatization might have become necessary as a process of national adaptation to international developments received relatively little attention. It appears that this relative neglect was not only a sign of a lack of attention to the changing environment, but also provided a way of reducing the complexity of the reform issue.

Notes

1   An earlier version of this chapter was presented at a workshop on 'German public-sector reform in the light of the British experience', London School of Economics and Political Science. I would like to thank the organizers and the participants of the workshop and, in particular, the discussant, Vincent Wright, for their helpful comments. I am also indebted to my colleagues Edgar Grande, Philip Manow, Volker Schneider and Raymund Werle. Last but not least, I would like to thank my interview

partners for their time and frankness. The manuscript was submitted in September 1994, and developments are described until that date.

2 See Grande (1989) for a detailed comparison of telecommunications liberalization in the UK and Germany. Werle (1990) provides an account of the development of telecommunications throughout the Federal Republic's history. Scherer (1985) is an older, but very comprehensive treatment of the German law and politics of telecommunications. Jäger (1994) is based on the studies by Grande and Werte but extends the analysis up to December 1993. For a shorter discussion in English, see Humphreys (1992) and, with regard to the 1989 reform only, Schmidt (1991).

3 Bundesgesetzblatt, Part 1, Z 5702 A, No. 37, Bonn 21 July 1989.

4 The following account of the second reform is based principally on newspaper reports and interview data, but see also Jäger (1994). For ease of presentation, only the most relevant reports are cited.

5 See Robischon (1994) for a detailed account of the initial stages of East German network construction and integration with the west.

6 The postal branch was also put under considerable pressure through unification, experiencing a rise in inter-German traffic of some 655 per cent in the first quarter of 1991. But investment here was lower, and the major step towards integration was the introduction of new post codes in July 1993.

7 An initial move for change had already been made by the Federal government in November 1990, partly in response to the rising criticism of Telekom, when a study group was set up by the government to assess the possibilities for the partial privatization of the DBP within the constraints of the Basic Law. This move was predominantly motivated by fiscal considerations and was not pursued further after Telekom's intensified investment in the East (FT, 1990).

8 The legal situation remained somewhat unclear. Although the activities of a Federal administration are inherently tied to the territory of the Federal Republic (with the exception of embassies), Telekom struck a deal with the US carrier Sprint in 1994 while it was still constituted as a Federal administration. The predominant perception was, however, that Telekom's legal status implied a significant constraint on commercial initiative and that private law subsidiaries were only an imperfect substitute for full corporatization (Scherer, 1992; von der Heyden and Werksnies, 1991).

9 A report of the US investment bank Salomon Brothers put the value of Telekom at between DM28bn and DM85bn, depending on the general public policy obligations which it would have to fulfil (DZ, 1992).

10 The DPG has now achieved a cooperative agreement with the IG Metall union, as the competitor for the telecommunications branch, which as such signifies the end of its previous monopoly. With regard to the postal service, the DPG fears that the public service and transport union, ÖTV, will become increasingly important, while, for banking, the HBV trade union is the most likely competitor. In the negotiations with the employers, the DPG has been designated as the partner for pay negotiations for future years.

11 This was achieved through the insertion of a new Article 143b into the Basic Law, which left the general constitutional foundations of the civil service, laid down in Article 33 (4), intact. The model differs from the one chosen for the railways, as the Federation takes on more limited financial obligations and allows the corporatized companies greater freedom of action.

References

Bock, E. (1992) 'Erfahrungen mit dem ordnungspolitischen Modell der Telekommunikation in der Bundesrepublik Deutschland: Vorschläge der Deutschen Postgewerkschaft für eine "Reform der Reform"', in F. Arnold (ed.), *Telekommunikation in Europa: Quo Vadis?* ONLINE '92, 15. Europäische Kongressmesse für Technische Kommunikation, Symposium I-1. I/05, Hamburg: Online.

Börnsen, A. (1992) 'Erfahrungen mit dem ordnungspolitischen Modell der Telekommunikation in der Bundesrepublik Deutschland: Handlungszwang für die Politik?', in F. Arnold (ed.), *Telekommunikation in Europa: Quo Vadis?* ONLINE '92, 15. Europäische Kongressmesse für Technische Kommunikation, Symposium I-1. I/03, Hamburg: Online.

Broß, P. (1992) 'Die bisherige Entwicklung der Telekommunikationsregulierung: Eine Bestandsaufnahme', in B. Bauer (ed.), *Telekommunikationspolitik in Deutschland – Perspektiven für die Zukunft*, Bad Honnef: Wissenschaftliches Institut für Kommunikationsdienste.

BT-Drucksache 12/6717 (1994) *Gesetzentwurf der Fraktionen der CDU/CSU, SPD und FDP-Entwurf eines Gesetzes zur Änderung des Grundgesetzes*, Bonn, 4 February.

BT-Drucksache 12/6718 (1994) *Gesetzentwurf der Fraktionen der CDU/CSU, SPD und FDP-Entwurf eines Gesetzes zur Neuordnung des Postwesens und der Telekommunikation (Postneuordnungsgesetz - PTNeuOG)*, Bonn, 4 February.

BT-Drucksache 12/8060 (1994) *Beschlußempfehlung und Bericht des Ausschusses für Post und Telekommunikation (18. Ausschuß)*, Bonn, 27 June.

BT-Drucksache 12/8101 (1994) *Beschlußempfehlung und Bericht des Rechtsausschusses (8. Ausschuß)*, Bonn, 23 June.

CEC (1987) 'Towards a dynamic European economy. Green Paper on the development of the common market for telecommunications services and equipment (COM(87) 290 final)', reprinted in J.C. Arnbak and M.C. Werner (eds), (1989) *Telecommunications for Europe 1992. The CEC Sources*, Amsterdam: IOS.

CWI (1993a) 'Schwarz-Schilling leaves liberal legacy', *Communications Week International*, 18 January.

CWI (1993b) 'Germany: unity at all costs', *Communications Week International*, 22 March, 1993.

Council (1993) 'Council Resolution of 22 July 1993 on the review of the situation in the telecommunications sector and the need for further development in that market (93/C 213/01)', *Official Journal of the European Communities*, no. C 213/1.

Czada, R. (1988) 'Bestimmungsfaktoren und Genese politischer Gewerkschaftseinbindung' in M.G. Schmidt (ed.), *Staatstätigkeit – International und historisch vergleichende Analysen*, Opladen: Westdeutscher Verlag.

Dyson, K. (1982) 'West Germany: the Search for a Rationalist Consensus', in J.J. Richardson (ed.), *Policy Styles in Western Europe*, London: Allen & Unwin.

DZ (1992) 'Wer bleibt auf der Strecke?', *Die Zeit*, 4 December.

FAZ (1992) 'Postminister droht SPD und Gewerkschaft', *Frankfurter Allgemeine Zeitung*, 10 December.

FAZ (1993) 'SPD-Länder dringen auf eine Einigung über die zweite Postreform', *Frankfurter Allgemeine Zeitung*, 13 January.

FAZ (1994a) 'Die Pensionslasten sind die größte Hürde bei der Postreform', *Frankfurter Allgemeine Zeitung*, 8 March.

FAZ (1994b) 'Postarbeitgeber schlagen neue Gespräche vor', *Frankfurter Allgemeine Zeitung*, 11 June.

FT (1990) 'Bonn May Sell Telecom Stake', *Financial Times*, 21 November.

Goetz, K.H. (1993) *Public Sector Change in Germany and the UK: Differences, Commonalities, Explanations*, manuscript.

Grande, E. (1989) *Vom Monopol zum Wettbewerb? – Die neokonservative Reform der Telekommunikation in Großbritannien und der Bundesrepublik Deutschland*, Wiesbaden: DUV.

HB (1993) 'Schwarzer Peter liegt bei Bötsch', *Handelsblatt*, 12 December.

Heyden, G. von der and S. Werksnies (1991) 'Unternehmensbeteiligungen der Deutschen Bundespost TELEKOM', *Archiv für das Post- und Fernmeldewesen*, **14**, 95–109.

Hollingsworth, J.R. and W. Streeck (1994) 'Countries and sectors: concluding remarks on performance, convergence and competitiveness', in J.R. Hollingsworth, Ph. Schmitter and W. Streeck (eds), *Governing Capitalist Economies*, New York: OUP.

Humphreys, P. (1992) 'The politics of regulatory reform in German telecommunications', in K. Dyson (ed.), *The Politics of German Regulation*, Aldershot: Dartmouth.

Jäger, B. (1994) *'Postreform I und II'. Die gradualistische Telekommunikationspolitik in Deutschland im Lichte der Positiven Theorie staatlicher Regulierung und Deregulierung*, Cologne: Institut für Wirtschaftspolitik.

Kohler-Koch, B. (1991) 'Inselillusion und Interdependenz: Nationales Regieren unter den Bedingungen von "International Governance"', in B. Blanke and H. Wollmann (eds), *Die alte Bundesrepublik – Kontinuität und Wandel*, Leviathan Sonderheft 12, Opladen: Westdeutscher Verlag.

Königshofen, T. (1992) 'Die rechtliche Stellung der Deutschen Bundespost TELEKOM und ihre Einbindung in die öffentliche Verwaltung', in C. Schwarz-Schilling and F. Görts (eds), *Jahrbuch der Deutschen Bundespost 1991*, Erlangen: Georg Heidecker.

Lehmbruch, G., O. Singer, E. Grande and M. Döhler (1988) 'Institutionelle Bedingungen ordnungspolitischen Strategiewechsels im internationalen Vergleich', in M.G. Schmidt (ed.), *Staatstätigkeit-International und historisch vergleichende Analysen*, Opladen: Westdeutscher Verlag.

Mayntz, R. and F.W. Scharpf (1975) *Policy Making in the German Federal Bureaucracy*, Amsterdam: Elsevier.

Meckel, H. and O. Kronthaler (1967) *Das Bundesministerium für das Post- und Fernmeldewesen und die Deutsche Bundespost*, Frankfurt a.M.: Athenäum.

Monopolkommission (1991) *Zur Neuordnung der Telekommunikation, Sondergutachten 20*, Baden-Baden: Nomos Verlagsgesellschaft.

Ostrom, E. (1986) 'An Agenda for the Study of Institutions', *Public Choice*, **48**, 3–35.

Plagemann, J. and U. Bachmann (1987) 'Die verfassungsrechtliche Zulässigkeit einer privatrechtlichen Organisation der Deutschen Bundespost – Die niederländische Lösung als Vorbild?', *Die Öffentliche Verwaltung*, **40**, 807–13.

Püttner, G. (1985) *Die öffentlichen Unternehmen*, Stuttgart: Boorberg.

Ricke, H. (1991) 'Telekom 2000 – Infrastruktur für die fünf neuen Bundesländer', in W. Effelsberg, H.-W. Meuer and G. Mueller (eds), *Kommunikation in verteilten Systemen*, Berlin: Springer.

Robischon, T. (1994) 'Transformation Through Integration: the Unification of German Telecommunications', in J. Summerton (ed.), *Large Technical Systems in Radical Reconfiguration*, Boulder: Westview.

Scharpf, F.W. (1988) 'The Joint-Decision Trap: Lessons from German Federalism and European Integration', *Public Administration*, **66**, 239–78.

Scharpf, F.W. (1993) 'Positive und negative Koordination in Verhandlungssystemen', in A. Héritier (ed.), *Policy-Analyse – Kritik und Neuorientierung*, Opladen: Westdeutscher Verlag.

Scherer, J. (1985) *Telekommunikationsrecht und Telekommunikationspolitik*, Baden-Baden: Nomos Verlagsgesellschaft.

Scherer, J. (1992) 'Die Zulässigkeit der Organisationsprivatisierung des Mobilfunkbetriebs der Deutschen Bundespost Telekom', *Archiv für das Post- und Fernmeldewesen*, **15**, 5–11.

Schmidt, S.K. (1991) 'Taking the Long Road to Liberalisation – Telecommunications Reform in the Federal Republic of Germany', *Telecommunications Policy*, **15**, 209–22.

Schneider, V. and R. Werle (1990) 'International Regime or Corporate Actor? The European Community in Telecommunications Policy', in K. Dyson and P. Humphreys (eds), *The Political Economy of Communications*, London: Routledge.

Schneider, V. and R. Werle (1991) 'Policy Networks in the German Telecommunications Domain', in B. Marin and R. Mayntz (eds), *Policy Networks – Empirical Evidence and Theoretical Considerations*, Frankfurt a.M.: Campus.

Simon, H.A. (1990) 'The Architecture of Complexity', in O.E. Williamson (ed.), *Industrial Organization*, Aldershot: Edward Elgar.

Streeck, W. (1993) 'Beneficial Constraints: On the Economic Limits of Rational Voluntarism', in J.R. Hollingsworth and B. Boyer (eds), *Contemporary Capitalism: The Embeddedness of Institutions*, New York and Cambridge 1996: Cambridge University Press.

Vogelsang, I. (1988) 'Deregulation and Privatization in Germany', *Journal of Public Policy*, **8**, 195–212.

Webber, D. (1986) 'Die ausbleibende Wende bei der Deutschen Bundespost', *Politische Vierteljahresschrift*, **27**, 397–414.

Werle, R. (1990) *Telekommunikation in der Bundesrepublik – Expansion, Differenzierung, Transformation*, Frankfurt a.M.: Campus.

Werle, R. (1994) *Institutionelle Entwicklungen als pfadabhängige Prozesse – Bedingungen, Verläufe und forschungsmethodische Implikationen*, Cologne, mimeo.

4 Privatizing to Keep it Public? The Reorganization of the German Railways

Dirk Lehmkuhl

Introduction

Attempts to take into account the dual character of the railways as a mode of transport have been characteristic of the development of the rail network in Germany (see Witte, 1932: 1). On the one hand, railways are commercial enterprises located within the transport industry and, as such, they are subject to competition. On the other hand, they touch upon vital social and public interests, including economic, social, environmental, territorial planning and security policies, which by their very nature encourage state intervention in the railways. Consequently, it was for a long time an almost universally accepted assumption that rail transport should be provided by publicly owned monopolies. In Germany, the transfer of the railways from private to public ownership during the latter half of the nineteenth century formed the basis for subsequent developments which culminated, in 1920, in a far-reaching centralization by which the various nationalized Länder railways were combined. The history of rail transport organization in Germany has thus been inherently linked to the evolution of the German nation-state, for example in regard to national security strategy, functional centralization, social welfare provision and fiscal policy.

Transport policy during the inter-war years has had decisive consequences for the organization and structure of the transport sector up to the present. The starting point of this development was the emergence of motorized vehicles as an alternative means to transport goods and persons, which ended the de facto monopoly of the railways. In order to counteract the fall in the railways' share of overall transport services, and the loss of state

71

revenue which this implied, progressively more stringent market regulations for other carriers were introduced to protect the railways. These 'regulations for controlled competition' (*kontrollierte Wettbewerbsordnung*), stipulated in particular to quantitative restrictions (licensing and permit systems) and pricing regulations (Monopolkommission, 1990; Deregulierungskommission, 1991) and, as regards their main features, they were to remain in place until the early 1990s.

The Deutsche Bundesbahn (DB) was constituted as the national state railway after the foundation of the Federal Republic, and operated in the context of strict transport market regulations which were based on structures dating back to the prewar period. It soon became apparent, however, that this was not sufficient to solve the dilemma posed by the officially defined role of the railways as set out in its company charter, namely to act as 'as an economic enterprise' which fulfils 'public service obligations' (*gemeinwirtschaftliche Aufgaben*), including, for example, public service provision and environmental policy and planning (Article 28 I of the Federal Railway Act). All attempts to grant the railways greater entrepreneurial freedom were thwarted by provisions contained in Article 87 (1) of the Basic Law, which stipulated that the railways had to be run in the form of a Federal administration (see Fromm, 1994a: 62f). This status as a public authority entailed the application of legislation governing the public service, industrial relations and budget regulations, which many considered too restrictive. Moreover, the DB was not only subject to the influence of the Federal government and Parliament. Through their representation on its Administrative Council, the Bundesrat, the trade unions and industry also took part in its decision making. The legal–budgetary regime established, whereby the railways constituted a special Federal fund without independent legal personality (*nicht-rechtsfähiges Sondervermögen*), helped to act as a buffer for the inherent conflict of objectives in the railways' constitution. Thus the costs resulting from efforts to fulfil conflicting goals built up as deficits in the special Federal fund outside the main Federal budget.

During the 1980s, however, the elaborate network of regulations surrounding the national railways began to come under greater pressure from various quarters. Transport experts and economists increasingly questioned the basic justification for regulation, and correspondingly argued for a strengthening of inter- and intramodal competition (see Willeke and Aberle, 1973; Drude, 1976; Soltwedel *et al.*, 1986). Demands for deregulation and liberalization were also supported by leading business associations, partly with reference to the positive effects of deregulation in other countries (see, for example, BDI, 1988). The need for change was also the product of EC legislation on the freedom to operate transport services and the opening up of transport markets. Accordingly, issues such as the vertical integration of rail infrastructure and operation, the monopolies of national railway companies and the lack of transparency in financial relations between member states and their national railways were all put on the agenda. Moreover, the shift in the political balance of power towards a more liberal economic approach was crucial in helping to promote the reduction of state intervention in the market. At the same time, the negative consequences of the existing arrangements were becoming increasingly apparent. The continuous decline of the railways was forcing the Federal government to provide steadily increasing subsidies. The Länder and local authorities, too, were having to bear greater costs as a result of the unsatisfactory state of local transport by rail and road, while the trade unions could not prevent the steady decline in jobs. Finally, stringent domestic regulations were causing growing competitive disadvantages for the German transport industry in a progressively integrating Europe.

The Reform Process

From the mid-1980s onward, the factors described above combined to stimulate the emergence of a basic parliamentary consensus between the governing Christian Democrat–Liberal coalition parties and the opposition Social Democrats in favour of changes in rail policy. A Government Railway Commission (*Regierungskommission Bahn*), established by a cabinet resolution of 1 February 1989, was charged with preparing proposals for reform. Against the background of growing financial risks for the railways, the Commission's brief was to create 'a sustainable basis for the development of the DB in terms of transport policy, territorial planning, environmental policy, and economic and fiscal criteria' (Regierungskommission Bahn, 1991: 4). The Commission's task was substantially affected by German unification and the opening up of Eastern Europe. The Commission took into account the calamitous financial situation of both the DB and the Deutsche Reichsbahn (DR), the GDR's state railways, the latter's specific problems, the anticipated increase in competition resulting from the prospective completion of the internal market and the prediction that Germany would become a key transit country. Against this background, the Commission concluded that existing problems could not be resolved without fundamental structural reform, nor would the railways be capable of meeting new challenges in the future.

The Commission's final report, published in December 1991, represented the most radical approach to the reorganization of the railways up to then. The first proposal advocated regionalization, that is the transfer from the Federal to the Länder level of functional and financial responsibilities for local rail passenger transport, in order to put an end to decades of conflict between the Federal government, on the one side, and the state governments and local authorities, on the other. Moreover, the Commission broke a taboo by proposing amendments to the Basic Law as part of its recommendations for legal and organizational reform.[1] In turning the Commission's recommendations into concrete proposals, the Federal transport minister became convinced that the desired improvements in productivity and financial performance depended on the extent to which the DB and DR would be transformed into enterprises under private law (see Bundesminister für Verkehr, 1992).

On the basis of the Commission's framework plan, the Federal government decided in July 1992 to institute a structural reform of the German railways to come into effect on 1 January 1994. The need for a fundamental redefinition of the relationship between the state and the railways, and especially a redefinition of the railways' status on the way to privatization, was generally acknowledged. The dramatic financial forecasts of the costs of maintaining the existing arrangements, coupled with Ministry of Transport estimates according to which the proposed reforms could save up to DM105bn by the year 2002, did not fail to impress. Nonetheless, the Federal government's resolution met with criticism from the SPD, the Länder, local government associations, trade unions and business associations. This criticism centred, in particular, on the reservations of Theo Waigel, the Federal finance minister, regarding the future financing of accumulated debt, regionalization and the responsibility for infrastructural rail facilities investment, and led to a polarization between the Federal government and the other key actors required to ratify any amendment to the Basic Law, namely the SPD opposition in the Bundestag and the Länder in the Bundesrat. Their agreement was imperative since a constitutional amendment requires two-thirds majorities in both the Bundestag and the Bundesrat. Waigel's attempt in early 1993 to include the amount which would have to be transferred to the Länder as a result of regionalization in the parallel negotiations on intergovernmental fiscal relations and equalization represented the negative climax in the clash between the Federation and the Länder. Even though railway restructuring and intergovernmental fiscal relations were later again decoupled during the negotiations on the Solidarity Pact, the immediate effect was not only a reinforcement of existing conflicts, but also considerable delay. As the railway reforms were still supposed to come into effect on 1 January 1994, the parliamentary legislative process was initiated while talks on contested issues were simultaneously being held between all parties involved. During these talks, the Länder, in particular, gave no quarter when confronting the Federal government with their demands. Thus it was not until a final meeting in December 1993 between Chancellor Kohl and SPD leader Rudolf Scharping, in his capacity as head of the conference of Länder Minister–Presidents, that agreement on the last points of contention could be reached. This enabled the railway reform legislation to be passed in the Bundestag and the Bundesrat on 2 and 17 December 1993, respectively.

The most important measures of the reform act can be summarized as follows.[2] On 1 January 1994, the DB and DR merged. In so doing, a distinction was drawn between the exercise of sovereign authority (*hoheitliche Aufgaben*) and commercial operation. For the exercise of sovereign powers, a newly formed administration, the Federal Railways Office (*Eisenbahnbundesamt*), was granted exclusive authority over planning, licensing and supervision. Competences for matters relating to personnel, debt and management of estate assets fell to the Federal Railways Asset Fund (*Bundeseisenbahnvermögen* – BEV), as a body without independent legal personality. As a special fund, the BEV took over both the accumulated inherited debts of the DB and DR, which totalled some DM67bn by the end of 1993, and responsibility for acquired pension rights. The commercial part of the enterprise was relieved of its debts and transformed into a joint stockholding company, the *Deutsche Bahn Aktiengesellschaft* (DB AG). Its basic organizational and legal subdivisions include rail track infrastructure (*Fahrwege*), local passenger transport, long-distance passenger transport and freight transport. At the end of a transitional period of three to five years, the DB AG is to be split into three separate companies under the direction of a holding company which can, in turn, be dissolved within a five-year period. For this last transition step, the agreement of the Bundesrat is needed.

The ownership of the railway tracks is transferred to the DB AG, including the building, maintenance and operation of railway guidance and security systems. If, in the future, parts of *Fahrweg AG* were to be sold off, the majority of shares must remain in the hands of the Federal government. Legislation relating to the expansion of the railway network provides that the funding for new investment, extensions or renovation is to come from the Federal government. With the implementation of EC Directive 91/1440, which guarantees non-discriminatory access and use in return for payment, the railway networks are to be opened up to third parties, so-called 'international groupings of railway undertakings'.[3]

A special problem was posed by the civil servant status (*Beamtenstatus*) of many railway staff. With regard to the transitional arrangements for civil servants, hitherto untested arrangements were introduced. Thus it was not only possible for civil servants to transfer to the DB AG by leaving the civil service or by taking temporary leave of absence, but an amendment to Article 143a (1) to the Basic Law also created the possibility of having staff compulsorily assigned from the BEV to the DB AG. Finally, financial and functional responsibility for local passenger rail transport was transferred to the Länder from 1 January 1996. At the same time, the 'subscription principle' *(Bestellerprinzip)* was to be applied to the provision of public service-oriented transport services, as set out in EC Regulation 91/1893. This means that if regional and local governments desire to operate a given service, they must ensure that operating deficits are covered. Overall, it is expected that, compared with the pre-1994 status quo, the reforms will yield savings of some DM247bn between 1994 and 2003 (see Graichen, 1993: 247).

In assessing these structural forms, the first point to note concerns the extent to which the far-reaching framework recommendations of the government Railway Commission were adopted and the speed with which they were translated into legislation. This is all the more remarkable in light of the numerous, long-drawn-out and essentially fruitless efforts at restructuring in the past, not only of the railways, but also in other policy areas, such as health policy or posts and telecommunications (see Rosewitz and Webber, 1990; Grande, 1989; Schmidt in the present volume). However, this should not obscure the fact that the transformation process was also characterized by sometimes bitter disputes and, upon closer examination, many of the final decisions bear the clear marks of compromise solutions.

Key Influences

In trying to explain the course and outcome of the reform process, four main actors or actor constellations are of particular significance. First, it is necessary to examine the influence of the Federal finance minister, especially with regard to the questions of debt relief, regionalization and future Federal responsibility for infrastructural rail track investment. Moreover, the types of conflicts which resulted from the need for two-thirds majorities for constitutional amendments in the Bundestag and the Bundesrat must be analyzed. Here it is useful to distinguish relations between the Federal government and the SPD-led opposition in the Bundestag (second) on the one hand, and the government and the SPD-dominated Bundesrat (third) on the other. Fourth, one actor seemed conspicuously absent from the headlines – the trade unions. This apparently low profile is all the more remarkable since the transformation of the railways from public to private status entailed significant legal change in personnel and industrial relations issues, especially as far as the status of civil servants was concerned.

The Trade Unions' Learning Process

The trade unions had proved capable in the past of exerting a significant influence on decisions relating to personnel policy and basic organizational issues within the rail industry. As the DB could not go bankrupt, the trade unions consistently managed successfully to push through pay and conditions settlements that ignored the railways' commercial failings (see Drude, 1976: 207). Nonetheless, unavoidable rationalization meant that the number of jobs declined significantly over the years. Thus, in 1958, the DB employed some 516 000 staff, this number had fallen to 226 854 by 1992 and 217 000 by 1993 (excluding the staff of the DR). Owing to the major influence of the unions, however, this reduction was achieved through natural wastage and retirement rather than compulsory redundancies (see Drude, 1976; Baum, 1985: 182).

Since the constitutional protection afforded by Article 87 of the Basic Law had proved insufficient in the past to stem either the steady stream of job losses or the shrinking market share of the railways, the largest relevant union, the German Railwaymen's Union (GdED), took a positive stance towards the proposed reforms at least since autumn 1991, provided the 'social terms' were favourable. The union's attitude can be explained as a result of a fundamental reorientation. In a keynote speech at the November 1992 union congress, GdED President Schäfer asserted that changes to the legal status of the railways would also necessitate change in the GdED's perception of its own character and purpose (*Frankfurter Allgemeine Zeitung*, 26 November 1992: 16). The Railwaymen's Union had always stood in the shadow of the much larger Public Services, Transport and Traffic Union (ÖTV). The relatively tight-knit milieu of a public-sector industry meant that railway staff were heavily unionized, with some 81 per cent of staff being members of the GdED. Not least as a result of President Schäfer's insistence, decision makers in the GdED came to accept that, in order to secure the future of railwaymen's jobs, new avenues had to be explored (see Schäfer, 1992).

As the GdED endeavoured to play a constructive role in the reform process, it was able to pursue, in addition to the call for the protection and maintenance of acquired social rights and privileges, a number of issues which served to reinforce its own position in the longer term. Thus, in accordance with the 1976 codetermination law, the DB AG's supervisory board, with a total of 20 members, now contains seven staff and three trade union representatives. Moreover, the reform afforded the GdED an opportunity to develop pay and conditions systems specifically tailored to the rail industry, and thus to sever the links with the general public sector pay rounds conducted until then by the ÖTV. Owing to the high degree of unionization, the GdED enjoys a strong bargaining position in its negotiations with DB AG.

Of course, the GdED could not avoid making concessions, in particular in relation to personnel transfer. After initially rejecting the notion of the compulsory transfer of civil servants, the union later went on to accept it, recognizing that the issue of the status of civil servants would decline in importance with the passing of the years. At the same time, the new situation allows the GdED to develop into an industrial trade union. The union's willingness to play a constructive role in shaping the reform of the railways can thus be interpreted as the result of a learning process in which 'the lessons of the past' were combined with 'the signs of the times'. The former involved acceptance of the fact that traditional Railwaymen's Union methods were unable to prevent the decline of both the railways and the union itself, while the latter related to the anticipation of profound change affecting the railways.

Reservations Concerning Financing Arrangements

As mentioned above, delays in the reform process can be explained in part by the influence exercised by Theo Waigel, the Federal finance minister. The strain on the Federal budget that resulted from the coincidence of the transformation crisis in East Germany with economic recession in the West served to reinforce Waigel's already powerful position within the Federal government's cabinet hierarchy. Fiscal problems forcefully underlined his contention that the reform of the railways must not be allowed to become 'a vehicle for shunting the financial burden of the railways onto the Federal budget' (see dpa-Hintergrund, 1993: 17). In contrast to the Federal transport minister, and also contrary to the views of opposition Social Democrats and the Länder, Waigel rejected a long-term credit-financed programme to relieve the DB of the debts that had built up over the years. In order to avoid the creation of an ever-growing 'unofficial' budget, the BEV was to be prohibited from conducting independent net borrowing.

Waigel's insistence on methods of financing that did not impose additional burdens on the budget was primarily aimed at developing new sources of revenue from the transport sector. While Waigel favoured an increase in the excise fuel duty, Krause (CDU), the then transport minister, developed a graded plan for the introduction of charges on road use. Krause would have been prepared to put his proposals into immediate effect; but vehement public opposition, primarily in protest at the hefty charges envisaged for the planned introduction of motorway tolls from 1994 (see *Die Zeit*, 19 February 1993: 13ff), led more and more politicians from the ruling coalition to distance themselves from Krause's plans, not least in view of the fact that

1994 was to be a 'bumper election year'. The conflict was not finally resolved until June 1993, when Finance Minister Waigel and Wissmann, the new minister for transport, agreed to raise the taxes on petrol and diesel by 16 pfennigs and 7 pfennigs per litre, respectively, from 1 January 1994 (see *Handelsblatt*, 23 June 1993: 1; *Frankfurter Allgemeine Zeitung*, 12 August 1993: 1f). Nevertheless, this agreement merely represented an interim solution, as the debt-relief compromise forged between the two ministers envisaged that the question of road tolls would be raised again by 1996. In return, Waigel made the concession, at least for the time being, to service the accumulated railways debt from the BEV rather than from the Federal budget, and granted the BEV a limited borrowing capacity for 1994 and 1995 of DM9.5bn. This concession was on condition that, from 1996, the railway deficit would be entirely funded from fees and other forms of revenue (see *Handelsblatt*, 10 February 1993: 1).

Waigel also had reservations about the future responsibility of the Federation for infrastructure investment in the railways. In his opinion, the transfer of ownership of the rail tracks to the DB AG was an essential and integral part of their reorganization, without which entrepreneurial objectives could not be realized. He rejected the suggested method of financing, according to which the Federal government would have had to foot the bill for new construction and line extensions, while the DB AG would merely have had to pay back the cost of depreciation over a lengthy period of time and without any interest, arguing that this was tantamount to 'subsidization in perpetuity' (see *Der Spiegel*, 6 July 1992: 83). The solutions eventually found to these contentious issues bear the marks of a compromise between the finance minister, on the one hand, and the Social Democrats and Länder, on the other. Ownership of rail track infrastructure was transferred to the DB AG, and there is a strong possibility that shares in the rail track company to be founded, the *Fahrweg AG*, may at some stage be sold off to third parties, but the Federation would have to retain the majority holding were this to occur. At the same time, the Federal government continues to be responsible for infrastructure rail investment in the future, but the new legislation explicitly acknowledges that this responsibility is subject to available Federal budgetary resources.[4]

The Confrontation at Federal Level

While opposition SPD MPs recognized the need for changes in railway policy, they criticized the fact that the debate could not just be restricted to the proposed amendment to Article 87 of the Basic Law. From the SPD's point of view, the key problem of the railways was less a function of their formal organization as such and more a question of the disadvantages in infrastructure development and investment the railways had suffered in the past. In advocating an integrated national transport system, the SPD was echoing the predominant views of experts in the field. Thus misguided decisions on, or inadequate investment in, the transport infrastructure were considered to have direct implications for the share of individual transport providers in the overall provision of transport, that is the 'modal split', and these consequences were difficult to reverse (see Ostrowski, 1993: 49). Second, infrastructure investment was perceived to be a highly effective means of influencing the demand for transport services and the modal split (see Baum, 1991: 7). As an opposition party, the SPD was under fewer constraints than the government to take into account budgetary limitations in formulating its policy demands. Thus, whereas the governing coalition parties, under budgetary pressure, had to accept increasing restrictions on their policy proposals, the SPD parliamentary party was free to develop ambitious plans for an integrated transport policy with a strong ecological component. In this manner, the SPD set the reform of the railways within the broader context of transport policy and transport regulation. This included, for example, demands for a legal parity of rail and road infrastructure, equitable user charges and the taxation of vehicles according to ecological criteria.

These dynamics were evident with regard to the question of debt relief. After initial agreement between the transport minister and the SPD that the repayment of accumulated debts should be achieved over the long term, the minister was eventually forced by Waigel's objections to look for other solutions. His plans for the privatization of the motorways and the introduction of road toll charges on lorries and cars were, however, rejected by the SPD. The Social Democrats complained that such isolated approaches were ineffective, since they were not part of a broader concept for an ecologically aware transport policy. While the SPD accepted the debt relief compromise set out above, the party successfully used its institutionalized veto position in constitutional legislation to guarantee the state's responsibility for railway infrastructure. By the summer of 1993, the Federal government had not yet complied with demands that rail and road provision be put on an equal legal footing, primarily through legislation on railway construction similar to that governing the construction of highways. While the construction of Federal highways is decided by Parliament, and is thus guaranteed once a parliamentary decision has been taken, investment in rail track infrastructure had been confined to the realm of non-obligatory declarations of intent, which were often later disregarded in the face of mounting Bundesbahn deficits. In the course of talks later, both in the Bundestag Transport Committee and between the Federal government and the Länder, a legal base for such equal treatment was finally agreed.

The Regionalization Issue

The main confrontation during the process of railway reform was between the Federation, on one side, and the Länder and local government associations, on the other. The proposed merging of functional and financial responsibility for local public passenger transport in the hands of regional and local authorities was presented as the solution to problems that had for decades been igniting conflicts and blocking reform. Accordingly, the issue of regionalization became the primary focus of controversy.

The Federation had initiated discussions on regionalization both in the mid-1970s and at the beginning of the 1980s (see Bundesverkehrsminister, 1975; 1977; 1983) with a view to transferring financial responsibility for local passenger transport deficits. Before any agreement was reached between the Federation, the Länder and local governments, the Federal government had embarked upon a strategic withdrawal, described by critics as 'regionalization by stealth', whereby Länder or local authorities had to shoulder costs if they wanted to maintain particular local services. In the late 1980s, in light of the worsening consequences of this Federal withdrawal strategy, the Länder eventually changed their stance towards regionalization. Since they could do nothing about the Federation's tactics of a creeping transfer of financial responsibility, the Conference of the Länder Transport Ministers (VMK), which serves as an institutionalized committee for horizontal inter-Länder coordination, demanded in October 1989 a new framework for local public transport (see *Vermerk über die VMK* of 16 and 17 October 1989). The Länder agreed to assume responsibility for local passenger rail transport,[5] which should be part of a comprehensive railway reform package, but combined this with substantial demands vis-à-vis the Federation. These demands concentrated, in particular, on the prospective scope of regionalization, its financial implications, operational matters, formal provisions for Länder influence and future Federal responsibility for infrastructure (this last point has already been discussed above). Within this context, the Länder unequivocally asserted that Bundesrat assent to the railway reform package was dependent on a postitive Federal reponse to the demands formulated unanimously by the Transport Ministers' Conference (see *Vermerk über die VMK* of 16 and 17 October 1989).

The cost and scope of regionalization   The Länder were opposed to the Federal government's proposal to restrict the scope of regionalization to local passenger rail transport. They advocated, instead, a unified legal framework, that is a regionalization act, which would integrate the disparate legal and institutional regulations governing competences (see, for example, Kübler, 1982; Kons, 1985) within the sphere of both local passenger rail transport and local public passenger transport in general. To compensate for the costs of regionalization, the Länder demanded a total of DM14bn[6] per annum from the Federal government. This sum was to be provided in the form of a Länder share of 25 per cent of excise fuel duty revenues, which had previously accrued exclusively to the Federation. The Länder argued that the reclassification of the tax on petrol as a shared tax would provide them with a direct and constitutionally guaranteed source of income, which would enable the Länder to determine for themselves the use to which the revenue would be put.[7] The Federal government rejected both the amount and the proposed means of financial transfer and, instead, emphasized the 'normal constitutional means' of a redistribution of value added tax revenue between the Federation and the Länder (see Bundestagsdrucksache 12/5015: 36).

After tough negotiations, an understanding was finally reached, according to which the Länder would receive DM8.7bn of Federal excise fuel duty revenues in 1996, and DM12bn per annum thereafter. The latter sum is to be index-linked to the growth in VAT revenues from 1998. In 1997 and 2001, both the rate of increase in compensation payments and the source from which the Federation is to provide the transfer compensation payments are to be reassessed. In return for this compromise, the Länder were obliged to make concessions concerning the method and level of the transfer compensation payments. However, they were successful in securing fixed Federal contributions for local passenger rail services in the new Länder and they were granted an integrated regionalization act to restructure local passenger transport services in general.

The operation of rail track infrastructure and the Länder's guaranteed right to future influence   The Länder and the local government associations feared that if Deutsche Bahn AG were run according to purely commercial criteria, and especially if it were to enjoy a rail track monopoly, this might detrimentally affect local passenger rail services in the face of competition from the more profitable freight transport and long-distance passenger services. To counter this possibility, the local government associations demanded in a joint declaration that local passenger rail services be given preferential status (see Bundesvereinigung der kommunalen Spitzenverbände, 1993). In addition, the Länder demanded a legally guaranteed right of participation in all rail-related laws and ordinances, since all future rail legislation would have implications for the Länder's new functional responsibilities. The amendments suggested by the Länder, as contained within the official Bundesrat statements on the Federal government's legislative proposal (see Bundesratsdrucksache 131/93), were rejected by the Federal government. The Federation argued that the Länder's demands would undermine the underlying principle of the reforms, namely the transformation of the railways into an independent commercial enterprise free from political interference (see Bundestagsdrucksache 12/5015: 38).

The Länder's uncompromising attitude – based on cross-party consensus, as expressed in the unanimous resolutions of transport ministers' conferences and in the Bundesrat – left the Federal government with no option but to accommodate to a large extent the demands of the Länder and local government associations. Thus a distinction was drawn between local and long-distance passenger transport services. Although local passenger rail transport was not granted a general preferential status as such, it has to be given special consideration in the allocation of rail track use (see Bundestagsdrucksache 12/6269: 58). The crowding out of local transport by the needs of long-distance users is avoided. Significantly, the Länder also succeeded in securing far-reaching participatory rights in future decision making, as all major future legislation or ordinances concerning the railways now require Bundesrat approval (see Articles 80 (2) and 87e (5) Basic Law). This provision covers, for example, legislation concerning the principles of the fee structure for the use of rail infrastructure and the sale, merger and demerger of railway enterprises. In return, the Länder gave up their original intention to gain influence over future rail policy through their representation on the DB AG supervisory board or their participation in an 'Infrastructure Council', to be modelled on the example of posts and telecommunications.

The Process Assessed

In analyzing the complex sequence of events relating to the transformation of the German railway system, it is apparent that the major lines of conflict were the result of the functional dispersal of competences along departmental lines and within the intergovernmental system (see Scharpf *et al.*, 1976: 18). The main cause of the Federal government's internal immobility was the stance of the finance minister, who sought to avoid at all costs the imposition of any further financial burdens on an already overstretched Federal budget. This approach resulted in problem postponement and problem segmentation, as was evidenced, for example, by the Federal government's attempt to decouple decision taking on the principle of regionalization from the issue of compensatory payments to the Länder. Intergovernmental fragmentation reflected the need for Bundesrat approval for any constitutional amendment. This constitutionally safeguarded veto position meant that the Länder were able to confront the Federation with stringent conditions in respect of regionalization.

It is also striking that the confrontation over railway reform did not produce intense party political conflict, despite the fact that the Bundestag and the Bundesrat were dominated by different parties. One reason was that the Länder's institutional self-interest in finding a favourable solution to the regionalization issue was stronger than party political constellations at both Federal and Länder levels. At the same time, the Social Democrat parliamentary party in the Bundestag lost its function as an advocate of union interests once the Railwaymen's Union had, in principle, accepted formal privatization.

The relative insignificance of the party political dimension of conflict concentrated the discussion on technical issues. In particular, the division of the now merged Deutsche Bundesbahn and Deutsche Reichsbahn into a commercial operation and a sovereign authority helped to reduce the potential for conflict. The far-reaching debt relief of the DB AG as a commercial enterprise laid the ground for fundamental decisions on market order and competition policy. At the same time, the retention of a residual special fund, the Federal Railways Asset Fund (BEV) increased the scope for consensual problem solving, in so far as the costs of political compromise would be borne largely by this fund. In this manner, a series of potential quarrels and blockages were successfully resolved. In this respect, it is worth recalling that the BEV assumed responsibility for inherited accumulated debts and pension payments. Similarly, the eventual compromise between the finance and transport ministers on the subject of debt relief only became possible after the BEV had been granted the right of net borrowing. Finally, possible conflicts over personnel transfers could be defused through solutions involving the BEV. This applied, for example, to union demands for guaranteed job security for East German railwaymen threatened with redundancy. The BEV was also used to finance the difference between salary levels of civil servants and the salaries paid according to collective agreements concluded by the Deutsche Bahn AG.

In addition to the general lines of conflict described above, the Federal transport minister's role in the reform process invites comment. The dominant position of the finance minister required the transport minister to adopt a pragmatic approach in trying to resolve the role-specific conflict of a minister in charge of a technical department. Thus he needed to reconcile his responsibilities for transport policy with the collective responsibility of a member of the government. As a result, the transport minister acted increasingly as a mediator between the finance minister, who was arguing according to the imperatives of limited budgetary resources, and the Länder and SPD, with their proposals for an integrated transport system encompassing Federal, regional and local levels.

Privatizing to Keep it Public?

If one tries to assess the most significant results and the medium- and long-term consequences of the reform of the German railways, a differentiated picture emerges. First, the unusually fast pace of the overall reform process deserves highlighting. Only five years lay between the appointment of the Government Commission in 1989 and the structural reform finally coming into force on 1 January 1994. Given the far-reaching reform intentions, this was a remarkably short period. The speed of reform may be explained in terms of the urgency of the problem, which was reinforced by the need to implement relevant European legislation. Only the combination of internal and external factors explains satisfactorily the speed and substance of the changes.

At the same time, the necessity of reconciling partly institutionalized conflicts of interest between numerous actors within a short space of time created a need for compromise. However, the resulting compromises were in some cases only partly suited to the problem at hand or were prepared so quickly that implementation problems would appear inevitable. Of course, many durable solutions were found. They included, for example, the transfer of responsibilities for old debts and pension payments to the BEV (see, however, Laaser, 1994: 23–5), the harmonization of employment regulations, which removed the distinction between workers and salaried employees, and the special transitional provisions relating to the status of civil servants working for the DB AG. At the same time, however, the closely interrelated areas of privatization, regionalization and liberalization require closer examination.

EC Directive 91/440, which was supposed to have been transposed into national law by 1 January 1993, aimed at guaranteeing independent management and greater cost transparency by distinguishing between rail track infrastructure and operation. Plans for privatization in Germany have been by no means as extensive as those in the UK, for example. Nevertheless, in the context of enacting binding EC restrictions, the Federal government has signalled that it intends to adopt the optional variants proposed by the EC Commission in granting autonomy to individual sectors through a gradual reorganization. As described above, the method of transition, that is the creation of a holding company, was the result of 'practical considerations' since, in view of the required broad political consensus, a stage-by-stage restructuring process 'would create considerably less friction and resistance' (Bundesminister für Verkehr, 1992: 31).

For the moment, however, only structural reorganization has been undertaken, that is the organizational division within the DB AG into the following branches: local passenger transport, long-distance passenger transport, freight transport and rail track infrastructure. For the time being, privatization by means of transformation into a joint-stock company under private law has been limited to a change in legal form, rather than in substance, as ownership relations have remained unchanged. There is widespread doubt as to whether the third stage of reform will ever be realized. In other words, there is a question mark over the dissolution of the holding company to be created during a future second reform phase and the granting of full autonomy to the four branches transformed into separate joint-stock companies. Resistance to these plans grows both in the trade unions and the DB AG itself. Moreover, in December 1993, during the hectic final phase of the legislative process, the Länder were able to impose a requirement whereby the realization of this third stage will require a separate piece of legislation subject to Bundesrat approval. The agreement of the Bundesrat to such a law may ultimately depend on the implementation of regionalization over the next few years and, in particular, access to rail track infrastructure for local passenger services.

The controversial nature of the regionalization issue has been highlighted in the preceding sections. Since the uncertainties and implementation problems associated with the transfer of functional responsibility to the Länder and local authorities could not be resolved within the general legislative process, it was agreed that regionalization should only come into force on 1 January 1996. Until then, the Länder would not invite tenders for the provision of transport services. Rather, they accepted an offer by the DB AG which guaranteed to operate local passenger rail services on existing terms. In return, the Länder agreed to transfer their corresponding allocation of Federal funds to the DB AG. This agreement could only be of a transitional nature, however, arising from the mutual uncertainty of the Länder and the DB AG as to their future course of action.

In the present transition and implementation process, the Länder have had to recognize that the funds that are transferred by the Federal government are insufficient to realize their ideas of an integrated local passenger transport system. So far, the much-vaunted 'AG effects', that is the effects of corporatization, have failed to materialize, notably improvements in the cost structures of regional transport resulting from the concentration of functional responsibility at a decentralized level. It is therefore to be expected that the legal deadlines for the reassessment of the amount of the Federal transfer payments to the Länder, at the end of 1997 and 2001, will rekindle the regionalization-related distributional conflicts between the Federation and the Länder (see for current developments and problems Herr and Lehmkuhl, 1996).

Finally, one needs to consider the central aspect of the intended liberalization, namely the abolition of the monopoly in rail services provision. The deregulation of the European transport market has been the subject of discussion ever since the 1985 European Court of Justice ruling against the Council of (Transport) Ministers, on the grounds of inactivity in regard to transport liberalization. In the course of this debate, it has come to be accepted that the provision of railway transport constitutes a service subject to liberalization according to internal market provisions (see Knieps, 1992: 283f). Ending the vertical integration of rail track infrastructure and operational management implies a distinction between the provision of rail infrastructure and the provision of railway transport services. At the same time, national rail systems are supposed to be opening up to competition from other railway enterprises, whether domestic or foreign, primarily through the granting of rights of access and transit. The result of this unprecedented exposure of the railways to competition has been the creation of new state responsibilities. The latter involve the establishment of licensing and registration requirements for railway companies as well as the harmonization of regulations governing the use of rail networks by third parties (see Pliquett and Wickert, 1992: 515).

As a result of railways reform in Germany, these duties have been split up between public authorities and the organizationally privatized DB AG. The Federal Railways Office has, accordingly, assumed the role of sovereign planning and licensing body, while the DB AG, as the owner of the rail track infrastructure, is charged with ensuring the application of EC measures demanding non-discriminatory access to railway networks. It has been the exercise of the latter function that has sparked off much criticism (see, for example, Laaser, 1994). Thus the official fee schedule for rail track use published in July 1994 envisaged a sixfold increase in per kilometre charges (see DB AG, 1994; *Bus & Bahn* 9/1994: 1). In addition, the small differences in fees between high-volume major routes and low-volume local services disadvantage private regional operators, who are unable to balance their losses against the revenue from other (more profitable) services. Moreover, the 13 per cent bulk discount guaranteed to the DB AG's commercial branches by the rail track infrastructure division undoubtedly discriminates against other operators. The DB AG's individual subdivisions also seem destined to enjoy an inherent mutual competitive advantage, as long as organizational division is not followed by full legal separation of the DB AG's branches (for a review and further literature see Herr and Lehmkuhl, 1996: 15ff). However, in view of the objections highlighted earlier, it seems doubtful whether such a separation, envisaged as the third stage of reform, and necessary to assure improved competition, will actually be put into effect. Furthermore, the example of the official fee schedule highlights the need for effective regulation in order to prevent the DB AG from abusing its monopoly position. Thus liberalization and privatization cannot be achieved merely by 'rolling back the state'; on the contrary, state involvement is essential in order to supervise effectively the operation of services (see Lehmkuhl and Herr, 1994).

There remains, then, the final question of how to judge the results of railway reform in Germany. Has the transformation been a historic achievement, as some politicians maintain? Or did the institutional particularities of the German political system, in combination with prevailing circumstances, resulting from the coincidence of unification, European integration and the opening up of East European markets, result in half-hearted compromises? From the above discussion it should be apparent that the reality lies somewhere in-between.

Undoubtedly, railways reform has entailed 'one of the largest commercial redevelopment projects in the history of the German economy', as it was put by former Transport Minister Krause (quoted in *Neue Zeit*, 17 February 1993: 1). Complete debt relief and the transfer of accumulated pension rights both represent major advances. In addition, internal reorganization of the DB AG and massive investment in infrastructure and rolling stock suggest that promising attempts are being made to reclaim lost ground. Similarly, there are clear signs of savings in procurement and construction, and a management orientation towards commercial objectives (see *Frankfurter Allgemeine Zeitung*, 14 November 1994: 21). Railway privatization meant that the instrument of a public enterprise, which has been described as 'one of the most pronounced instruments of state intervention' (Ambrosius, 1993: 266), has been relinquished. This approach represents a reversal of earlier trends towards centralization, nationalization and regulation. However, until a change in ownership relationships comes about, this trend reversal must remain incomplete.

Doubts concerning such a positive appraisal focus above all on the still unanswered questions relating to reform implementation and the future role of the state in the transport sector. The right of influence guaranteed to the Länder, coupled with unchanged ownership, is at odds with the attempt to free the railways from politically motivated interference. At the same time, the measures contained in the railways reform for reducing state intervention have not been linked to any reconceptualization of the state's role under changed circumstances. Just as the prevention of monopolistic abuse to ensure liberalization and market access requires state regulation, the overriding commitment to permanently sustainable mobility relies on the state's steering capacities.

In all this it must be kept in mind that the railways do not operate in a closed system. Indeed, the role of the railways is influenced to a much greater degree by competition between roads, rail, inland waterways and air transport than by the intramodal competition among individual rail service operators. The application of free market-oriented paradigms to the running of the railways represents merely one, albeit an important, aspect of a reorientation of the transport system as a whole. This step marks a departure from the basic belief in 'the unique nature of transport' that had for decades served to justify the extensive regulation of transport markets.

This departure will not be complete, however, until the conditions for competition applying to individual transport carriers become harmonized, for example with regard to liability for infrastructure costs or the internalization of external costs. Further progress will also require a clearer definition of the role of the state in deregulated and privatized transport markets. So far, proposals on a new regulatory basis for transport markets, which are both compatible with European regulations and help to exploit fully the benefits and dynamics of intra- and intermodal competition, have remained fragmentary. Indeed, these views continue to be characterized by contradictory commitments to unfettered competition, on the one hand, and the need to take account of general public policy objectives, in particular in the field of environmental protection, on the other.

Notes

1   The refusal of the Federal President in 1991 to sign legislation relating to the privatization of air traffic control services without prior amendment to the Constitution provided another argument in favour of the method advocated by the Government Commission. See Riedel and Schmidt, 1991.
2   See Eisenbahnneuordnungsgesetz – ENeuOG, 27 December 1993, BGBI I, pp.2378–2427.
3   For the relevant EC/EU legislation see COM(93)678 in. – SYN 488-490.
4   See Bundesschienenwegeausbaugesetz (SchWAG), of 15 November 1993, as contained in the version of article 6 of the Eisenbahnneuordnungsgesetz (ENeuOG), of 27 December 1993.
5   This fundamental reorientation was set out in written form for the first time in August 1991, in the concluding report of a group comprising representatives from the Federal government, the Länder and local bodies. See Arbeitsgruppe ÖPNV, 1991.
6   This sum included approximately DM7.7bn provided by Federal government for local passenger rail transport to the DB and DR on the basis of EC regulations (EC reg. 69/1191 as amended by EC reg. 91/1831); some DM2bn of annual local passenger rail transport deficit not previously covered by the Federation; DM1.1bn for investments that should have been made; some DM1.5bn for additional expenditure for the new Länder; and the costs of index-linking local passenger rail transport funds and other local transport funds of approximately DM1.5bn.
7   See AG Bahnpolitik, 1992: 29f; see also *Vermerk über die VMK* of 29 and 30 October 1992, p.55.

References

AG Bahnpolitik (1992) *AG Bahnpolitik der Verkehrsabteilungsleiterkonferenz, Konzept zur Regionalisierung des ÖPNV, Anlage 3 zum Vermerk der Verkehrsministerkonferenz am 29./30. 10. 1992.*

Ambrosius, G. (1993) 'Abbau und Ausbau der öffentlichen Wirtschaft in den 80er Jahren', in R. Voigt (ed.), *Abschied vom Staat – Rückkehr zum Staat*, Baden-Baden: Nomos Verlagsgesellschaft, 265–83.

Arbeitsgruppe öffentlicher Personennahverkehr der Verkehrs- und Finanzressorts von Bund, Ländern und kommunalen Spitzenverbänden (1991), *Bericht über die Regionalisierung des Öffentlichen Personennahverkehrs (ÖPNV)*, Stuttgart, 19 August.

Baum, H. (1985) 'Eisenbahnsanierung, Verfügungsrechte und Ordnungspolitik', *ORDO – Zeitschrift für die Ordnung von Wirtschaft und Gesellschaft*, **36**, 181–209.

Baum, H. (1991) 'Infrastrukturpolitik als Mittel zur Steuerung des Verkehrsträger-wettbewerbs', *Zeitschrift für Verkehrswissenschaft*, **60**, 125–59.

Bericht der Regierungskommission Bahn, December 1991, manuscript.

Bundesminister für Verkehr (1975) *Zielsetzungen des Bundesministers für Verkehr für die Unternehmenspolitik der Deutschen Bundesbahn und für den öffentlichen Personennahverkehr*, Bonn: Schriftenreihe des Bundesministers für Verkehr, no. 49.

Bundesminister für Verkehr (1977) *Vorschläge für eine nachhaltige Verbesserung des öffentlichen Personennahverkehrs in der Fläche, Bericht der Arbeitsgruppe im Bundesverkehrsministerium*, Bonn, September.

Bundesminister für Verkehr (1983) *Leitlinien zur Konsolidierung der Deutschen Bundesbahn, Kabinettsvorlage E 10/20.0011/29Va83*, Bonn, 17 November.

Bundesminister für Verkehr (1992) *Kabinettsache, Datenblatt-Nr. 12/12074-05*, 6 June.

Bundesverband der Deutschen Industrie – BDI (1988) *Liberalisierung der Verkehrsmärkte. Erfahrungen des Auslands – wissenschaftliche Erkenntnisse, politische Konsequenzen*, Cologne.

Bundesvereinigung der kommunalen Spitzenverbände (1993) *Stellungnahme der Bundesvereinigung der kommunalen Spitzenverbände zu den Bundesrats-beschlüssen vom 7. Mai 1993 (Bahnstrukturreform und Regionalisierung des ÖPNV), AZ:66.41.11.* Cologne, 14 May.

Deregulierungskommission (1991) *Marktöffnung und Wettbewerb (Unabhängige Expertenkommission zum Abbau marktwidriger Regulierungen)*, Stuttgart: Poeschel.

Deutsche Bahn AG (1994) *Die Bahn öffnet den Fahrweg für Dritte. Kurzinformation zum Trassenpreissystem*, Frankfurt, July.

dpa-Hintergrund (1993) *Bundesbahn und Reichsbahn – Neuanfang auf dem Privatgleis, verantwortlich: A. Nürnberger*, 16 February.

Drude, M. (1976) 'Sanierung der Deutschen Bundesbahn durch Privatisierung? – Eine Problemskizze', *Zeitschrift für Verkehrswissenschaft*, **47**, 195–221.

Fromm, G. (1994a) 'Die Reorganisation der deutschen Bahnen – Voraussetzung für eine Neubestimmung des Standorts der Eisenbahnen in der Verkehrspolitik', in W. Blümel (ed.), *Verkehrswegerecht im Wandel*, Berlin: Duncker & Humblot, 59–78.

Fromm, G. (1994b) 'Juristische Probleme der Reform der Eisenbahnen. Verfassungsrecht, Eisenbahnrecht, Wettbewerbsrecht', *Internationales Verkehrswesen*, **45**, 97–102.

Graichen, R. (1993) 'Wirtschaftlicher Neubeginn der Bahn in Deutschland', *Zeitschrift für öffentliche und gemeinwirtschaftliche Unternehmungen*, **17**, 237–49.

Grande, E. (1989) *Vom Monopol zum Wettbewerb? Die neokonservative Reform der Telekommunikation in Großbritannien und der Bundesrepublik Deutschland*, Wiesbaden: DUV.

Herr, C. and Lehmkuhl, D. (1996) *Was zu erwarten war und ist. Aktuelle und zukünftige Probleme des öffentlichen Personennahverkehrs*, Bremen/Florence, March, unpublished.

Knieps, G. (1992) 'Konkurrenz auf den europäischen Eisenbahnnetzen', *Jahrbuch für Nationalökonomie und Statistik*, **209**, 283–90.

Kons, W. (1985) *Die Finanzierung der ÖPNV-Betriebe in der Bundesrepublik Deutschland*, Düsseldorf.

Kübler, K. (1982) *Die öffentlich-rechtlichen Grundlagen des öffentlichen Personennahverkehrs*, Düsseldorf.

Laaser, C.-F. (1994) *Die Bahnstrukturreform. Richtige Weichenstellung oder Fahrt aufs Abstellgleis?*, Kiel: Institut für Weltwirtschaft, Kieler Diskussionsbeiträge no. 239.

Lehmbruch, G., O. Singer, E. Grande and M. Döhler (1988) 'Institutionelle Bedingungen ordnungspolitischer Strategiewechsel im internationalen Vergleich', in Schmidt, M.G. (ed.), *Staatstätigkeit: International und historisch vergleichende Analysen* (PVS Sonderheft 19), Opladen: Westdeutscher Verlag, 251–83.

Lehmkuhl, D. and C. Herr (1994) 'Reform im Spannungsfeld von Dezentralisierung und Entstaatlichung: Die Strukturreform der Deutschen Bahnen', *Politische Vierteljahresschrift*, **35**, 631–57.

Monopolkommission (1990) *Wettbewerbspolitik vor neuen Herausforderungen, Hauptgutachten 1988/89 (VIII)*, Baden-Baden: Nomos Verlagsgesellschaft.

Ostrowski, R. (1993) 'Neue Wege der Infrastrukturfinanzierung', *Zeitschrift für Verkehrswissenschaft*, **64**, 49–66.

Pliquett, B. and P. Wickert (1992) 'Die Beschlüsse der Europäischen Gemeinschaft zur Weiterentwicklung der Eisenbahnunternehmen', *Die Deutsche Bahn*, no. 5, 511–16.

Riedel, N.K. and A. Schmidt (1991) 'Die Nichtausfertigung des Gesetzes zur Privatisierung der Flugsicherung durch den Bundespräsidenten', *Die Öffentliche Verwaltung*, **44**, 371–5.

Rosewitz, B. and D. Webber (1990) *Reformversuche und Reformblockaden im deutschen Gesundheitswesen*, Frankfurt a.M.: Campus.

Schäfer, R. (1992) 'Die Gewerkschaft der Eisenbahner will keine Schrumpfbahn', *SPD-Bundestagsfraktion, Fraktion Aktuell No. 18*, 5 October.

Scharpf, F.W., B. Reissert and F. Schnabel (1976) *Politikverflechtung: Theorie und Empirie des kooperativen Föderalismus in der Bundesrepublik Deutschland,* Kronberg/Ts.: Scriptor.

Schmidt-Aßmann, E. and H.C. Röhl (1994) 'Grundpositionen des neuen Eisenbahnverfassungsrechts', *Die Öffentliche Verwaltung,* **47**, 577–85.

Soltwedel, R. *et al.* (1986) *Deregulierungspotentiale in der Bundesrepublik,* Kieler Studien 202, Tübingen: J.C.B. Mohr (Paul Siebeck).

Verkehrsministerkonferenz, *Vermerke der VMK der Länder, Geschäftsstelle – K20.10 – seit 1975,* various volumes, Bundeshaus, Bonn.

Willeke, R. and G. Aberle (1973) 'Thesen zur Sanierung der Deutschen Bundesbahn', *Zeitschrift für Verkehrswissenschaft,* **44**, 38–50.

Witte, B. (1932) *Eisenbahn und Staat. Ein Vergleich der europäischen und nordamerikanischen Eisenbahnorganisation in ihrem Verhältnis zum Staat,* Jena: G. Fischer.

5 The Treuhandanstalt and the Transition from Socialism to Capitalism

Roland Czada

The transition from socialism to capitalism in East Germany has proved to be a highly demanding task for politicians and businessmen and a major challenge to the adaptive capacities of the administrative system. The Treuhandanstalt, the Federal agency established as institutional trustee (Trust Agency, or THA), was at the centre of this historical transformation process. This quasi-non-governmental organization was set up by a government order of the penultimate Council of Ministers of the German Democratic Republic (GDR) and, on 1 March 1990, it took over the entire nationalized economy of East Germany. Thus it started to operate before the economic integration of the former socialist system into the West German market economy was set in motion and made irreversible with the Treaty on Monetary, Economic and Social Union of 18 May 1990.

At the time of its establishment, the THA was said to be the world's largest industrial enterprise. It owned approximately 45 000 permanent establishments, which belonged to some 8500 industrial enterprises with approximately 4 million employees. In the following months, demergers further increased the total number of enterprises to 13 000. Little more than four years later, by the end of 1994, only about a hundred of them were left in the THA's possession, the others having been privatized, transferred to local governments or closed down. At that time, apart from the remaining firms, vast land holdings, representing some 40 per cent of the former East German territory, also still awaited privatization (Sinn and Sinn, 1993: 123).

The German path from socialist economic planning to a market economy was very distinct when compared to the transition experiences in the Czech Republic, Poland, Hungary or Russia. By joining a highly industrialized

Western European country, East Germany became a high-wage region with low industrial productivity. Monetary union exposed its industries to the global market and, as a result, both politicians and managers were quickly forced to realize the weakness of the productive base. The GDR's national accounts and industrial statistics turned out to have been manipulated in order to portray the country as a leading industrial economy and it became clear that many, though not all, East German enterprises were practically worthless. The whole region threatened to become an industrial wasteland, unable to compete with the low-wage neighbouring countries to the east or with the highly productive and technologically advanced producers in the west. In order to maintain competitive jobs and harmonize standards of living in a united Germany, the former socialist economy had to be completely modernized. However, faced with this daunting task, very few private investors seemed willing to acquire firms in the five new German Länder, despite the low prices at which the THA offered firms, some of which had previously enjoyed a worldwide reputation for quality and reliability. German Federal and Länder governments therefore had to support the THA's privatization policy by providing loans, guarantees, subsidies, social overhead capital and other incentives in an effort to win over private investors. Altogether, more than 700 public programmes were put into place to support economic development in Eastern Germany.

The Political Importance of the THA

The goal of establishing a market economy was given both a legal and an organizational foundation in the form of the THA. Its legal bases included the Trusteeship Act (*Treuhandgesetz*) of 17 June 1990, the Unification Treaty, the Property Act (Vermögensgesetz) and the Trust Agency Borrowing Act (*Treuhandanstalt Kreditaufnahmegesetz*), which provided it with far-reaching regulatory powers and controls. The former Federal Chancellor Helmut Schmidt called it a 'most powerful second national government' (H. Schmidt, 1993: 32, 110) and a Bundestag representative of the Alliance 90/Greens described it as a 'superministry for the economic development of East Germany'. As a huge development agency, the THA had no predecessor. Not surprisingly, the centrality of its position made it the target of intense political pressure and contradictory demands. Political parties, Federal and Länder parliaments and governments, local governments, interest groups, businesses, former property owners (the so-called *Alteigentümer*),[1] the Federal Antitrust Office (*Bundeskartellamt*) the Federal Audit Office (*Bundesrechnungshof*) and many other interested parties all attempted to gain influence over the organization as a whole or over particular decisions.

In some cases they also sought to exercise supervisory powers over the THA and limit its discretionary scope. The network of relationships that emerged between the THA and these actors reveals much about the functioning of the political system of the Federal Republic.

From the outset, the THA operated under great uncertainty, which derived from the diverse and contradictory character of its mission and was accentuated by the constantly changing problems it faced. It was these factors which largely accounted for the extraordinary overburdening of the THA with what its last president, Birgit Breuel, described as 'completely exorbitant demands' (quoted in H. Schmidt, 1993: 108). Certainly, the THA was taken by surprise by economic developments which it could not influence. In this respect, the breakaway of Eastern European markets and the global economic crisis, with all their implications for the sale of problem-ridden East German companies, were of special importance. In the face of growing problems, the THA's means of response became increasingly limited. In addition, there were the constraints associated with the need for political negotiation and coordination involving Federal and Länder governments, trade unions and business associations. It is therefore very difficult to separate objective problems from those caused by institutional constraints that arose from the complicated and time-consuming procedural requirements imposed by the governmental system. Since the Federal government had raised high hopes of quick economic success in the new Länder, there was a very real danger that the blame for failure would be laid at the door of the political institutions. Thus an important additional task fell to the THA: to direct public disappointment and anger towards itself and away from the elected governments at the Federal and Länder levels. This was the 'lightning-rod function' or scapegoat role of the THA as an autonomous administrative agency which has been stressed by many commentators (R. Schmidt, 1991: 125).

Uncertainty also resulted from the information and communication gap between the THA and the individual enterprises it owned. Plant managers and staff often felt that they were subject to arbitrary decisions of the THA central office and its regional branches; the latter, in turn, frequently did not know what exactly was happening in the companies that still tended to be managed by the old cadres – often under the influence of prospective buyers from the West. The market value of the enterprises typically had to be assessed by West German economic consultants and auditors who might be tempted to act in collusion with plant managers and investors to mislead the THA. Thus the THA itself has estimated that there were about 1000 cases of dubious contracts and fraudulent gain. Of course this represents a relatively small share of the approximately 50 000 contracts concluded by the THA within a three-year period, which included not only the price of purchase (with total proceeds of DM43bn), but also job pledges (1.5 million jobs), investment pledges (DM180bn), details on the execution of contracts, arrangements in respect of inherited ecological burdens (*Altlasten*) and provisions relating to outstanding debts of GDR firms. In this connection it is interesting to note that, when the THA was first set up, it was still assumed that the conversion of GDR enterprises into private companies would involve little more than an act of bookkeeping, which could be managed by 150 lawyers and financial experts from the former finance ministry of the GDR in cooperation with West German consultants.

The THA between Länder and Federal Governments

Through the formation of formal and informal networks, an encompassing and complex system of interrelationships evolved around the THA. Of special interest were the problems that a centralized body of institutionalized trusteeship, created by the GDR government, faced in adjusting to the federal structure and the pattern of relationships between the state and interest groups that predominates in the Federal Republic. The THA further complicated the interlocking political nexus of Federal and Länder governments in Germany and put to the test the 'neo-corporatist' integration of economic interest groups into the Federal Republic's political processes.

Overlapping Federal and Länder jurisdictions have always been a characteristic of the German federal state, and they place powerful constraints on the political negotiating process (Lehmbruch, 1978; Scharpf, 1993: 35). The Federal Republic has been called a 'semi-sovereign state' (Katzenstein, 1987: 371f) because of its complex interlocking of domestic powers – an arduous political gearbox that has been lubricated by effective rules of compromise and consensus democracy. These rules have evolved during the postwar period and proved highly adaptive in the face of the political conflicts and economic crises of the 1970s and 1980s. Even by the mid-1990s, however, it is still an open question whether they can also meet the challenge of the conversion of a socialist planned economy into a market economy (H. Schmidt, 1993: 105ff; Hankel, 1993: 179f; Lehmbruch, 1991: 592f; M.G. Schmidt, 1993: 448f).

In the run-up to German unification – notably in the negotiations on the Unification Treaty, the Treaty on Electrical Power (*Stromvertrag*), the Trusteeship Act and the legislation concerning municipal property – the Federal Republic's intergovernmental negotiating system was temporarily bypassed in order to reach prompt decisions (Lehmbruch, 1991: 586). Only after the new Eastern Länder had been established and their resource needs could no longer be ignored, did the question arise as to the future shape of the intergovernmental system in unified Germany. At issue here were both the political and fiscal status of the Federal government vis-à-vis what were now 16 Länder and the horizontal redistribution of revenues (fiscal equalization) between the old and new Länder (Mäding, 1992). The THA, directly subordinate to the Federal government, played a decisive role in this respect, since it was confronted by tasks that fell under the jurisdiction of the new Länder, notably as far as implications of THA activities for regional structural development policy were concerned. In view of the centralist intentions of the Trusteeship Act and the fiscal problems of the new Länder, the situation in 1990 understandably gave rise to concerns about the possibility of greater centralization in intergovernmental relations (Seibel, 1992; Mäding, 1993; Lehmbruch, 1991: 592f; M.G. Schmidt, 1993: 453).

THA President Rohwedder, who was murdered by terrorists in April 1991, had anticipated this political development, and signalled his willingness to the Länder to make concessions while, at the same time, he sought to stake out areas of autonomy vis-à-vis the Federal government. This is also the context for the creation of a permanent presence for the THA in Bonn. Established in April 1991, the chief of this office was to represent the interests of the THA before Parliament. Thus, during its first two years, the THA Bonn office responded to some 2000 requests for information, mostly from members of parliament, and held more than 30 events to provide information on the THA's activities.[2] The Bonn office thus occupied the curious position of a lobbying institution of a Federal agency at the seat of the Federal government and Parliament.

Institutions of THA–Länder Coordination

The constitutional position of the Länder vis-à-vis the THA was made particularly clear in the Principles for the Cooperation of the Federal Government, New Länder, and Trust Agency in the Economic Upturn of East Germany of 15 March 1991 (Principles) (*Grundsätze zur Zusammenarbeit von Bund, neuen Ländern und Treuhandanstalt für den Aufschwung Ost*, in: Treuhand Informationen No. 1, May 1991; see also R. Schmidt, 1991: 31ff). These principles stated, 'The radical change of systems in the new Länder requires unusual measures in a concerted collaboration of the Federal government, the new Länder and the Trust Agency.' Furthermore, the Principles established the role of the THA as a 'service-provider' in the development of regional economic structures in the new Länder. The THA agreed to provide the Länder with all relevant information concerning enterprise closures and redundancies, including what particular measures would be taken (demolition, recycling, and land conservation and rehabilitation); what their employment effects would be; what contribution THA enterprises would make to job creation programmes; and what their land holding assets were. All of these data would be conveyed to the relevant Länder ministries. In addition, the seats reserved for the new Länder on the THA governing board (*Verwaltungsrat*) were to be filled by the Länder Minister–Presidents themselves; in this way, they would be kept informed of organizational developments, the general plan of action and all major decisions.

In addition to the governing board, the Principles also specified some additional institutional linkages between the THA and the new Länder, including THA economic cabinets (*Treuhand Wirtschaftskabinette*), advisory boards for the branch offices and direct contacts between government and administrative offices, on the one hand, and the THA's enterprise divisions, charged with privatization, on the other. THA economic cabinets were constituted in April 1991 on the basis of paragraph 8 of the Principles in each of the new Länder. The sixth session of the THA cabinet in Saxony provides a typical example of the range of participants. They included, on behalf of the THA, the division for the State of Saxony, representatives of the enterprise divisions affected by particular items on the agenda and the THA regional branch offices. For the State of Saxony, participants included representatives of the ministries of economics, finance and agriculture, the director of the Office for the Regulation of Unresolved Property Questions (*Amt zur Regelung offener Vermögensfragen*, or Property Office), the chair of the economics committee of the Landtag and other members of the Land parliament.

The monthly talks (*Monatsgespräche*) between the Land economic ministries and the representatives of the THA enterprise divisions, as well as the sectoral talks (*Branchengespräche*) and the company reorganization talks (*Sanierungsgespräche*) were closely related to the economic cabinets. They convened either directly after economic cabinet meetings or separately, with their own list of participants. The sectoral talks usually followed a uniform pattern in that they provided information on, first, enterprises, their starting position and situation, and their appraisal by the Supervisory Committee (*Leitungsausschuß*) of the THA; second, the state of privatization and interested parties; third, investment plans; fourth, means of funding; and, finally, further procedures.[3] Consultations with Länder parliaments and committee members were also part of the sectoral talks. By means of this preliminary provision of information, the Land divisions of the THA hoped to minimize the number of necessary responses to parliamentary requests for information. Länder governments were informed first, and on a regular basis, of any business closures or staff redundancies in the framework of an 'early-warning system', which was a product of the framework Principles adopted in the spring of 1991.

Länder aid for THA enterprises became an increasingly prominent part of the collaboration between the THA and Länder governments. The latter attempted to prevent further job losses, especially by using funds of the traditional Federal-Länder joint task programme for the promotion of regional economic development and funds of the European Commission designated for regional economic aid and by means of a diverse range of special programmes. Agreements with individual Länder show that the THA thoroughly approved of such initiatives as a way of reducing its own responsibilities. Thus, in the Breuel–Schommer agreement of 24 April 1992, the Saxon government pledged 'to support regionally important business enterprises, which it defines as such, with its entire set of instruments, and especially with GA[4] funds and with guarantees ... to promote the necessary public infrastructure measures and to make its labour market policy instruments available for specific purposes'.[5] In return, the THA intended to grant the enterprises supported by the Land government 'the necessary entrepreneurial and financial room for manoeuvre', even if the approved plan 'requires a modernization process of several years'.[6] The collaboration with the Länder resulted in various programmes for the joint promotion of regionally important enterprises, of which the Saxon ATLAS Project became the best known.

The THA as a 'Second East German Government'

The extent to which the THA's activities should be assigned to the fields of economics, politics or public administration is debatable. According to the Trusteeship Act of 17 June 1990, the Agency was set up as a concentration of stock companies under the supervision of a governing board. Another open question concerns the degree of autonomy it enjoyed vis-à-vis the Federal government, the Länder governments, the European Commission and the major interest groups.

Even before unification the stock company model had been replaced. A few stock companies which owned almost the whole economy would have carried on the old socialist combine structure. This approach threatened to preserve the GDR as an economic entity. Another factor was that the stock companies would have come under the German codetermination act of 1976. It is true, the THA owned a great number of legal stock corporations which have been codetermined by union and workers representatives. However, these were not powerful groups of affiliated companies. In accordance with the Trusteeship Act a plan of July 1990 provided for only four huge stock companies covering the fields of heavy industry, the capital goods industry, the consumer goods industry and services with a portfolio of up to 2,500 subsidiaries each.

On 24 August 1990, immediately after taking office as president, Rohwedder outlined the key features of a completely different organizational structure. Instead of a few sectoral stock companies below the THA office, responsibilities became divided between the central office in Berlin and 15 regional offices, with the former responsible for big firms and the latter for medium-sized and small ones. This was a violation of law and in September 1990 Rohwedder apologized in front of the GDR parliament using a traditional proverb: 'Real life comes before the letter of law'.[7]

In legal terms, the THA was not a business enterprise and, in factual terms, it was not a conventional state agency. Certainly, its legal form as an agency of public law directly accountable to the Federal government permitted no conclusions to be drawn about the actual role it played in the political system of the Federal Republic. Its mission and its way of operating placed it at the interface between state and economy. Speaking in legal terms, it could be defined as an 'organization in the area of overlap of two legal spheres' in which a mandate under public law and its discharge under private law coincide (Schuppert, 1992: 186). It functioned as an agent of the state for developing the private economy. In this sense – and in its legal form – it was reminiscent of the Reconstruction Investment Bank (*Kreditanstalt für Wiederaufbau*), which emerged after the Second World War out of the administration of the Marshall Plan funds of the European Recovery Programme. Both were in control of a special fund of the Federal government and under the supervision of a governing board that consisted largely of representatives of industry. The THA, of course, was conceived as a government agency, but, with the coming into force of the Trusteeship Act, its entrepreneurial character became more prominent, although when the Act was passed no one anticipated the political role it was gradually to assume. The THA's growing engagement in labour market policy, in particular, reflects the extent of its political involvement.

Between 1991 and 1993, the THA progressively lost much of the autonomy and room for manoeuvre that it had initially enjoyed. This occurred in the context of the increasing diversity of its tasks, the growing need to coordinate its actions with the Länder, and tighter controls by the Federal Antitrust Office, the Federal Audit Office, the Bundestag and Federal ministries. In 1993, the division responsible for company liquidations alone estimated that 1000 man-days were spent on answering requests for information from ministries, the Federal Audit Office, and Federal and Länder parliaments (*Süddeutsche Zeitung*, 22 July 1993: 17). When, in 1993, THA directors, branch managers and divisional heads were surveyed on external restrictions in the exercise of THA tasks, 58.8 per cent reported an increase in external influences on the activity of the THA between 1991 and 1992, 31.5 per cent reported no change, and 9.7 per cent answered that external influences had decreased.

The Supervisory Committee, the Ludewig Round and the Bundestag

Leaving aside, for the moment, the requirement of official approval for certain financial and policy-shaping decisions and the informal understandings reached in daily contacts with the Bonn ministries, especially the Ministry of Finance, there were two key institutions linking the THA and the Federal government: the Supervisory Committee (*Leitungsausschuß*) of the THA and the so-called 'Ludewig Round', named after Johannes Ludewig, the head of division in the Federal Chancellery entrusted by the Chancellor to deal with questions regarding the development of East Germany.

The institution of a Supervisory Committee can be traced back to the time of currency conversion in the GDR. At that time, a first group of auditors was sent to Berlin by the Federal Ministry of Finance to check on the use of funds. The start of currency union on 1 July 1990 allowed 8000 industrial enterprises to submit applications to the THA, specifying the operating funds they required in Deutschmarks, broken down according to wage payments, social insurance contributions, completion of orders, investments and so on. Since the THA was not, at the time, directly accountable to the Federal government, these applications had to be examined primarily in terms of business management criteria rather than legal prerequisites. Auditors and business consultants were commissioned to carry out this assessment exercise. After unification, they provided the core of the THA Supervisory Committee under the chairmanship of Horst Plaschna. The decision of the Federal government to approve only 41 per cent of the requested operating funds in the first phase was based on their expert appraisal. This constituted an early disappointment, and many managers of GDR firms laid the blame at the door of the central office of the THA. From this time on, the Supervisory Committee – as an autonomous advisory body to the Federal Ministry of Finance which was active in the THA but not incorporated into it – examined all entrepreneurial schemes submitted to the central office and issued recommendations on how they should be acted upon.

The prime function of the Ludewig Round was to act as a high-ranking political coordinating body. It convened for the first time on 13 May 1991 and then at intervals of several weeks (and sometimes more frequently), usually in the Berlin branch office of the Federal Chancellery. Its mission was to attend to, and also to monitor, the implementation of the resolutions on the development of East Germany passed in the first months of 1991. From the beginning of 1992, the meetings also served to prepare the talks of the Federal Chancellor with the Minister–Presidents of the new Länder and the governing mayor of Berlin. The participants in the Ludewig Round included the THA executive manager (*Generalbevollmächtigter*), the heads of the Minister–Presidents' offices of the new Länder, and the Federal

Chancellery, represented by Johannes Ludewig and the director of the Chancellery's Berlin office. The chief issues discussed included the financial requirements of the new Länder, current economic questions, initiatives for the development of East Germany, administrative assistance, trade with Eastern Europe, Federal export credit guarantees ('Hermes' credits), job-creation programmes and other controversial questions, such as the transfer of Federal land holdings to the Länder or the operations of the criminal prosecuting authorities at the THA.

The Ludewig Round was set apart from other coordinating bodies in which the THA took part by its multilaterality, its high rank and binding character, and the frequency and regularity with which it met. It linked the political control centres at a working level below that of the heads of governments and the THA executive (*Präsidium*). Unlike the Chancellor's Round on the development of East Germany in Bonn, which met informally and much less frequently, the political executives in the Ludewig Round coordinated their plans and interests in a small circle without the participation of societal interest groups. In those instances where talks were held in coordination with the meetings of the Chancellor and the Minister–Presidents of the new Länder, important decisions were often agreed, concerning, for example, the criteria for the award of Hermes credit guarantees and a draft of the Property Transformation Act (*Vermögensänderungsgesetz*). In this way, as well as through direct contacts with the Bundestag and the individual Federal ministries, the THA played an active role in shaping legislative initiatives. Thus the THA initiated, for example, a number of regulations of the Property Allocation Act (*Vermögenzuordnungsgesetz*), the Investment Priority Act (*Investitionsvorranggesetz*), the amended Jobs Development Act (*Arbeitsförderungsgesetz*) and the Trust Agency Borrowing Act (*Treuhandanstalt-Kreditaufnahmegesetz*).

Parliamentary oversight of the THA was initially assigned to a subcommittee of the budget committee of the Bundestag. In comparison to Federal and Länder governments, this committee played a minor part in the monitoring and regulation of the THA. Partly this was because the normal regulatory mechanisms and conditions of approval that are granted to Parliament under its budgetary powers were not fully applicable to the THA as an entity enjoying the legal status of an incorporated public law institution (Spoerr, 1991: 15). Partly the committee's lack of impact reflected the prevailing affirmative attitude vis-à-vis the THA on the part of the majority of its members. This may, in part, have been a reaction to the early severe criticism of the THA by the Alliance 90/Greens, which, in June 1991, went as far as presenting a draft for a new Trusteeship Act. The committee did not want to be seen to encourage in any way their demands for organizational reform, greater parliamentary controls, debt reduction and reorganization of

THA companies, especially since what influence the committee possessed was largely dependent on the agreement of the THA. The Trust Agency Borrowing Act of 3 July 1992 set a credit ceiling of DM30bn per fiscal year for the THA, and required approval by the Bundestag budgetary committee for this facility to be fully used in 1993 and 1994. In response, the THA expanded its briefings of the committee, frequently inviting the committee members to on-site inspections in Berlin or at industrial locations in the new Länder.

It was only in February 1993 that a separate Bundestag committee to deal with the Trust Agency was created, which covered the entire scope of THA activities. This committee was regularly informed by the THA of its operations, contract supervision activities, company reorganization plans, new approaches to privatization and THA expenditure. On 16 June 1993, the THA informed the THA committee that it wanted to raise DM8bn more on the capital market than its established credit limit and sought – through the Federal Ministry of Finance – the approval of the budget committee. This amount had already been agreed upon in negotiations between the Länder and Federal governments on the Federal Consolidation Programme, that is the Solidarity Pact on the development of East Germany. The money was intended, above all, to secure and renew industrial centres.

However, the budget committee of the Bundestag only approved DM7bn, a decision which prompted the THA to announce that it intended to curtail its participation in companies subsidized for purposes of job maintenance (*Beschäftigungsgesellschaften* or job maintenance companies) in the metal and electrical industries. This announcement also had a collective bargaining component to it. It was designed to induce the metal workers' union to extend the application of the so-called 'hardship clause' to THA enterprises (*Frankfurter Allgemeine Zeitung*, 3 July 1993: 12), which allowed for the reduction of wages in enterprises that suffered acute economic difficulties. The union had previously refused the use of this clause in the case of THA enterprises, since THA firms were maintained by public funds. In this situation, the budget committee's resolution was to be understood as a signal that THA firm managers, works councils and the trade unions would not be allowed to prevent the application of the hardship clause at the expense of taxpayers, without having to bear the consequences in terms of factory closures and unemployment. Here the interlocking of the parliamentary arena with the THA and interest group politics became especially clear. The THA responded to the parliamentary limitation of its financial discretion by threatening to cut back its job maintenance measures. This decision immediately raised a problem for trade union policy. In 1993, collective bargaining and employment policy became the politically most significant and explosive problems facing the THA.

Interest Groups and Public Administration in the Trust Agency Complex

The privatization activities of the THA resembled a balancing act, in that it had to balance investment and employment objectives, the assumption of inherited debt, participation in environmental clean-up projects and privatization receipts in such a way that the greatest possible consideration was given to the interests of the respective Federal and Länder ministries, business associations and trade unions. Of course no ideal solutions existed, particularly when the aims of job preservation and the promotion of investment became embroiled in conflicts of interest between trade unions and business associations. In addition, the representatives of industry, who held the majority of seats on the THA governing board (Table 5.1), were also concerned about the level of investment assistance the THA gave their potential competitors in the new Länder and the industrial structure which would emerge as a result of the THA privatization approach.

Table 5.1 Representation on the Treuhandanstalt's governing board (*Verwaltungsrat*) (number of seats)

Industry	9
Länder governments	6
Trade unions	4
Federal government	2

Source: *THA Organisationshandbuch*, rule no. 1.1.1.1.

Representatives of industry were, at times, the most uncompromising opponents of an entrepreneurially active trusteeship policy. They criticized key marketing concepts of THA enterprises (such as the Leipzig Trade Fair 'Made in Germany') and expressed their fear that government assistance in the east might jeopardize companies in the west, especially in the precarious economic situation of 1992 and 1993. On the other hand, the new Länder and the trade unions occasionally advocated highly risky modernization strategies, primarily for reasons of regional and social policy.

All major privatization plans had to be approved by the governing board,[8] as did certain executive decisions in such areas as organization, privatization guidelines, financial dealings and annual economic plans. Most resolutions tended to be unanimously approved after preliminary clarification, though they were also subject to approval by the Federal minister of finance and the

European Commission. Originally, the governing board was not supposed to be a vehicle for the representation of interests. The Trusteeship Act mentioned neither representatives of interest groups nor the participation of the Länder; instead, economic expertise was laid down as the sole appointment criterion. Formal regulations calling for the representation of Länder governments were first found in Article 25 (2) of the Unification Treaty, which established additional seats on the governing board. By contrast, trade union representation was solely at the discretion of the Federal government.

As part of the process of providing Länder, social groups and local authorities with better access to the THA, advisory boards to the regional branch offices were created in March 1991 on the basis of a directive of the THA central office. According to the directive, the aim was to 'bring about accord with the political, economic and societal forces of the region'. The composition of the advisory boards differed greatly from one regional branch office to the other. In Chemnitz, Cottbus, Dresden, Berlin and Halle, industry was particularly strongly represented; in Frankfurt/Oder, Leipzig and Rostock, the trade unions; in Erfurt and Frankfurt/Oder, the churches; in Gera, the municipalities; and in Neubrandenburg, citizen action groups played a major role (see Table 5.2).

Table 5.2   **Representation on the 15 regional branch office advisory boards of the THA (in number of seats and percentages), as of March 1991 (June 1991 for Berlin)**

Industry, chambers of commerce	45 (33%)
Local governments	28 (20%)
Trade unions	18 (13%)
Länder governments	14 (10%)
Churches	14 (10%)
Agriculture	9 (7%)
Citizen action groups	9 (7%)
Total	137 (100%)

Sources: THA-Office in Bonn, Appendix to the Report, 'Co-operation between Länder, the Federal Government and the THA' of 28 November 1991. Data on Berlin: Protocol of the constitutive meeting of the advisory board of the THA branch office in Berlin of 11 June 1991.

Labour Market and Industrial Relations

In the Principles for the development of East Germany, mentioned above, the establishment and funding of job maintenance companies were made the exclusive responsibility of Länder governments and the Federal Labour Office.[9] This created problems, since such companies could usually only be accommodated in the buildings of THA enterprises, make claims on the established subsidies of these enterprises and, in part, perform clean-up and reorganization operations on their behalf. Also, by implementing redundancy plans, the THA could trigger job maintenance measures at any time. The political conflict over job maintenance companies – involving the Federal government, the THA, Länder governments, trade unions and business associations – intensified until the middle of 1991, when the THA agreed to a compromise. Its basic features were adopted by the THA and representatives from the two sides of industry on 1 July 1991. The compromise resulted in a formal framework agreement between the trade unions, employers' federations and the THA, which was signed on 17 July 1991 and was to serve as the basis for the creation of Companies for Job Development, Employment and Structural Development (*Gesellschaften zur Arbeitsförderung, Beschäftigung und Strukturentwicklung*, or ABS companies).

From the very beginning, the THA would only take part in job-securing measures if they did not jeopardize its privatization mandate. For this reason, the THA insisted, in agreement with the business associations, on ending job maintenance employment in THA enterprises and on 'establishing a new legal relationship of a special kind' in ABS companies, which would reduce its responsibilities as an employer. Moreover, the legal construct of these companies would also make it easier to release employees. The THA declared its willingness to pay the managers of ABS companies for up to six months (and in special cases for up to a year) and to provide consulting and management assistance. The same held true for initial administrative tasks such as wage and salary accounting or social insurance payments. Finally, the THA had prefinanced numerous ABS companies, which resulted in reimbursement claims against the Länder governments. The latter, in turn, called for a stronger financial commitment on the part of the Federal government and the Federal Labour Office.

A completely new perspective opened up with the insertion of paragraph 249h into the Jobs Development Act. The new regulation, which came into being as a result of the efforts of the THA, made it possible for the Federal Labour Office to provide wage subsidies for a period of up to five years to those companies in the new Länder that contributed to environmental improvement, youth welfare services or other social services. On this basis, the

THA pledged, in an agreement with the Chemical Workers' Union, to endow an accreditation programme for chemical workers (*Qualifizierungswerk Chemie*) with DM75mill. and to administer it in close cooperation with the Chemical Workers' Union. Thus the THA made available earmarked funds to equip the companies taking part in the retraining programme with materials. The social compensation plans (*Sozialpläne*) of THA companies in the chemicals sector were to ensure that employees received compensation in the form of wage payments after being assigned to a company subsidized for purposes of reorganization (*Sanierungsgesellschaft*, or reorganization company). These reorganization companies received assistance from the employment authorities according to paragraph 249h of the Jobs Development Act.

The THA concluded a similar framework agreement with the Miners' and Energy Workers' Union. Here mine workers from the potash and lignite mines were to be retrained as landscape gardeners and employed in large-scale land rehabilitation programmes. The two initiatives, covering as many as 40 000 jobs, demonstrated the willingness of the THA to support job creation programmes if they were primarily investment-related, facilitated the privatization of THA enterprises and did not prevent a return to normal conditions. In the second half of 1993 alone, the THA earmarked a total of DM1.2bn for measures in accordance with paragraph 249h of the Jobs Development Act.

The politics of interest groups and wage agreements represents a further area that provides clear evidence of the close involvement of the THA in labour market and social policy issues. From the very beginning, the THA had trouble preventing its plant managers from making concessions to their employees. Only a few months after unification, it became clear that, with the help of West German consultants, many company agreements on redundancy protection and social compensation plans had been agreed upon which, in some cases, provided for extraordinary settlement sums. In one instance, the full salary was to be guaranteed until retirement age, while, in another, severance pay was set at DM156 000 for every worker to be made redundant. In both cases, the THA was expected to bear the full costs (Hanau, 1993; *Frankfurter Allgemeine Zeitung*, 29 January 1991). Only the first framework agreement, concluded on 13 April 1991 by the THA with the Federation of German Trade Unions (*Deutscher Gewerkschaftsbund*) and the German Union for Employees (*Deutsche Angestellten-Gewerkschaft*) provided for consistent provisions regarding redundancy. However, this agreement only became possible after the Federal Ministry of Finance had approved an endowment of DM10bn to fund social compensation plans.

THA guidelines on company wage and pay agreements and on the membership of THA enterprises in employers associations aimed to prevent the proliferation of company agreements.[10] According to the guidelines, its enterprises should join employers associations which were able to create an effective social consensus with the trade unions. Clearly, the THA preferred industry-wide collective bargaining agreements to company wage and pay contracts. Membership of an employers association was thus almost obligatory for THA enterprises, especially since in some businesses – for example, in the steel and shipyard industries – the works councils had such membership contractually guaranteed. Moreover, THA enterprises promoted the establishment of employers associations in the new Länder in so far as they paid their dues on time, in contrast to some privatized companies, but did not demand a strong voice in association matters. The THA also worked with the trade unions to try to ensure that foreign investors would maintain the employers association membership of privatized companies and did not enter into wage and pay agreements at the company level.

Municipalities, Former Property Owners and the Priority of Investment

The THA executive always endeavoured to present itself as its companies' executive management. That a public enterprise was involved was obvious, not only from the THA's array of relationships with external institutions and the impact of political considerations, but also from the public powers which had been bestowed on the THA. This applied, in particular, to its legal powers concerning the restitution of municipal properties and the property rights of former private owners, where priority was accorded to investment rather than restitution. In both cases, legally binding administrative acts were carried out by the THA, in particular its legal affairs division in the executive sector (*Präsidialbereich*) and the division for municipal properties and water regulation.

The directorate for municipal property had its own sections for each of the new Länder which were independent from the executive level, and there was also a liaison office for contacts with the main local government associations. The head of the division for municipal property was delegated from the German Association of Cities (*Deutscher Städtetag*) and maintained close contacts with this organization and with the cities and also with the Association of Counties (*Deutscher Landkreistag*) and the Association of Towns and Municipalities (*Deutscher Städte- und Gemeindebund*). Moreover, the municipal property division maintained close links with the Federal and Länder interior and justice ministries whose administrative regulations largely shaped its activities.

The municipal property division was also integrated within a wider relational network with Parliament and other parts of public administration. Requests for information were frequently received from the THA Committee of the Bundestag, there were daily calls from the Federal Ministry of Finance and frequent requests for information from local, regional, Länder and Federal politicians. In addition, the division, together with other THA divisions and the regional finance directorates (*Oberfinanzdirektionen*), which had local jurisdiction under the Property Allocation Act, was repeatedly represented at local government conferences, which were held by the Federal Ministries of Finance and the Interior. Finally, the municipal property division itself also organized its own local government conferences at the district level in order to report on the procedures and state of property restitution. These conferences focused on the west–east transfer of institutional know-how and problem-solving approaches related to the local provision of basic social services in the new Länder. These multiple links allowed the THA to take part in the development of the new Länder's local and state administrations.

Former property owners (*Alteigentümer*), their interest representatives[11] and local governments frequently turned to the THA in connection with Article 3a of the Property Act. At issue here was the suspension of THA restraints on the disposal of landed holdings and enterprises on which former owners had entered a claim. The Property Act, in its original version of 23 September 1990, turned out to be an impediment to investment. Accordingly, at the hearings to prepare a Federal Act on the Removal of Impediments to Investment (*Hemmnisbeseitigungsgesetz*), the THA called for the right to reject reprivatization claims in cases where former owners were only interested in property holdings and not willing, or able, to continue to run a business. As early as March 1991, with the insertion of Article 3a in the Property Act, the THA was empowered to establish the priority of investment over restitution. This provision transformed the claim to the return of property into a claim for compensation. Once the THA instigated investment priority proceedings, the restitution process by the responsible Land government Office for the Regulation of Unresolved Property Questions was legally discontinued.

In the conflict between the investment, employment and development interests of the THA and decisions on restitution claims by the property authorities, administrative competition arose which was supposed to be defused by means of joint working sessions between the THA and the property authorities. Nonetheless, in the eyes of several property authorities, the THA was their greatest enemy. Others were more open in their response to the priority of investment, especially since, in the assigning of property to former owners, they were dependent upon the previous work of the THA, notably the reprivatization division. Despite precautions, both legal and informal, restitution rulings sometimes conflicted with decisions by the THA, and the THA usually took legal action against decisions of property offices if they conflicted with THA privatization plans. This was especially the case if former owners attempted to stop important, large-scale projects in an attempt to increase the amount of compensation they would receive.

Amongst the public powers of the THA, mention should also be made of the Special Assignments unit of the THA, which was vested with the powers of an investigative department of a public prosecutor's office. It was staffed primarily by prosecuting attorneys and police detectives delegated by Federal and Länder governments. In close cooperation with district attorneys and auditors, its four departments investigated cases of managerial abuse of trust, the unlawful dismantling of enterprises, subsidy fraud, unification-related criminality, corruption, breach of entrepreneurial secrecy, defamation and environmental offences. They were also involved in the internal audit of the THA. Prompt investigative work made it possible to secure some 90 per cent of the total of DM3bn at issue in the investigations of fraud up to December 1992.

Conclusion: Privatization in Interwoven Decision Making Structures

The major goal of the THA was to create efficient property rights through what might be called 'negotiated privatization'. Neither auctions nor direct sales in favour of former socialist managers played any significant role in the East German road from socialism to capitalism. Even restitution to former property owners was conditional on the THA's assessment of their entrepreneurial abilities. Thus, from July 1992 onwards, the THA could authoritatively allocate property rights to competent investors if former owners were not willing to invest or not able to present appropriate business plans. This power was based on the Investment Priority Act.

In one sense, the THA did not really sell its firms; rather, it bought business plans and investments. Many THA firms achieved only negative contract prices and, in five years, the Agency ran up enormous debts, amounting to DM270bn (including DM70bn in old debts, which had been converted into Deutschmarks through monetary union). Since 1 January 1995, these debts have had to be met by the Federal budget, together with other unification costs, amounting to some DM450bn. Thus the German taxpayer will have to finance interest and capital repayments of about DM40bn per annum for an estimated 30 years.

With only minor exceptions, unification policies tried to preserve the system of government, public administration and political economy of West Germany by transferring it to the new eastern Länder. This has turned out a risky but promising endeavour. As far as the political economy is concerned, the 'German model' (Scharpf, 1987) had proved itself in West Germany. It is characterized by collective bargaining autonomy and cooperative interest group politics, monetary stability, free trade, a consensus on industrial competitiveness, and welfare state provisions, including codetermination in industry or social security schemes which are mostly linked to labour contracts. The transition from socialism to a market economy in East Germany was a process of rapid and comprehensive institutional adjustment to the functional conditions and customary patterns of problem solving found in West German politics.

This process of institutional transfer can be seen very clearly in the evolution of the THA from a central economic agency of transformation created by the GDR government into part of the complex political system of the Federal Republic. As an intermediate institution between the Federal government and the new Länder, it functioned as a third level of cooperation in Germany's intergovernmental system. Thus both Federal and Länder governments were represented on its governing board and numerous coordinating committees, as were representatives of industry and the trade unions. The THA's scope for manoeuvre and the conditions of success were shaped by this relational network. Early assessments of the THA, which assumed that it would strengthen central state power because of its dominant economic role in East Germany (Seibel, 1992: 194), therefore need to be qualified. How did the THA's intermediary position in the bargaining arenas of federalism and of interest group politics affect its success? This question is not easily answered, as technical restrictions need to be distinguished from institutional ones. Undoubtedly, many of the THA's problems simply resulted from the diversity and contradictory character of its responsibilities. Conflicts between different substantive goals and economic constraints that hampered the policy transformation existed independently of the institutional configuration of the agents of transformation. As problems, time constraints and the pressure to succeed grew, the THA's room for manoeuvre shrank. Accordingly, the correct question to ask is whether, in the words of former Chancellor Helmut Schmidt, its 'condition, which was overburdened in any case, really worsened by the large number of bodies interfering with the agency', or whether, on the contrary, the THA's network of external relations helped it to cope with its excessive responsibilities.

In answering this question, it should first be noted that the interlocking of decision makers in the transformation process lessened the legitimation problems of the THA. This was, in fact, the effect the THA aimed for with its strategy of cooption and the opening to political and interest groups. Of course, this strategy raised the danger of capture by pressure groups, and many critics complained of the privileged position of business interests within the THA. However, the cooption of all relevant actors contributed to checks and balances between political, economic and trade union interests and to the better coordination of objectives.

The Trust Agency complex is a classic example of the way an encompassing network of coordination and control arises out of the confrontation of mutually dependent political and interest group actors. Ultimately, it was the THA itself that linked much of this network of transformation policy making together. Its legal status and the strategy of cooption it consistently pursued allowed it to gain the commitment of powerful actors and, at the same time, helped to create common areas of action. Where it entered into relationships – whether on the basis of the Principles for the economic recovery of East Germany, framework agreements with unions, internal guidelines, or through the many coordinating committees – the THA relied on the common interest of all participants in the success of economic reorganization and tried to garner the widest possible support for its line of action.

There was a constant danger of conflict inherent in the precarious dual role of the THA as an employer and agent of transformation, on the one hand, and a key player in labour market and social policy, on the other. The only realistic option open to the THA was to meet this challenge in the spirit of compromise, as it would otherwise have quickly been destroyed in the clash of forces between the Federation, individual Länder, business associations and the trade unions. A process of mutual accommodation, which from the outside might have looked like helpless 'muddling through' (see Lindblom, 1959), was the only promising solution in the confusing situation that posed a constant threat to the very existence of the organization. Such 'muddling through' can be understood as a logical consequence of the interlocking nature of the institutions of the German system of government. Even in a situation characterized by far simpler problems, it would have been difficult to attain a greater degree of control in this differentiated system. Nonetheless, programmatic coherence and calculable procedures remain the aim of all rational attempts at problem solving, especially in the internal realm of major organizations. Such coherence and reliability, however, proved unattainable. This was in part the result of the network of political relations in which the THA had to operate, the complexity of the problems it faced and the need for flexibility in dealing with investors. Perhaps more importantly, almost all participants in the transformation process shared the notion that the path from the plan to the market could not itself be planned, and that there were, accordingly, limits to a rationally calculated and routinized mode of problem management.

Where governance through markets or hierarchies does not yet function, or cannot guarantee satisfactory solutions to specific problems, the principle of political compromise to be found in informal social networks and interlocked decision making structures can be invoked. In the face of a severe economic and political crisis – when it was evident that most of its firms were not saleable – the Trust Agency moderated its strict market approach and learned to take advantage of semi-bureaucratic, informal procedures, and its organizational boundaries became blurred. The THA did not really sell its firms any more, but bought concepts of private investors and subsidized their rescue operations to the extent of negative net contract prices. Thus the THA came to act as a development agency.

If it is true that governments cannot plan, but only support, the way a market economy functions, then the Federal Republic was better designed to face the risks involved in the transformation of socialist economic systems than a unitary state. Its political institutions are geared to negotiations and the balancing of political interests (Czada and Schmidt, 1993). They are not hierarchically structured, but are oriented towards the constant mutual readjustment of their parts. The THA of the GDR government represented a

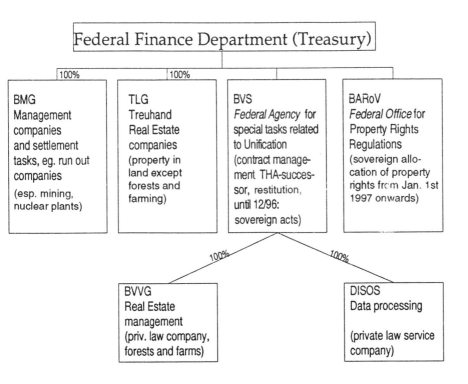

Figure 5.1   THA successor organizations

'faulty construct' (Helmut Schmidt) for this system, which first had to free itself from its set 'planning targets' in order to find its place within the bargaining democracy of the Federal Republic. When it had succeeded in this task, it was time to consider ending its institutional life.

By 1 January 1995, the THA itself was transformed and organizationally restructured into a new political body called the Federal Agency for Special Tasks Related to Unification (*Bundesanstalt für vereinigungsbedingte Sonderaufgaben* – BVS) and several smaller administrative units (Figure 5.1). The control of contracts, future privatizations of public lands, the handling of several closed-down nuclear power plants and many other tasks will remain for a longer period.

The Treuhandanstalt did not break up the ordinary framework of German administrative law. The unique and sovereign nature of its tasks, however, made it an autonomous though not independent body of political decision making and administration. Its operations were not so much determined by law or by governmental order nor by parliamentary oversight as one should assume in view of its legal foundations and vital political importance. So far, the Treuhandanstalt could possibly serve as a model for a project-oriented public administration operating in informal, network-like structures which go beyond the public-private boundary. Although informal policy making has been ubiquitous due to overlapping political responsibilities for a long time, the infiltration of a private sector culture into government is weakly developed in Germany compared to other industrialized countries. In this respect, the THA has to be considered as an exception. This is also indicated by the fact that it lost some of its flexibility because of growing demands for coordination and a process of bureaucratization imposed by the Federal Audit Office, Federal ministries and the European Commission. To conclude, the Treuhandanstalt revealed considerable adaptive capacities of the German political and administrative system. Yet for the same reason it did not significantly change the operating principles of this system.

Notes

1   These are former owners of property in the territory of the former GDR who filed claims for the restitution of their erstwhile property.
2   See THA-Büro Bonn, 'Zwei Jahre "Büro Bonn der Treuhandanstalt"', Ms, 29 April 1993.
3   See 'Schwerpunktaufgaben der Länderabteilung Sachsen-Anhalt', 17 January 1992, THA-Archiv, SAN 5: 49.
4   GA funds consist of Federal and Länder monies allocated to the Joint Task Regional Economic Development (Article 91a of the Basic Law).
5   The Breuel–Schommer Agreement of 24 April 1992 (named after the THA president, Birgit Breuel, and the Saxon economics minister, Kajo Schommer), quoted in the letter

from THA President Breuel to Saxon Minister–President Kurt Biedenkopf, 27 April
1992, on 'Cooperation Between the Trust Agency and the Free State of Saxony', THA-
Archiv, SACH: 198–201.
6   Ibid.
7   Volkskammer der Deutschen Demokratischen Republik, 10th legislative period, 35th
session, 13 September 1990, shorthand report, page 1680.
8   According to the THA's rules of procedure (paragraph 15), governing board consent
was obligatory if any two of the following criteria applied: the total balance involved
exceeded DM100mill., turnover value exceeded DM300mill., or the enterprise had
more than 2000 employees.
9   *Grundsätze Aufschwung Ost*, Treuhand Informationen no. 1, May 1991: 11, paragraph
5.
10   See *Richtlinie für Betriebsvereinbarungen und Haustarifverträge*, vol. 1, September
1992: 1.
11   They included the Association of Central Germans (*Bund der Mitteldeutschen*), mainly
refugees from the former GDR living in West Germany and the Organization of
Owners of Berlin Wall Land Plots (*Organisation der Besitzer von Berliner
Mauergrundstücken*). In addition, the Diet of German Industry and Commerce
(*Deutscher Industrie- und Handelstag*) and other business associations also played a
limited role.

References

Benz, A. (1985) *Föderalismus als dynamisches System*, Opladen: Westdeutscher
Verlag.
Benz, A. (1993) 'Reformbedarf und Reformchancen des kooperativen Föderalismus
nach der Vereinigung Deutschlands', in W. Seibel, A. Benz and H. Mäding (eds),
Verwaltungsreform und Verwaltungspolitik im Prozeß der deutschen Einigung,
Baden-Baden: Nomos Verlagsgesellschaft, 454–73.
Czada, R. (1993) 'Das scheue Reh und die Kröte. Investition und Beschäftigung im
Kalkül der Treuhandanstalt', in G. Bosch, B. Reissert and H. Heinelt (eds),
Arbeitsmarktpolitik nach der Vereinigung, Berlin: Sigma, 214–33.
Czada, R. and M.G. Schmidt (eds) (1993) *Verhandlungsdemokratie, Interessen-
vermittlung, Regierbarkeit: Festschrift für Gerhard Lehmbruch*, Opladen:
Westdeutscher Verlag.
Eichener, V., R. Kleinfeld, D. Pollak, J. Schmid, K. Schubert and H. Voelzkow
(eds) (1992) *Organisierte Interessen in Ostdeutschland*, Marburg: Metropolis.
Hanau, P. (1991) 'Sozialverträgliche Gestaltung bei der Umstrukturierung und
Auflösung von Unternehmen', in P. Hommelhoff (ed.), *Treuhandunternehmen
im Umbruch. Recht und Rechtswirklichkeit beim Übergang in die Marktwirtschaft*,
Cologne: Kommunikationsforum, 101–20.
Hanau, P. (1993) 'Soziale Regulierung der Treuhandtätigkeit', in W. Fischer and
H.K. Schneider (eds), *Treuhandanstalt – das Unmögliche wagen*, Berlin: Akademie
Verlag, 444–80.
Hankel, W. (1993) *Die sieben Todsünden der Vereinigung*, Berlin: Siedler.

Hesse, J. and W. Renzsch (1990) 'Zehn Thesen zur Entwicklung und Lage des deutschen Föderalismus', *Staatswissenschaften und Staatspraxis,* 4, 262–78.

Hommelhoff, P. (ed.) (1991) *Treuhandunternehmen im Umbruch. Recht und Rechtswirklichkeit beim Übergang in die Marktwirtschaft,* Cologne: Kommunikationsforum.

Katzenstein, P. (1987) *Politics and Policy in West Germany. The Growth of a Semi-Sovereign State,* Philadelphia: Temple University Press.

Kern, H. and C.F. Sabel (1992) 'Zwischen Baum und Borke – Zur Unsicherheit der Treuhand, was sie als nächstes sagen sollte', *Sofi-Mitteilungen,* 1, 61–78.

Lehmbruch, G. (1978) 'Party and Federation in Germany: A Developmental Dilemma', *Government and Opposition,* 13, 151–77.

Lehmbruch, G. (1991) 'Die deutsche Vereinigung. Strukturen und Strategien', *Politische Vierteljahresschrift,* 32, 585–604.

Lindblom, C.E. (1959) 'The Science of "Muddling Through"', *Public Administration Review,* 13, 79–88.

Ludwig Erhard Stiftung (1993) *Wirtschaftliche und soziale Ausgestaltung der deutschen Einheit,* Bonn.

Mäding, H. (1992) 'Die föderativen Finanzbeziehungen im Prozeß der deutschen Einigung – Erfahrungen und Perspektiven', in H.-H. Hartwich and G. Wewer (eds), *Finanz- und wirtschaftspolitische Bestimmungsfaktoren des Regierens im Bundesstaat – unter besonderer Berücksichtigung des deutschen Vereinigungsprozesses,* Opladen: Leske & Budrich, 183–214.

Olsen, J.P. (1993) 'Political Science and Organization Theory. Parallel Agendas but Mutual Disregard', in R.M. Czada and A. Windhoff-Héritier (eds), *Political Choice: Institutions, Rules and the Limits of Rationality,* Frankfurt a. M.: Campus, 87–120.

Ouchi, W.G. (1980) 'Markets, Bureaucracies, and Clans', *Administrative Science Quarterly,* 25, 129–41.

Pilz, F. and H. Ortwein (1992) *Das vereinte Deutschland. Wirtschaftliche, soziale und finanzielle Folgeprobleme und die Konsequenzen für die Politik,* Stuttgart: Enke.

Powell, W. (1990) 'Neither Market nor Hierarchy: Network Forms of Organisation', *Research in Organizational Behavior,* 12, 295–336.

Priewe, J. and R. Hickel (1991) *Der Preis der Einheit,* Frankfurt a. M.: Fischer.

Rosenthal, U. and B. Pijnenburg (eds) (1991) *Crisis Management and Decision Making,* Dordrecht: Kluwer.

Scharpf, F.W. (1972) 'Komplexität als Schranke der politischen Planung', *Politische Vierteljahresschrift,* Sonderheft 4, 168–92.

Scharpf, F.W. (1987) *Sozialdemokratische Krisenpolitik in Europa,* Frankfurt a. M.: Campus.

Scharpf, F.W. (1993) 'Versuch über Demokratie im verhandelnden Staat', in R. Czada and M.G. Schmidt (eds), *Verhandlungsdemokratie, Interessenvermittlung, Regierbarkeit,* Opladen: Westdeutscher Verlag, 25–50.

Scharpf, F.W., B. Reissert and W. Schnabel (1976) *Politikverflechtung. Theorie und Empirie des kooperativen Föderalismus in der Bundesrepublik,* Kronberg/Ts.: Scriptor.

Schmidt, H. (1993) *Handeln für Deutschland. Wege aus der Krise*, Berlin: Rowohlt.

Schmidt, M.G. (1992) *Regieren in der Bundesrepublik Deutschland*, Opladen: Westdeutscher Verlag.

Schmidt, M.G. (1993) 'Die politische Verarbeitung der deutschen Vereinigung im Bund-Länder-Verhältnis', in W. Seibel, A. Benz and H. Mäding (eds), *Verwaltungsreform und Verwaltungspolitik im Prozeß der deutschen Einigung*, Baden-Baden: Nomos Verlagsgesellschaft, 448–53.

Schmidt, R. (1991) 'Aufgaben und Struktur der Treuhandanstalt im Wandel der Wirtschaftslage', in P. Hommelhoff (ed.), *Treuhandunternehmen im Umbruch. Recht und Rechtswirklichkeit beim Übergang in die Marktwirtschaft*, Cologne: Kommunikationsforum, 17–38.

Schuppert, G.F. (1992) 'Die Treuhandanstalt – Zum Leben einer Organisation im Überschneidungsbereich zweier Rechtskreise', *Staatswissenschaften und Staatspraxis*, **3**, 186–210.

Seibel, W. (1992) 'Necessary Illusions: The Transformation of Governance Structures in the New Germany', *The Tocqueville Review*, **13**, 177–97.

Seibel, W. (1993) 'Lernen unter Unsicherheit. Hypothesen zur Entwicklung der Treuhandanstalt und der Staat-Wirtschaft-Beziehungen in den neuen Bundesländern', in W. Seibel, A. Benz and H. Mäding (eds), *Verwaltungsreform und Verwaltungspolitik im Prozeß der deutschen Einigung*, Baden-Baden: Nomos Verlagsgesellschaft, 359–70.

Sinn, G. and H.-W. Sinn (1993) *Kaltstart. Volkswirtschaftliche Aspekte der deutschen Vereinigung*, Tübingen: Mohr.

Spoerr, W. (1991) *Treuhandanstalt und Treuhandunternehmen zwischen Verfassungs-, Verwaltungs- und Gesellschaftsrecht*, Cologne: Kommunikationsforum.

6 The Regional Districts in Search of a New Role

Dietrich Fürst

Germany's public administration is organized on both territorial and functional principles. Although, historically, territorial forms of organization dominated, industrialization and modernization have shifted the emphasis towards the functional principle. Districts (*Bezirksregierungen, Regierungspräsidien*) are intermediate administrative authorities which represent the territorial dimension and act as intermediaries between the Länder governments and local government. One of their chief functions is to coordinate Länder sectoral policies at the regional level. Districts exist in Bavaria, Baden–Württemberg, Hesse, Lower Saxony, North Rhine–Westphalia, Rhineland–Palatinate, Saxony and Saxony–Anhalt, and in most cases the Land territory is subdivided into three or four districts (five in the case of North Rhine–Westphalia and seven for Bavaria). Districts are administrative bodies without popularly elected political representatives and, as dependent Land authorities, they receive their resources from the Länder ministries of the interior and are subject to the directives of the Land governments. By contrast, counties are upper-tier local governments which comprise several independent municipalities and cooperate with these municipalities on the basis of a division of labour that follows, in principle, the idea of subsidiarity.[1] Counties and municipalities perform their functions separately, while larger 'county-free' cities (*kreisfreie Städte*) combine the functions of both in one body. Both counties and municipalities have directly elected councils.

Districts have only been treated very selectively in the German public administration literature. Most analyses have been written by lawyers or practitioners with close links to district authorities. Thus, while we know much about what tasks districts are supposed to carry out, there are few assessments of their actual performance and their ability to cope with a changing environment which increasingly calls into question the need for district authorities.

From the start, districts were confronted by the conflict between increasing state intervention, on the one hand, and decentralization pressures, on the other. As local government became more powerful, the conflict between districts and local governments intensified. At the same time, with the improvement of transport infrastructures and communication, the central Länder administrations centralized government functions by expanding into the sphere of implementation, which challenged the *raison d'être* of the districts. Therefore the districts' role was questioned at an early stage (Hillmann, 1969: 70f) and, following both world wars, there were proposals for their abolition, supported by the *Städtetag,* the Association of County-free Cities. Yet it was only in the context of the administrative and territorial reform debate that began in the 1960s that the existence of districts was more widely discussed. Following the territorial reforms of the late 1960s and early 1970s, the administrative system became more decentralized, with stronger local governments, more regionalized, with larger counties, but also more politicized (Wagener, 1982: 157). In response, doubts further increased as to the future role of districts. They had to face growing competition from other administrative organizations, such as larger counties, regional associations of local governments and special authorities, all of which were beginning to encroach on traditional district functions.

Against this background, the following discussion focuses on three questions. First, what are the dominant contextual changes that challenge the traditional role of districts? Second, how do districts cope with these challenges? Third, what does the future hold for the districts?

The Historical Functions of Districts

In normative terms, the territorial component is still regarded as the dominant aspect of the German administrative structure. As Frido Wagener (1982: 156) put it: 'The well-known principles of the German administrative system – the universality of the political domain; the unity of administration at the levels of counties and districts; the regional coordinating function – they all belong to the historical orientation of our administration towards territory.' Accordingly, the main attempts at functional administrative reform have all tried to strengthen the territorial component in order to improve intersectoral coordination at the levels of counties, districts and, at times, even the central Land administration.

Historically, the districts have been important in organizational terms because they combined functional and territorial structures. In the Prussian territories, districts were introduced by Stein and Hardenberg shortly after 1800, in order to counterbalance the growing functional specialization of the ministries and to regionalize central state policies (see Jacob, 1963; Hillmann, 1969: 45ff; Faber, 1985; Köstering, 1991; Lottermoser, 1992). Under the influence of the Prussian reforms, intermediary institutions resembling the Prussian districts were also established in Bavaria through the administrative reforms of Montgelas (Hillmann, 1969: 49f). While both Bavaria and Prussia were influenced by French–Napoleonic ideas, other Länder, including Württemberg and Baden, did not adopt that model, and it was only after the Second World War that Baden–Württemberg came to establish districts.[2]

Districts represent the Land government at the regional level, a role similar to that of commissioners or governors. As a result, they are not mere administrative bodies, but tend to enjoy considerable political weight. It is for this reason that the district chiefs have always been political appointees, with the exception of Bavaria, where the district chief must not have any party political affiliations. In addition to districts, there are some special authorities (*Sonderbehörden*) with executive and implementation functions which operate outside the control of the district chiefs. They tend to include, for example, authorities for road construction, statistics, the protection of the environment, agrarian land reform, revenue collection or the supervision of mines. These special authorities are directly responsible to their respective ministries, and districts exercise no control over them.

In all policy areas not covered by special authorities, policy implementation is channelled through the district offices. The main functions of districts include coordinating sectoral policies at the regional level, supervising and advising local governments, supporting policy preparation at the Land level and resolving conflicts between local governments, and between citizens and local administrations. In terms of their internal organization, district offices closely reflect the sectoral structure of the Land ministerial bureaucracy, although some ministries, including Justice, Science and Culture, and Finance have few direct links with district authorities, but operate through special authorities. Each district department does, however, have to serve more than one ministry in order to facilitate policy coordination. Districts are directly responsible to the Land ministries of the Interior as far as legal controls are concerned, but are subject to the substantive control of sectoral ministries in the implementation of sectoral policies.

Districts vary considerably in terms of their territory, population and the size of district offices (see Schrapper, 1994). Some Länder are big (North Rhine–Westphalia has five districts, 17 million inhabitants and a territory of 34 071 square kilometres) others are very small (for example, Saxony–Anhalt has three districts, 3 million inhabitants and an area of 20 444 square kilometres). The largest district in terms of inhabitants is Düsseldorf, with a population of 5 million, and the smallest Trier, with 500 000 inhabitants. In terms of territory, the largest district is Upper Bavaria, with 17 529 square kilometres, the smallest Dessau, with 4254 square kilometres. The number of employees in district offices also differs markedly, depending on the range of functions performed by the district, which is decided by the Land government, and the number of inhabitants within a district. The size of district administrations ranges from about 800 employees, such as in Arnsberg in North Rhine–Westphalia, to more than 1200 in Lower Saxon offices. The latter figure reflects the range of functions performed by Lower Saxon district administrations. Thus, of a total of 41 different district functions identified by Schrapper (1994: 161), the Lower Saxon authorities carry out 37, while the figure for their counterparts in Bavaria and Rhineland–Palatinate is 34, in North Rhine–Westphalia and Saxony–Anhalt 33, in Baden–Württemberg 32, in Hesse 31 and in Saxony 29.

To summarize, the districts' main function is to coordinate or 'bundle' sectoral policies within their region. The importance of such horizontal coordination was well illustrated by the administrative problems caused by the absence of districts when the new eastern Länder were established in 1990. Huge amounts of financial assistance poured into the regions without adequate coordinating bodies at the regional level (Hoffmann, 1992: 694). Yet, given their history and traditional purpose, districts have also always been instruments of power and hierarchical control. This is a legacy which they have not been able to overcome and which limits the willingness of local governments to cooperate with district authorities.

Contextual Changes: Challenges to the Districts' Role and Functions

Since their creation, districts have had to compete with the increasing political and administrative weight of local government. Local authorities became more important as the central state changed from being a controlling state (*Herrschaftsstaat*) to a service and welfare state. As part of this development, more functions accrued to local government and, by means of territorial reforms, local authorities were partly converted into the lower executive level of central government. Even more important were the general political processes of democratization and the creation of the welfare state, which began after the First World War and gained momentum after the Second World War. As a consequence, local government became pivotal in supplying social welfare services and public goods.

At the same time, districts were challenged by the tendency of Land governments to centralize policy implementation. They lost much of their former power when politicians started to channel popular demands directly to central government, thereby further reinforcing centralizing tendencies. The larger local authorities followed suit in bypassing the districts, and increasingly turned directly to the Land ministries for resources and guidance. The ministries were usually only too eager to respond since direct contacts allowed them to enhance their own influence without becoming overly dependent on the districts.

These trends were already clearly in evidence at the beginning of the twentieth century, and after the First World War they provoked sporadic demands for the abolition of districts in favour of politically directly accountable institutions (Hillmann, 1969: 70ff). Nonetheless, even after the Second World War, when all the newly founded Länder had the chance to rebuild their administrative structures, the discussion on whether to abolish the districts was muted. Only Schleswig-Holstein, and later the Saarland, rejected the district model, as both were considered too small to warrant an additional general level of administration between the Land ministries and local government. Instead, both Länder relied on the counties and on special authorities to perform functions which elsewhere were carried out by district authorities.

Territorial reform in the late 1960s and early 1970s prompted a new round of discussions on the role of districts. The Länder ministries of the interior established a commission to consider the future of the districts, which reported in 1973 (Mittelinstanz-Bericht, 1973), but a vote against the districts was never expected, as the commission consisted entirely of government officials. The difficulty of abolishing districts was clearly demonstrated in Baden–Württemberg where they lacked a firm basis in tradition. In 1971, the parliament of Baden–Württemberg passed a law to abolish the districts, but before it could be implemented the law was amended, in 1976, and the districts' future existence secured. As a consequence, although economic, technical, political and administrative conditions have changed profoundly in the last 160 years, districts have remained remarkably unchanged (Ellwein, 1993a). A casual observer may take this as just another instance of administrative inertia, but an organizational analysis of a district in North Rhine–Westphalia, formerly Prussian territory, came to the conclusion that the structure and processes of its offices were more or less functionally appropriate (Zündel, 1991). This assessment could be generalized to apply to all North Rhine–Westphalian district authorities, as they follow a common organizational pattern. This finding is not altogether surprising, given that the key arguments put forward in support of districts by the Mittelinstanzbericht in 1973 still apply today. Thus, the report emphasized the following points:

- Districts allow continuity in the representation of regional interests in administrative policy preparation and implementation. This is of growing importance since the territorial dimension tends to be neglected in a political world which defines and resolves problems along segmented sectoral lines and organizes political groups and parliamentary committees accordingly. By strengthening the territorial component within the largely sectoralized political–governmental structure, districts provide a kind of 'matrix organization' that combines territory and function.
- By supervising and controlling local governments, districts alleviate the burden on Länder ministries.
- The dominant role of district chiefs is coordination (*Bündelungsfunktion*). Again, this role is gaining in significance since the number of policy areas cutting across the institutional boundaries of sectoral ministries is growing.

Despite the continued validity of these arguments, districts are undoubtedly challenged by a changing environment that tends to destabilize their fragile position as intermediary organizations. The main challenges are similar to those which underlie the discussion on 'meso-level politics' (Sharpe, 1993; Fürst, 1993). They include a pervasive tendency of governments to decentralize and regionalize politics; the increasing competition of regions within a 'Europe of regions'; and economic and political pressure on regions to enhance regional decision making capacities. These pressures put strains on the adaptive capacities of districts.

The Growing Need to Organize Regions and the Districts' Limited Capacities to Satisfy that Demand

In the past, while Länder governments increasingly centralized steering and control, implementation functions were decentralized. This division of labour enforced interlinkages between local and Länder governments, with Länder governments defining rules and regulations and local governments influencing the policy making process 'from below'. This development accentuated the need to define regional interests more precisely and posed the question of how districts could contribute to this definition of regional interests. There has been a great deal of scepticism about the districts' capacity to take on this task. First, the districts are hierarchically embedded in the Land administration and they are primarily the representative of the Land government in the region rather than a representative of the region at the Land level. Second, the decentralization of implementation renewed the discussion about the need for elected political bodies at the district level.

Such considerations gained in importance when, in the mid-1970s, regional planning gradually came under the control of the Länder. While different models were adopted, the general direction was very similar: the districts were to provide the technical basis for planning, while an attached body of representatives of local authorities would take decisions on regional plans. Thus the attached bodies provided the districts with political support and led to an institutional nucleus of 'parliamentarization' at the district level. 'Parliamentarization' of the intermediary level, accordingly, became a central topic in the reform discussions towards the late 1970s (Benz, 1983; Wagener, 1982: 164). A weak, but politically acceptable substitute for elected councils were the advisory bodies (*Beiräte*) through which regional political groups and actors could be incorporated into Land policy making.

Economic change has tended to increase the regions' importance. The reasons are, first, that since the beginning of the 1980s, business firms have no longer been satisfied with single locations, but have increasingly branched out to form multi-site firms and even 'production clusters' (the key jargon here is flexible specialization, out-sourcing, lean production and just-in-time production). Second, the growing regional differentiation in implementation conditions has meant that public policies also have had to be differentiated regionally. Third, with the increasing influence of the EU and the change in the EU's regional policy towards programme-oriented funding, the regions have enjoyed increased prominence. The EU Commission now requires regions to define regional programmes to be submitted for funding, and the NUTS 3 regions correspond to the districts' territorial boundaries. Fourth, since the beginning of the 1990s, the Länder's fiscal crisis has made them switch to strategies of 'endogenous development', thus regionalizing their policies and shifting more responsibility for economic development to the regions under the banner of 'regional structural policy'.

These developments would seem to give the districts an active role in regional development and might be seen as an opportunity for expanding their functions of regional planning, provided the Länder transfer the necessary competences. However, the more regional development tasks have gained in significance, the more the districts have come under pressure to change. In particular, their hierarchical control functions have proved counterproductive as they try to adopt a more active role in organizing and moderating regional cooperation.

Changes in Local and Länder Governments Reduce the Districts' Capacity to Supervise Local Government

It was already recognized in the early 1970s that the growing importance of urban renewal, regional economic development and environmental protection required new modes of coordinated policy making (Mittelinstanz-Bericht, 1973: 15). In the beginning, these challenges were not met by new coordinating devices. By the end of the 1980s, however, they came to be associated with institutional innovations such as 'regional conferences', regional councils and even regional associations, as, for example, in the Stuttgart region. These initiatives have been based on an awareness of the growing competition amongst European regions and have been reinforced by new mechanisms for the regionalization of sectoral policies. Certainly, in a situation where power is shifted away from the centre, where public authorities are becoming more dependent on the willingness of the private sector to comply, and where the state is restricted by the high costs of consensus building, financial pressures and implementation deficits, administrative structures which are based on the principle of hierarchical intervention, such as the districts, appear increasingly outdated.

Political and Institutional Changes Hamper the Coordinating Function of Districts

As noted above, the general trend towards sectoral verticalization has long affected the districts. The different divisions of district offices adapted to this trend and developed strong ties with their respective sectoral ministries (Woike, 1983). 'Accordingly, there is a tendency on the part of sectoral ministries to keep the districts' divisions on a short leash. Instead of directives given by the minister to the district chief, one frequently encounters senior officials in the ministry giving instructions, often by phone, to the district office divisions. By cutting lines short, this behaviour threatens to undermine the coordinating function of the districts' (Wagener, 1982: 157).

In the process of centralizing steering and control functions, many Länder ministries even centralized implementation functions and started to regulate in detail the operation of local governments or built up close direct contacts with local authorities. Länder ministries were thus bypassing the districts, again reducing their coordinating powers (Woike, 1983: 37f). Finally, with local governments emerging as powerful administrative bodies in the wake of the territorial reforms of the 1960s and 1970s, the larger cities, in particular, became very critical of the districts. They claimed to benefit little from districts and saw them primarily as an unnecessary restriction on their own scope of action.

To conclude, districts have for some time been under growing pressure to improve their institutional performance and justify their existence. First, they have strongly felt the frictions of a changing state that has been moving away from the hierarchical mode of intervention towards the cooperative state, a development which has blurred the boundaries between public and private spheres. Second, districts have not been able to meet fully the increasing demand for horizontal coordination and to overcome the growing sectoralization and centralization of policy making. Thus districts find it difficult to respond to the growing demand for intersectoral coordination, regional cooperation and decentralized decision making capacities, and the role and functions of districts have become ambiguous. This has lent support to calls for their abolition, for example by the associations of cities and counties (Thränhardt, 1978) and, in the past, reform proposals often focused on this issue (see Mattenklodt, 1976: 23ff), rather than the possibility of organizational change.

Reform Perspectives Under Contemporary Conditions

With the accession of the East German Länder to the Federal Republic, a new round of administrative reform has been opened in both east and west. The dominant objectives have been to reduce the number of special authorities outside the control of the district chief; to redraw the dividing lines between, on the one hand, steering and control functions of the ministries and, on the other, district implementation functions with an emphasis on the decentralization of tasks and functions; and, more generally, to redefine and reorganize administrative functions according to changing societal needs.

Although these objectives are by no means novel, current attempts at reform appear more ambitious than those during previous administrative reform waves. Especially in the western Länder, the thrust is towards 'lean administration' designed to reduce public expenditure, to deregulate administrative processes, to speed up administrative decision making and to render public administration more flexible in accordance with the requirements of international competition. The latest round of administrative reform is partly a reaction to economic pressures and to the international competition of 'home environments' (Porter, 1990) and most of the reform proposals borrow freely from the language of business management concepts in the shape of the New Public Management (Stewart and Walsh, 1992).

While fiscal stress and the need for retrenchment have certainly been important catalysts for recent reform proposals, other sources of pressure for change must not be overlooked. They include, in particular, the following:

- the partial political withdrawal of citizens (*Politikverdrossenheit*), which underlies demands for more transparent and responsive governmental–administrative structures; and
- the trends towards horizontal networking, informal bargaining processes and an increasing number of public–private partnerships. These

trends intensify the interlocking of policy making and threaten to have a delegitimizing effect since they diffuse responsibility and blur the dividing line between the public and private spheres.

Reform discussions are constrained by the growing influence of the EU, which not only adds a further layer of government, but also results in a steeper hierarchy of control levels. As a result, decision making tends to become not only more complicated, time-consuming and conservative, but also more opaque, with the attendant risk of alienating the citizens from public administration.

Although these developments could well be expected to weaken the districts and reinforce demands for their abolition, the current reform discussion in the Länder, notably in Baden–Württemberg, Brandenburg, Lower Saxony, North Rhine–Westphalia, Saxony and Saxony–Anhalt, does not point in that direction. None of the old Länder appears intent on abolishing the districts, but there are signs that the role of districts might be formally redefined. In the first instance, districts seem set to lose some of their competences in service provision and the issuance of permits to the counties. At the same time, districts may gain in importance as regional–territorial coordinators. Second, rather than reduce the number of districts, reform endeavours focus on improving and rationalizing administrative processes within existing authorities.

The State of Reform

What are the reform strategies adopted by the old and new Länder, and have the new Länder been able to profit from the relative freedom they have enjoyed in establishing new administrative structures? The new Länder were hesitant to revive the former districts (*Bezirke*), since they were regarded as the embodiment of the Communist Party (SED) regime (Hoffmann, 1992: 691). However, there was broad agreement that the territorial component in the organizational structure of public administration needed to be strengthened and, under the influence of West German models, the new Länder had, in effect, to choose between two options: either the institutionalization of districts or the establishment of large counties (*Regionalkreise*) which would be strong enough to take over most of the districts' functions.

The solutions adopted in the new Länder show a variety of mixed approaches. Districts were adopted in Saxony and Saxony–Anhalt, while Mecklenburg–West Pomerania modelled its territorial administrative system on Schleswig-Holstein, with large counties. Brandenburg introduced a combination of special agencies and large counties, and Thuringia disguised the intermediate authority under the label of a State Administrative Authority (*Landesverwaltungsamt*) with regional branches (Becker, 1993). In addition, all of the new Länder set up special regional bodies for regional planning which may, over time, become nuclei for the regionalization of Länder policies. These regional associations consist of local government representatives who decide on proposals submitted by either district officials (as in the case of Saxony–Anhalt and Thuringia), special authorities (in Mecklenburg–West Pomerania and Saxony) or the regional association itself (in Brandenburg).

In contrast, the reform debate in the old Länder has concentrated on four central issues:

1   The future role of districts is seen primarily in terms of vertical communication, horizontal coordination and the moderation of regional development processes for which new types of regional cooperation and networking are required. In the Länder where the districts also provide the technical infrastructure for regional planning, district chiefs often initiate round-table discussions of regional actors to define regional programmes and action plans for the restructuring and development of their region. A very advanced concept was introduced by North Rhine–Westphalia at the end of the 1980s in reaction to the grave unemployment crisis suffered by the Ruhr area (see below: regional conferences).

2   Where regional planning takes place at the district level, there is also a tendency to enlarge the discretionary powers of districts in allocating financial grants. North Rhine–Westphalia had already adopted such arrangements in the 1970s, and other Länder, including Lower Saxony and Bavaria, seem set to follow suit. However, empirical evidence shows up practical problems, since the districts meet with strong opposition from sectoral ministries when they try to make full use of their discretionary allocational powers. Land ministries tend to interfere and attempt to recentralize decision making (Zündel, 1991: 31).

3   Growing importance is attached to improving the management capacities of districts and to replacing control with cooperation and consultation. This is an important concern in a number of Länder, including Saxony, Saxony–Anhalt (Projektgruppe Mittelinstanzbericht, 1992), Lower Saxony (Arbeitsgruppe Modernisierung, 1992), Baden–Württemberg (Regierungskommission Verwaltungsreform, 1993: 74f) and North Rhine–Westphalia (Zündel, 1991). The underlying logic follows the principle of 'least effort'. If districts are resistant to comprehensive reform initiatives, then reform objectives must be reduced and adjusted to what is feasible. In general this entails, first, unburdening districts of functions that could be performed more effectively by local

government or private suppliers; second, reorganizing the districts' internal divisional structure in order to combine those functions which interact closely and frequently; and, finally, improving procedures to create a more flexible and less time-consuming administration.

4   Contrary to the ambition of sectoral ministries to try to liberate themselves from the constriction of having to operate through district chiefs by setting up special authorities, there is a strong political will to maintain the principle of regional unity in public administration. Accordingly, attempts are made to reintegrate special authorities into district offices. However, many sceptics doubt whether the results will be long-lasting and point to the past successes of ministries in establishing their own implementing bodies.

While the general thrust of the reform debate clearly points in the direction of stronger districts, several Länder are also seeking to establish additional intermediary bodies to undertake tasks that districts seem ill-suited to perform. Since districts are organized on the basis of hierarchical controls, they find it difficult to cope with demands for decentralized and participatory decision making, the peripheralization of power, the pluralization of organized interests and horizontal networking. Consequently, districts have difficulty in meeting the need for regionally integrated environmental policies, the regionalization of state policies and the regional integration of local actors. A number of Länder have responded by seeking to institutionalize integrated authorities for environmental policy, new forms of intermunicipal cooperation and regional conferences.

Integrated Authorities for Environmental Policy

Regionally integrated authorities for environmental policy have been created in Lower Saxony (*Landesamt für Umweltschutz*), Saxony (*Staatliche Umweltfachämter*), Saxony–Anhalt and Baden–Württemberg (*Umweltfachämter*) and North Rhine–Westphalia (*Landesumweltamt*). While there is a convincing logic to support such a step, there are also obvious deficiencies, notably the fact that, with the exception of Saxony, none of the Länder mentioned has integrated regional planning into its regional environmental authorities. This separation clearly reduces the potential of regional planning to foster sustainable regional development. Moreover, the institutionalization of special environmental authorities has regularly been accompanied by the need for an additional environmental planning system, which adds a further complication to the already highly intricate German planning landscape.

Intermunicipal Cooperation

New models of intermunicipal cooperation are being discussed in Baden–Württemberg and Lower Saxony, with a view to strengthening the regions' competitive position within the European framework. Thus the region of Stuttgart has been organized as a new type of regional authority (*Regionalkreis*), which takes on the functions of regional planning, waste disposal, public transport and regional economic development (including regional marketing) and is controlled by a directly elected regional assembly. In Lower Saxony, the Land government is exploring the creation of new regions which would be endowed with functions taken from both districts and counties. Unsurprisingly, this idea has met with intense opposition from the county and district representatives.

Regional Conferences

A number of considerations make the option of regional conferences attractive. First, they can be created without major political conflict. Second, they are in line with recent developments at the district level to reconcile new control and supervisory functions, including environmental impact studies, regional impact control procedures (*Raumordnungsverfahren*) and planning approval procedures (*Planfeststellungsverfahren*), with the need for regional cooperation. Accordingly, new procedures are adopted by districts that enable them to interact with project developers in a consultative manner, thus making them 'procedural managers'. Third, the model corresponds to recent trends according to which regional planning is to be perceived, not so much as a regional control, but as a concept of moderating integrated economic development on the basis of regional networks.

North Rhine–Westphalia was the first Land to adopt the model of regional conferencing on a wide scale. This is probably due to favourable framework conditions that were already in place, which allowed the district chiefs greater room for manoeuvre than in other Länder, for instance in the distribution of special earmarked grants. Moreover, since 1975, North Rhine–Westphalian districts have provided the technical facilities for regional planning, while the political decisions have been taken by a special body of local representatives attached to the district (*Bezirksplanungsrat*).

However, the successful implementation of the model is partly contingent on conditions that are outside the control of the state. Thus regional conferencing is bound to meet with resistance if it is adopted in regions with strong local authorities that entertain effective direct political links to the Land government and are used to bypassing the districts. This has, for example, been the tradition in the Ruhr area. Moreover, the district may become subject to divided loyalties if it is responsible for authoritative allocational decisions while, at the same time, it is supposed to play the role of a neutral moderator.

Conclusion

German districts seem to count amongst the administrative institutions that are blessed with eternal life. Although they often appear to lack strong political supporters, their survival has rarely been seriously under threat. Politicians such as former North Rhine–Westphalian Minister Zöpel may denounce them as 'demigods', members of parliament may regard them as 'bureaucratic impediments' and many local authorities may question their usefulness, yet districts continue to survive, relatively unaffected by administrative reforms which tend to focus on other executive levels. Three main reasons help to explain this state of affairs.

1   Districts profit from a delicate balance of power. If they were to be abolished, the Länder ministries would be pitted directly against local government and local authorities would be free to deal directly with the ministries. This would not only unduly burden the ministries' administrative capacity; more importantly, it would require the ministerial administration to take full account of the ever-growing diversity of implementation contexts. There would be no filters to exclude individual local requests in favour of the generalized regional interest, and ministries would find it difficult to avoid being captured by strong local political influences.

At the same time, alternative organizational devices are politically very costly. They would require either the territorial enlargement and functional upgrading of the counties or the acceptance of a larger number of special authorities directly attached to the ministries. The first solution, the enlargement of counties, would be opposed by municipal governments and their political allies, since strong counties would reduce their autonomy. Enlargement would also, of course, imply the abolition of some smaller counties, which, in view of the political influence wielded by county chief executives, would inevitably meet with strong opposition. Moreover, larger and stronger counties with their own power base would find it easier to escape the control of Länder ministries, something which is evidently not in the latter's interest.

The alternative solution of transferring district functions to special authorities would be counterproductive, for two reasons. First, the proliferation of special authorities would not only multiply the overhead costs which, at present, are covered by the districts, but would also make the transfer of employees from one task to another very difficult – both arguments which are particularly persuasive in times of retrenchment. Second, intersectoral coordination costs would rise considerably at a time when the 'evolution of cooperation' (Axelrod) is the relevant political paradigm.

2 Districts are useful to the ministries because they help to deflect criticism from the ministerial bureaucracy in case of errors in policy programmes or implementation difficulties. Districts are supposed to find adequate solutions to implementation problems and accept responsibility for inadequate delivery.

3 Districts profit from the prevalence of coalition government at the Land level. Altering or abolishing districts would require the consent of all ministers, since each of them would be affected. The costs of consensus are, therefore, extremely high. However, since the 'golden rule of equal distribution of costs' tends to prevail, there is only a very slim chance of significant change.

District chiefs are well aware of the delicate position of intermediate bodies and recognize the importance of being more proactive in restructuring the regional economic bases. Nonetheless, they tend to prefer to keep a low profile in the current discussions on administrative reform. In general, they aim to preserve the established structures, but seek to extend their sphere of influence by changing procedures to make 'form follow function'. Their room for manoeuvre will, however, remain limited, since the contextual conditions do not seem to be changing in their favour. First, Länder ministries seem to be centralizing even more functions in order to compensate for influence lost to the Federal and EU levels. Second, the propensity of ministries to decentralize fiscal allocation powers has always been very limited, and will be even more so under the pressure of fiscal retrenchment. Third, the more district chiefs seek to act as regional moderators in economic development, the more they will be challenged either by the counties or by the newly established regional conferences, which are reluctant to concede a leading role to the district chiefs.

In response, an increasing number of district chiefs are discovering the value of environmental policies and, in part, the value of regional planning as a means of legitimately involving themselves in local issues. Consequently, some district chiefs have become the protagonists of environmental policies, while others try to increase their public profile by moderating regional conferences. What they share is an unwillingness to become relegated to the role of a mere 'messenger' between the Land government and the local level. Thus they discover regional politics as a new field of action and engage in it with the aim of improving the competitive position of their region within a 'Europe of regions'. In line with this development, the reorganization of district administrations might be increasingly influenced by the need for 'communication, coordination, concentration [of functions], cooperation, creativity and control, (Zündel, 1991: 3).

Might districts then become models of a modern version of form following function? Rather than pursuing politically costly reforms of institutional structures, districts seem to be adapting in terms of procedural rules, individual behaviour (negotiation, bargaining and networking) and changing cognitive patterns. To a certain extent, the restrictive powers of organizational structures seem to be lessening. In sum, districts may increasingly profit from a general societal need for a 'new bargaining arena based on territory rather than sector, where non-producer groups via communal institutions at the meso level may correct some of the distortions generated by universalistic egalitarianism and corporatism alike' (Sharpe, 1993: 17).

Notes

1   See Henneke (1994) for a survey of the counties after the latest territorial reforms.
2   The law on the organization of public administration of Baden–Württemberg of 1955 considered districts 'provisional', and it was only in 1958 that districts became permanently institutionalized.

References

Arbeitsgruppe Modernisierung der Bezirksregierungen (1992) *Zwischenbericht: Innere Aufbauorganisation*, Hanover: Innenministerium des Landes Niedersachsen.
Becker, B. (1993) 'Zum Thüringer Landesverwaltungsamt – Vivisektion einer Neuzüchtung', *Die Verwaltung*, **26**, 317–28.
Benz, A. (1983) *Parlamentarische Formen in der Regionalplanung. Eine politik- und verwaltungswissenschaftliche Untersuchung der politischen Vertretungsorgane in der Regionalplanung*, (Beiträge zum Siedlungs- und Wohnungswesen und zur Raumplanung, vol. 92), Münster.
Ellwein, T. (1993a) *Stellungnahme zur Anhörung im Ausschuß für Verwaltungs- strukturreform des Landtages Nordrhein-Westfalen am 16.06.1993*.
Ellwein, T. (1993b) *Neuordnung der staatlichen und kommunalen Arbeitsebene zwischen der Landesregierung und den Städten und Kreisen des Landes Nordrhein- Westfalen*, report.
Faber, H. (1985) '100 Jahre Bezirksregierung Hannover', *Die Öffentliche Verwaltung*, **38**, 989–97.
Fonk, F. (1967) *Die Behörde des Regierungspräsidenten*, Berlin: Duncker & Humblot.

Fürst, D. (1993) 'Raum – die politikwissenschaftliche Sicht', *Staatswissenschaften und Staatspraxis*, **4**, 293–315.

Glass, C.-P. (1967) *Die Realität der Kommunalaufsicht*, Cologne: Deutscher Gemeindeverlag.

Gross, R. and E. Laux (1992) *Denkschrift zum Aufbau der öffentlichen Verwaltung im Lande Sachsen-Anhalt*, report, Hanover/Düsseldorf.

Henneke, H.-G. (1994) 'Kreisebene in der Bundesrepublik Deutschland nach der Gebietsreform in den neuen Ländern', *Der Landkreis*, 145–52.

Hillmann, G. (1969) *Der Regierungspräsident und seine Behörde. Die allgemeine staatliche Mittelinstanz in der Verwaltungsreform*, unpublished doctoral dissertation, University of Göttingen.

Hoffmann, G. (1992) 'Die staatliche Mittelinstanz in den neuen Bundesländern', *Die Öffentliche Verwaltung*, **45**, 689–96.

Jacob, H. (1963) *German Administration since Bismarck. Central Authority versus Local Autonomy*, New Haven: Yale UP.

Keating, M. (1993) 'The Continental Meso: Regions in the European Community', in L.J. Sharpe (ed.), *The Rise of Meso Government in Europe*, London: Sage, 296–311.

Köstering, H . (1991) '175 Jahre Bezirksregierung', *Städte- und Gemeinderat*, 225–30.

Köstering, H. (1994) 'Grundlagen und Probleme einer Funktionalreform im Land Brandenburg. Ein Beitrag zum Aufbau der Verwaltung in den neuen Ländern', *Die Öffentliche Verwaltung*, **47**, 238–49.

Lottermoser, E. (1992) 'Nur gemeinsam bilden wir den Staat. Über Geschichte und Aufgaben von Bezirksregierungen', *Landkreis Hildesheim, Jahrbuch 1992*, Hildesheim, 83–93.

Mattenklodt, H.-F. (1976) *Gebiets- und Verwaltungsreform in Nordrhein-Westfalen*, Münster: Vilhasen.

Mittelinstanzbericht: Sonderarbeitskreis der Ständigen Konferenz der Innenminister der Länder (1973) *Neuordnung der staatlichen Mittelinstanz*, unpublished report.

Porter, M. (1990) *The Competitive Advantage of Nations*, New York: The Free Press.

Projektgruppe Mittelinstanzbericht (1992) *Verwaltungsaufbau in der Mittelinstanz und Erledigung staatlicher Aufgaben auf Ortsebene im Land Sachsen-Anhalt*, report, Magdeburg.

Regierungskommission Verwaltungsreform (1993) *Verwaltungsreform in Baden-Württemberg. Erster Bericht*, report, Stuttgart.

Rosellen, B.J. (1977) *Die Reform der Bezirksregierung*, unpublished doctoral dissertation, Speyer.

Schrapper, L. (1994) 'Bezirksregierungen in Deutschland: Die Bündelungsbehörde der Mittelinstanz im Vergleich', *Die Öffentliche Verwaltung*, **47**, 157–62.

Sharpe, L.J. (1993) 'The European Meso: An Appraisal', in L.J. Sharpe (ed.), *The Rise of Meso Government in Europe*, London: Sage, 1–39.

Stewart J.D. and K. Walsh (1992) 'Change in the Management of Public Services', *Public Administration*, **70**, 499–518.

Thränhardt, D. (1978) 'Funktionalreform als Politikinhalt und Politikdeterminante. Eine Einleitung', in D. Thränhardt (ed.), *Funktionalreform – Zielperspektiven und Probleme einer Verwaltungsreform*, Meisenheim/Glan: Athenäum.

Wagener, F. (1982) 'Die Regierungsbezirke im Gesamtaufbau der Verwaltung', *Verwaltungs-Archiv*, **73**, 153–66.

Woike, U. (1983) 'Die Bezirksregierungen in Niedersachsen. Gesetzliches Modell und Wirklichkeit', *Deutsche Verwaltungspraxis*, 31–8.

Zündel, G.J. (1991) *Gutachten zur Untersuchung der Organisation und Struktur des Regierungspräsidenten (RP) Arnsberg*, unpublished report, Nettetal.

7 The Transformation of Local Government in East Germany: Between Imposed and Innovative Institutionalization

Hellmut Wollmann

This chapter deals with the reconstruction and reorganization of local government in East Germany. In particular, it identifies central dimensions of the institutionalization process; highlights key factors that have shaped this process; and assesses to what extent the institutionalization of local government in East Germany has followed the West German model.[1] In analyzing institution building or institutionalization, the focus is on formal political and administrative structures, the legal, territorial and functional framework of local government and the organizational design of county and municipal authorities.

The following discussion distinguishes between 'exogenous' and 'endogenous' factors (see Lehmbruch, 1994; Wollmann, 1995; 1996b). This distinction is based on the assumption that the transformation process in East Germany was shaped, by, first, the 'old' Federal Republic as an external change agent and, second, internal factors, including East Germany's institutional and cognitive legacies from its GDR past and specific developmental patterns following the collapse of the communist system. In assessing the degree to which institutionalization followed the 'West German model', the following four key concepts are employed:

1 imposed institutionalization: here provisions and directives laid down in the Basic Law or in Federal legislation make certain institutional formations obligatory;

2   imitative institutionalization: the West German model is closely followed, even though there may be no strict requirement to do so;
3   adaptive institutionalization: institutional decisions have been shaped significantly by legacies or interests rooted in the East German context; and
4   innovative institutionalization: this represents institution building that goes beyond the existing institutional repertoire in place in West Germany.

Institutional Transformation in East Germany: a Case of Exogenous Determination?

At first sight, institutional transformation in East Germany appears to represent a case of 'institutional transfer' (Lehmbruch, 1993) in which the West German model was largely extended to, if not imposed upon, East Germany. This would seem to set the German transformation process apart from the other formerly socialist countries in Central and Eastern Europe. Under the provisions for 'accession' (*Beitritt*) contained in the Unification Treaty (see Derlien, 1993b: 320f; Wollmann, 1995: 502ff; Wollmann, 1996b), the constitutional and legal order of the old Federal Republic, together with the institutional–organizational models with which it is associated, was extended to East Germany. The GDR ceased to exist as a sovereign state and most of its constitutional–legal framework and its central government structures were abolished. This type of institutional transfer, that is the extension or transplantation of a 'ready-made state' (Rose *et al.*, 1993), and the suddenness with which it took place, clearly distinguish the transformation in East Germany from that in other post-communist countries in Central and Eastern Europe, where crucial decisions regarding political and administrative restructuring have been determined in the domestic arena.

   Institutional transfer was accompanied by a massive elite transfer of West German political and administrative personnel who moved to East Germany, often on a temporary basis. This influx of western personnel reflected the 'political and administrative elite vacuum' that resulted from the removal of much of the GDR's leading political and administrative personnel (Derlien, 1993a; 1993b). Personnel transfer highlighted the political implications of the GDR's integration into the old Federal Republic. At least at first sight, West German transferees, their orientation and conceptual 'luggage',[2] were bound to act as an additional external lever for facilitating institutional transfer from West to East Germany and underlined its exogenous thrust. Again, this was in marked contrast to Central and East European countries in which, notwithstanding the influx of foreign consultants, an elite import on such a scale was inconceivable.

To highlight the size and function of what came to be called 'administrative assistance' (*Verwaltungshilfe*), a term – perhaps revealingly – borrowed from assistance to developing countries, it might be useful to mention some basic facts and figures on the Länder and local government levels in the east.

The Länder Level

As early as 29 June 1990, the ministers of the interior of the old Länder agreed to close cooperation with the emergent new Länder and laid the foundations for inter-Länder partnership relations. Their main aim was to assist the establishment of functioning Länder structures in the east. Partnership agreements linked Mecklenburg–West Pomerania with Hamburg and Schleswig-Holstein; Brandenburg with North Rhine–Westphalia; Saxony–Anhalt with Lower Saxony; Saxony with Bavaria and Baden–Württemberg; and Thuringia with Hesse, Bavaria and Rhineland–Palatinate. At the heart of these partnerships was administrative assistance, to which the Federal and western Länder governments had committed themselves in the Unification Treaty, initially until 30 July 1991. Among the various forms of administrative assistance provided, two types of personnel transfer must be mentioned in particular. First, there were advisers (*Berater*), who travelled to East Germany on a short-term basis, essentially in a consulting or training capacity. Second, a major role was played by administrative aides (*Verwaltungshelfer*), who moved to East Germany for a longer period to work predominantly in leadership and senior management positions.

It is estimated that, by 1993, some 15 000 western officials had acted as advisers at the Länder level, while the number of West German administrative aides who had taken over operative functions reached some 5000 (Hansch, 1993: 290), of whom most worked in the judiciary and in revenue and tax administration (*Finanzverwaltung*). In Brandenburg, for example, of a total of 956 North Rhine–Westphalian administrative aides in 1993, 46 per cent were employed in the judiciary and 30 per cent in tax and revenue authorities (Diekelmann, 1994: 27). Regarding the new Länder's ministerial bureaucracy, the following data are worth highlighting. Although, after the formation of the new Länder, less than one-third of ministerial positions in the five Länder cabinets were being taken by West Germans,[3] a significant percentage of senior positions in the ministries was filled by Western officials. In Brandenburg, by the end of 1991, 52 per cent of posts in the higher service brackets (*höherer Dienst*) were occupied by West Germans. In some key ministries, the proportion was even higher, reaching 73 per cent in the Minister–President's Office, 72 per cent in the Ministry of Justice and 67 per cent in the Ministry of Finance (see Hansch, 1993: 291). These figures reflected the elite vacuum and the lack of qualified East German personnel. Except for the more 'political' executive positions, the administrative elite of the new Länder ministries was thus predominantly made up of West Germans.

The Local Level

Administrative assistance for local authorities was provided in different ways (see Scheytt, 1993), including west–east twinning partnerships (*Städtepartnerschaften*) and special programmes funded by the Federal government and the West German Länder.[4] A survey conducted by the Association of Local Authorities shows that, by the end of 1991, 100 per cent of East German local authorities with more than 20 000 inhabitants and 95 per cent of those with between 10 000 and 20 000 inhabitants were twinned with a West German authority; about half of these partnerships involved concrete assistance and consultancy (see Scheytt, 1993: 80f). Through twinning arrangements, western material assistance, advice and know-how were made available to East German local authorities, often on a daily basis over the phone. In a more systematic manner, and with financial support of both the western Länder and the Federal government, West German local officials transferred to the east to take up administrative positions with county and municipal authorities, mostly on a temporary basis. In 1993, approximately 4000 West German local governments experts and employees worked with East German local authorities (Keller and Henneberger, 1993: 183). Although this constituted a significant influx of personnel, it was a small figure compared to the relative weight of personnel transfer to the new Länder ministerial administrations.

Seen in the broader context of the unification process and the huge financial transfers from West to East Germany (amounting to some DM150bn per annum), institutional and elite transfer underline the extraordinary West German presence in the East German transformation. Against this background, it may indeed seem justified to interpret institution building in East Germany as being largely shaped by exogenous factors, that is West German institutions and elites. From this perspective, institutionalization could be expected to have largely followed a pattern of imposition and imitation. In this perspective, a 'photocopy' or 'blueprint' approach clearly predominated (Reichard and Röber, 1993).

The Role of Adaptation and Innovation

A number of factors qualify the impression of a predominantly exogenous determination of the institution-building process. First, while the essential principles of West Germany's 'ready-made state' were extended to East Germany, this related only to basic structures, including, for example, those of the federal system and the institutional imperatives following from Federal legislation. Beyond such areas of imposed institution formation, the institutional wasteland that resulted from the political and administrative demise of the GDR created great scope for institution building. In this situation, Länder parliaments and governments, and also local authorities, enjoyed considerable scope for developing institutional solutions.

Second, in most instances, there was no single West German model that could be transferred. The Federal Republic's political and administrative system is, at all levels and in all sectors, characterized by a very considerable institutional differentiation and variability, not least with regard to the organization of Länder administration, Länder–local relations and local authorities (Goetz, 1993). Thus the repertoire of institutional solutions on which institutional transfer could draw was diverse and well developed.

As far as the discretion of East German Länder and local actors in institution building is concerned, it is important to take account of the political dynamics generated by the local elections in May 1990, the Länder parliament elections in October 1990 and the subsequent formation of the Länder governments. At the Länder level, the new parliaments were made up almost entirely of East Germans (Derlien and Lock, 1994), who constituted a new East German political elite that has since been rapidly gaining in self-confidence and political assertiveness. Coalition politics, such as in Brandenburg, where, after the first elections, a coalition of Social Democrats, Greens and Free Democrats was formed, added a further important element to the process of institution building, particularly in politically controversial areas. Also, as mentioned above, East Germans dominated in the political executive. However, the administrative elite in the Länder ministries was predominantly made up of West Germans. Thus the political and administrative stage was set for controversies in which, through the Länder parliaments, and also through the Länder Minister–Presidents, East German particularities and interests could gain influence and restrained the direct impact of administrative aides.

Moreover, it is at least questionable whether West German transferees could primarily be seen as an exogenous elite pressing for the application of a West German model. There is evidence to suggest that in many cases West German administrators deliberately sought to avoid the mistakes and errors committed in the West German context and welcomed the *tabula rasa* situation in East Germany to implement innovative institutional solutions that might, at a later stage, be transferred to the west. There are also indications that many West German officials soon began to identify with their new Land and developed a political sensitivity to its specific needs, circumstances and cognitive legacies. A growing number of administrative aides have decided to stay in East Germany for good,[5] and they may well constitute a promising combination of professionalism, brought along in their 'luggage' from the west, and special sensitivity to the East German context.

Turning to the county and municipal level, similar dynamics shaped the processes of institution building. When, on 6 May 1990, the first democratic local government elections were held, a largely new political elite, eager to rebuild local administration and revive local self-government, won representation in the county and municipal councils. The newly elected councils expelled many of the former regime's administrative power holders in county and municipal administrations and elected or appointed a largely new set of administrative leaders: mayors, deputy mayors (*Beigeordnete*) and section heads (*Amtsleiter*). Thus the local administrative level in East Germany experienced far-reaching elite change. Although this held true for most of the former top position holders, particularly for the members of the Communist Party (SED), some members of the old elite, especially supporters of the former bloc parties, were successful in gaining elective and senior administrative offices.[6] While a significant percentage of the new administrative leaders already worked in state administration (in the narrow sense) before 1990, albeit mostly in subordinate positions, the vast majority are relative newcomers. It should also be kept in mind that, at least in quantitative terms, western transferees played a much smaller role in local administration than in the Länder ministerial bureaucracy (Wollmann and Berg, 1994: 248), although there were considerable regional variations (Berg and Nagelschmidt, 1994: 71).

The administrative newcomers form the most intriguing group when it comes to assessing the reformist potential in local administration. Most of them belonged to the technical and economic intelligentsia and previously worked in clerical and managerial positions in state enterprises before seeking or accepting administrative positions in 1990.[7] Their ability to cope with the new political, administrative and organizational challenges varied. On the one hand, in addition to their high political motivation and drive, they often brought with them the ability to act and operate flexibly on the basis of the experience and skill in improvising which was one of the crucial skills of survival in the socioeconomic reality of the GDR (Marz, 1992; Klinger, 1994: 72f). On the other hand, the newcomers were mostly not well-versed in administrative procedures and organizational strategies. They were used to solving concrete problems and trained to think individually and tactically rather than organizationally and strategically (Klinger, 1994). The same could be said of the 'old-timers' among the new administrative leaders, that is, those who had already worked in state administration prior to 1989, mostly in subordinate positions. As for the West Germans employed by East German county and municipal authorities, who made up some 10 per cent of the senior administrative personnel, most were engaged in building up and operating the legal offices (*Rechtsämter*) and economic promotion offices (*Wirtschaftsförderungsämter*) and tended not to be directly involved in crucial organizational decisions.

The factors influencing institutional formation by local leaders, then, suggest an ambivalent picture. On the one hand, West German organizational schemes and experiences clearly had an impact upon the organizational efforts of East German local governments. Of great importance in this respect were twinning partnerships with individual West German counties and municipalities and the authoritative, though not obligatory, organizational recommendations issued by the *Kommunale Gemeinschaftsstelle für Verwaltungsvereinfachung* (KGSt), a local government-funded institution with a major influence in local government organization. On the other hand, East German local authorities quickly developed into lively political arenas with actors and groups from different professional and political backgrounds as well as different political and personal ambitions. Taken together, this constellation of factors has had a major influence on the local decision making process regarding organizational matters.

Finally, in assessing the influence of endogenous inputs, it is necessary to distinguish different phases of the transformation process since late 1989. In particular, it seems important to pay attention to the period of 'the round tables' which, between October 1989 and March/May 1990, created a political self-understanding and institutional claims which may have constituted important legacies for subsequent developments. With regard to the counties and municipalities, a similar conclusion might emerge from a closer examination of the period between May and October 1990. During this time, the GDR central government was already destined to disappear, and the new Länder had yet to be established. As a consequence, the counties and municipalities represented the only operating institutional level in a heady upsurge of local democracy and autonomy, which was carried over, as another specific legacy, into later conflicts (Berg and Nagelschmidt, 1994, ch. 2).

Against the background of the differing perceptions of the role of exogenous and endogenous factors in the institutional transformation process, the remainder of the chapter will discuss crucial dimensions in the institutionalization of county and municipal government in East Germany. These dimensions include (1) the introduction of a new constitutional–legal framework for local government (local government charters) in East Germany since 1990; (2) the redrawing of county boundaries; (3) the rearrangement of municipal boundaries and functions; (4) the decentralization and delegation of administrative Länder functions to lower-level authorities (*Funktionalreform*, or functional reform); (5) the internal reorganization of county and municipal administrations; and (6) the organizational restructuring of county and municipal authorities under the influence of New Public Management concepts.

Towards New Local Government Charters

While the traditional Länder structure had initially been maintained in the GDR after its foundation in 1949, it was abolished when, in common with other Central and East European countries under Soviet control, the Stalinist organizational model was imposed. It was organized on a regional basis which acted as the administrative backbone for central party and state domination. Accordingly, the territory of the GDR was divided into 15 regions (*Bezirke*) that constituted the mainstay of territorial administration. At the same time, the number of counties was significantly increased, so that they could serve as bottom-line administrations in a centralized and hierarchically organized system. This massive reorganization resulted in a total of 191 counties and 27 county-free cities. At the lower local tier, the boundaries of the 7500 municipalities were left unchanged, although half of them had a population of fewer than 500 inhabitants (Hauschild, 1991; Wollmann, 1991).

The GDR's constitutional system ruled out any form of local autonomy as incompatible with the doctrine of the unitary state and established a strict hierarchical top-down system. This system was deceptively described, in the official terminology, as democratic centralism and 'double subordination'. Double subordination stood for subordination to both the elected county or municipal council and to the administrative body on the superior level. While the former was largely fictitious, hierarchical command and control represented the centralist top-down reality. After the collapse of the communist regime at the end of 1989, the creation of a new legal framework for local government was seen as an urgent task, a decisive step towards reestablishing democracy in East Germany. The results of the first democratic election to the GDR's parliament accelerated the pace towards unification (Bernet, 1993b: 33) and the preparations for legislative changes. These were largely planned through an intensive exchange between West German experts and their East German counterparts, and the debate was heavily influenced by the idea of making the GDR's local government structures compatible with the general West German model of local self-government.

In choosing concrete institutional designs, decision makers were, in essence, confronted by two variants of municipal organization found in West Germany: the North Rhine–Westphalian model, with a mayor elected by the council as its chairman and a city manager, who is appointed by the council; and the South German 'strong mayor model', in which the mayor is directly elected by the local population as both chairman of the council and the local authority's chief executive. The drafters of the new local government charter were influenced by the debate among West German experts on the merits and demerits of the two variants. In this long-standing debate, the North Rhine–Westphalian model has tended to be viewed very critically, whereas the South German strong mayor model has generally been credited with strengthening the executive and financial performance of local government. Despite much interest in the strong mayor model, the GDR's new Local Government Charter (*Kommunalverfassung*) of 17 May 1990 opted for an arrangement in which the mayor would act as the municipal chief executive to be elected by the municipal council. Thus the GDR parliament chose a variant of its own (Derlien, 1994: 55), opting for neither of the two dominant West German charter models. The Unification Treaty stipulated that this local government charter would remain in force as Land legislation, until the new Länder adopted their own individual charters.

Political and administrative change at the local level had already been set in train by the round-table talks after November 1989 and, for example, some turnover in senior administrative personnel and limited organizational adjustments. But it was only after the first democratic local elections of 6 May 1990 and the adoption of the new local government charter of 17 May 1990 that radical political and administrative restructuring of county and municipal authorities started in earnest. The period from May 1990 to October 1990 provided a particular challenge to the emergent new group of local leaders. The GDR's central administration was doomed to be abolished, the once powerful *Bezirke* were falling into disarray and the Länder administrations had yet to be established. In this situation, local government was expected to embark upon a fundamental political and administrative reconstruction. It should come as no surprise that the incoming new local decision makers, particularly the county chiefs (*Landräte*) and the mayors of big cities, swiftly established themselves as a group of self-confident local leaders ready to hold on to, and also fight for, their newly achieved local autonomy (Bernet, 1993a: 394). Together with the upsurge in political participation at the local level, the emergence of a new self-confident local elite can be identified as a specific legacy of the early transitional phase.

Once the new Länder were established in October 1990 and their parliaments were elected, the new Länder were swift to prepare new local government charters of their own, making use of the constitutional legislative prerogative that the Länder possess in this area. The local government charters which the new Länder enacted between late 1993 and early 1994[8] show broad similarities in their basic features, but also significant variation in important details. This can be illustrated with reference to the mode of election and the powers of the municipal mayors. All five new local government charters now provide for the mayor to be directly elected by the local population, with tenure varying between six years (Thuringia) and eight years (Brandenburg); in the majority of the new Länder, the county chiefs continue to be elected by the county council. In two Länder, however, Saxony–Anhalt and, after 1999, Mecklenburg–West Pomerania, the county chief is to be directly elected. With the exception of Brandenburg, the new legislation followed the South German strong mayor model, in that the mayor is both the chief executive of the local administration and chairman of the local council. To appreciate the strong position which this affords the mayor, it should be recalled that, in line with the German administrative tradition, the mayors of county-free cities (as well as the county chiefs) are given the responsibility, in their own right, of discharging all administrative tasks 'delegated' by the state to local level administration (*Pflichtaufgaben nach Weisung*). Local councils have no right to interfere in these matters; that is, their decision making is limited to local self-government affairs. In the new Länder, the new local government charters came into force after the first local elections,[9] with the exception of Mecklenburg–West Pomerania, where the direct election of the mayors and the county chiefs was postponed until the second round of post-unification local elections.

The legislative process concerning the new local government charters suggests that debates among West German experts on the western experience of local government organization had an important influence on political decision makers in the east, both during the adoption of the GDR's local government reform act of May 1990 and subsequently in the new Länder. Undoubtedly, the strong criticism voiced by many western experts in respect of the North Rhine–Westphalian model and the general preference in favour of the South German strong mayor model weighed heavily, even in Brandenburg, with its close partnership links to North Rhine–Westphalia. On the other hand, a number of endogenous factors also had a strong impact on the legislative process. First, the argument that the strong mayor model is conducive to decisive political leadership and budgetary discipline must have been attractive and persuasive to Länder policy makers who recognized the enormous problems of local government and its budgetary predicament. In Brandenburg, in particular, the mode of mayoral elections became a bone of contention between the three parties – Social Democrats, Greens and Liberals – that made up the government coalition. The junior coalition partners pressed for the direct election of the mayor, in the hope of increasing the chances of their own candidates, while the Social Democrats dragged their feet on the issue. Finally, a compromise typical of coalition bargaining was reached, according to which mayors would be popularly elected, while the county chiefs would continue to be chosen by county councils. In order to counterbalance the power of the strong mayor, and with an explicit reference to the experience with a strong council under the GDR's local government charter of May 1990, the new Brandenburg legislation did not give the mayor the additional function of chairing the council. Instead, the council chairman is elected from amongst the members of the council, thus creating a certain institutional counterweight to the mayor.

In summary, the drafting and adoption of the new local government charters can be described as a case of institutionalization in which West German experience played a major role in the legislative debate as a persuasive exogenous model. Yet the ultimate content of the charters adopted was strongly influenced by endogenous considerations and concerns, as regards both general organizational principles and, in particular, important institutional details. As a result, the institutional solutions which finally emerged tended to follow a pattern of adaptive institutionalization, while in some cases, such as Brandenburg's combination of a strong mayor with a council chairman elected by the council, political choice resulted in innovative institutionalization.

Territorial County Reform and Municipal Change

As mentioned above, the GDR, in 1952, abolished the Länder structure and created 15 regional districts. At the same time, the boundaries of the counties were redrawn to allow for greater centralist control, and their number increased to 191. The fragmented municipal map, with some 7500 municipalities, was left untouched.

When the negotiations on the Unification Treaty were still under way, it was already generally accepted that the small size of the eastern counties seriously hampered the ability of county authorities to cope with an unprecedented problem load. Yet the issue was not seriously pursued for the time being, in particular because territorial county reform was seen to be inextricably linked to comprehensive territorial reform at the municipal level. As regards the latter, however, policy makers showed a great hesitancy to act, as they feared that the local population would perceive and reject any reform attempt as a blow to local democracy, at a time when local self-government was beginning to be restored.

After the formation of the new Länder in October 1990, the new governments soon started to prepare territorial county reform, and also began to explore the possibilities for territorial municipal reform or some functional equivalent.[10] Without going into the details of the reform drives in the five Länder,[11] the pace and determination with which Länder governments and parliaments pursued reform initiatives should be noted. Within two years, the highly contentious redrawing of county boundaries was achieved and, at the same time, a territorial rearrangement of municipal administrative functions had been secured. The territorial county reform bills were passed by new Länder parliaments between 15 December 1992, in Brandenburg, and 15 July 1993, in Thuringia. They reduced the number of counties significantly, most radically in Brandenburg, from 38 to 14, and Mecklenburg–West Pomerania, from 31 to 12 (see Schmidt-Eichstaedt, 1994: 137ff)

Linked to territorial county reform, the problems posed by the multitude of small and very small municipalities inherited from the GDR were also tackled. East German policy makers were faced with the option of either reducing the number of small municipalities by amalgamation to form larger 'unitary communities' (*Einheitsgemeinden*) or retaining existing municipalities as political entities, while encouraging or even requiring the creation of joint administrative agencies, which would perform part or all of the municipal administrative functions. With the exception of Saxony, which pursued a course of amalgamation, the East German Länder favoured the creation of joint administrative authorities, which could take different forms (see Schmidt-Eichstaedt, 1994: 221ff).

If one tries to assess the relative influence of exogenous and endogenous factors in the territorial reform process, the influence of western concepts, personnel and know-how transfer clearly was of major importance. Particularly during the early phases, when Länder administrations had to be built from scratch and the new Länder parliaments were still finding their feet, West German experts and transferees formed an activist core in the fledgling ministries, including the ministries of the interior, which was central to the reform drive. A typical way of institutionalizing the 'import' of West German expertise on a temporary basis was the creation of working groups and expert commissions. In Brandenburg, for instance, an 'independent working group' on territorial county reform was established, which consisted of top level administrators from Brandenburg and North Rhine–Westphalia (and a single representative of the Brandenburg local authorities) (see Eisen, 1996: 139f). More generally, the West German experts community strongly argued for swift and radical territorial county and municipal reforms in numerous fora, including publications, meetings, workshops and conferences. If one takes these factors together, there seems to be good reason to conclude that the swiftness and momentum with which territorial county and municipal reform was put on new Länder's agenda can be explained by essentially externally initiated reform demands (see Bernet, 1993a: 395).

However, there are also clear indications that important procedural and conceptual aspects of the reforms reflect the specific conditions of the East German context. Again Brandenburg may serve as an illustration. As a matter of principle, the three coalition partners in Brandenburg had decided in their coalition agreement of late 1990 that the regional district level would be abolished. Thus Brandenburg opted for a basic two-level administration, consisting of the central Land administration and the local government level. In striking a decentralist note, this decision, taken in the arena of party and coalition politics that was mainly made up of East Germans, was bound to have important consequences for the entire subsequent administrative reform process (see Eisen, 1996). When the government subsequently encountered protest and resistance against county territorial reform, particularly from the county chiefs (see Hanisch, 1993: 84ff), it chose to avoid to push for any hard-line amalgamation of municipalities, as a political price for being able to pursue a more stringent course on the territorial county reform issue. The decision by four out of five Länder to retain the status as political bodies of even the smallest municipalities can be interpreted as an attempt to preserve and honour the many local identities, the boundaries of which can in most cases be traced back to the nineteenth century and to which, it has been argued (Bernet, 1993a), the East German population, under the communist regime, developed particularly strong ties.

In sum, the speed and momentum with which the territorial county and municipal reforms were placed on the new Länder's political agenda owed a great deal to exogenous pressure and persuasion. Furthermore, the pace at which reforms were politically and administratively advanced is largely accounted for by an effective coalition of West German administrative aides in senior ministerial positions, particularly in the Länder ministries of the interior, on the one hand, and East German politicians in the Länder parliaments, on the other. The lengthy discussions of West German aides with county and municipal authorities provided a context for their adjustment to East German socioeconomic and sociocultural circumstances and, in many cases, their gradual development into 'quasi-East Germans' (*Wossis*). Finally, the prevailing context of party politics and coalition politics was crucial in determining the degree to which endogenous considerations affected the reform process. Again adaptive institutionalization appears to have been the predominant pattern of institution building.

Functional Reform

The interinstitutional and, in particular, intergovernmental distribution of administrative tasks has been a central concern in some of the new Länder. This issue is typically dealt with under the heading of functional reform, which refers back to the West German reforms of the 1970s. At the centre of functional reform has been the decentralization, or at least deconcentration, of administrative functions by their transfer from higher-level Land authorities (*Landesoberbehörden*) or specialized lower-level Land agencies (*untere Sonderbehörden*) to counties and county-free cities and also, to some degree, municipal administrative authorities. The need for functional reform in East Germany has arisen mainly because, during the first phases of the creation of Land administrations, a large number of special Land agencies were created, often with their own field offices (Köstering, 1994). Compared to the West, Eastern Länder authorities have thus tended to carry out a greater number of functions. With the conclusion of local territorial reform, the dissolution of many special Land agencies and the transfer of their tasks to county authorities have been widely advocated. The central objective of functional reform is the strengthening of the general administrative level of the *allgemeine Verwaltungsbehörden* (Zöllner, 1993; Halstenberg, 1993: 14).

Brandenburg has taken the lead in functional reform in an impressive sequence of steps. The following briefly summarizes the main steps:

- 29 January 1991: only weeks after the re-establishment of Brandenburg, the cabinet requests the Minister of the Interior to prepare the territorial county reform.
- 16 December 1992: the Brandenburg parliament passes the Territorial County Act, finalizing the territorial county reform.[12]
- December 1992: the formation of joint municipal administrative authorities is completed.
- 29 April 1993: the Land government introduces the bill on the new local government charter.
- 24 June 1993: the Land government releases an official statement on the need for and principles of a functional reform. It stresses its intention to create 'an administration that is close and responsive to the citizens … particularly by transferring the discharge of public tasks, to the largest possible degree, to the counties, county-free municipalities, joint administrative authorities and communities'.
- 27 September 1993: the Land parliament adopts the new local government charter.
- 12 October 1993: the Land government establishes a government commission on functional reform.[13]

- 5 December 1993: local government elections are held.
- 3 March 1994: the Land parliament commences its first reading of the functional reform bill.
- 16 June 1994: the Land parliament passes the (first) Functional Reform Act.

The first Functional Reform Act provided the legislative basis for a comprehensive decentralization and deconcentration of administrative functions. In principle, Brandenburg committed itself to an extensive transfer of administrative functions to the counties and county-free cities by the end of 1997. Under the Act, an administrative function should remain with a Land agency only 'if it cannot be discharged by the county and municipal authorities adequately, economically and effectively' (for details see Uebler and Heinze, 1994). In establishing a general presumption of task allocation in favour of local government and in putting the 'burden of proof' on the Land, the new Act was without precedent in both the new and the old Länder.

A word of caution regarding the much-heralded communalization of tasks (*Kommunalisierung*) is, however, in order. The administrative responsibilities transferred to the counties and county-free cities are carried out by the county chiefs and mayors as obligatory tasks to be discharged under Land control (*Pflichtaufgaben zur Erfüllung nach Weisung*). They are not part of the tasks of local self-government that are decided by the local elected councils. Hence functional reform, implemented through communalization, amounts to administrative deconcentration rather than political decentralization. Yet it must also be noted that, following communalization, administrative responsibilities that were hitherto discharged by Länder agencies and Länder personnel are carried out by office holders who are either elected by the local population, in the case of the mayor, or by the county council, in the case of the county chief.

While initially functional reform may have been put on the agenda in response to exogenous factors, notably the intention to fall in line with the West German pattern of distributing administrative functions, the dynamics following the Brandenburg government's early decision in favour of a two-tiered administration and decentralization have been predominantly shaped by endogenous factors. The pace of reform, and the general presumption in favour of local provision, approximate innovative institutionalization.

The Organization of County and Municipal Administrations

Having examined institutionalization in terms of the legal, territorial and functional framework for the operation of county and municipal authorities, it is now time to examine their internal organization. Under the GDR regime, the internal organizational set-up of counties and county-free city administrations followed a uniform scheme. The councils of counties and county-free cities (*Rat des Kreises* and *Rat der Stadt*), as the administrative collegiate directorate, were composed of 19 councillors, each of whom was responsible for an administrative division (see Schubel and Schwanengel, 1991: 251). Even smaller municipalities had a considerable number of councillors and administrative divisions (see Berg, 1994: 194). This resulted in an organizational imbalance, with the administration consisting of a large number of administrative chiefs and administrative divisions, many of which had only a handful of staff (see Rapsch and Simanski, 1991: 196).

In many counties and municipalities, the transformation of local administration towards an organizational design modelled on West German examples took shape between October 1989, when the iron rule of the Communist Party collapsed, and the first democratic local government elections of 6 May 1990. During this time, often decisive political influence was exerted by new political groupings, particularly through local round tables (see Berg and Nagelschmidt, 1996, ch. 2). Many administrative office holders were forced to resign or chose to leave more or less voluntarily during this interim period and, in many cases, administrative divisions were abolished or organizationally regrouped (Schubel and Schwanengel, 1991: 251). With the local government elections 6 May 1990 drawing near, new organizational schemes were debated in the local authorities and preparations for organizational reforms to be implemented after the elections were undertaken. In bracing themselves for what was nothing less than a paradigmatic rupture (Wollmann, 1991), both organizationally and conceptually, and with very little knowledge and experience in such matters, the local actors turned, first of all, to the organizational designs and know-how available in West Germany. At this stage, East German local authorities sought the advice of their western partner authorities and the *Kommunale Gemeinschaftsstelle*, which, as mentioned above, had over the years established itself as an authoritative voice in local government organization.

Unlike the experience at the Länder level, where administrative structures had to be built up virtually from scratch, the principal organizational task at the local level was to effect a changeover from the existing organizational and personnel structures to a new design that reflected the new political, legal, territorial and functional framework of local government. Of course a number of responsibilities discharged by local government in the GDR were at least partly comparable to the tasks of local government in West Germany. Accordingly, organizational change involved a great deal of shifting and regrouping of administrative units, subunits or splinters (for a case-study, see Berg, 1994: 197). The task of reorganization was especially challenging in the many small and tiny localities which, under the GDR's administrative regime, had only exercised minimal administrative functions and, hence, possessed hardly any organizational and personnel resources worth mentioning.

In the early stages of transformation, many counties and municipalities seemed tempted to follow and more or less copy the organizational examples and recommendations of their western twin authorities, western administrative aides and the *Kommunale Gemeinschaftsstelle für Verwaltungsvereinfachung*. While for the counties and county-free cities the chief task consisted in restructuring and reorganizing the existing administrative institutions and personnel, smaller municipalities often had to build up effective administrative structures from their foundations and recruit administrative personnel. Available evidence indicates that, in most cases, this reorganization of local administrations was not, in fact, guided by an organizational master plan or blueprint. Western conceptual assistance was welcomed, but the practice in many local authorities tells the story of an organizational incrementalism rather than institutional reconstruction on the basis of comprehensive schemes. Most local authorities experimented with the number and the functional definition of divisions (*Abteilungen*) and sections (*Ämter*), partly as a result of learning processes and sometimes contradictory external advice, but partly also in response to the demands of local political parties and coalitions to be considered in the share-out of positions (Berg, 1994: 197f). The number of division heads, in particular, appears frequently to have been a bone of contention. Moreover, the fact that, in the GDR, local authorities often had administrative directorates with up to 20 senior positions seems to have predisposed local decision makers towards the creation of a large number of new, attractive leadership jobs. West German administrative aides soon came to regard this proliferation of senior posts as a major threat to the establishment of effective local administrations (Rapsch and Simanski, 1991: 196), which prompted Länder policy makers to restrict the number of heads of division by means of the new local government charters and executive directives.

It is not easy to assess the outcome of organizational development in East German county and municipal administrations. On the one hand, one still finds considerable organizational shortcomings, and often they seem to be of an elementary nature. For example, there is often a lack of clarity regarding the division of responsibilities between administrative divisions and sections and also between individual employees and office holders. It is by no means unusual for written documents on organizational structures, the distribution of tasks and responsibilities and instructions about how to keep files to be unavailable or, where they exist, to be ignored (see Bundesvereinigung der kommunalen Spitzenverbände, 1994; Grömig, 1994).

On the other hand, one has to bear in mind the enormous difficulties which local authorities have had to confront. Forced to cope with inadequate organizational structures and a shortage of qualified personnel and financial resources, East German local authorities had to tackle an unprecedented socioeconomic problem load, while at the same time trying to restructure their organization and to retrain their personnel. In addition, key components of local government were challenged at least twice within four years: first, following the reintroduction of local self-government after the collapse of the communist regime; and second, as a result of the adoption of new Länder local government charters, territorial reform, the creation of joint administrative authorities and, most recently, functional reform.

With a focus on the agents of change, it is clear that basic parameters and models for restructuring the internal organization of the local authorities were, by and large, defined by the West German model and transmitted by a large influx of administrative assistance from West Germany. However, within these exogenously defined parameters, the organizational practice of East German local authorities has shown a great deal of variability that can largely be explained by reference to endogenous factors. Among the latter, local political and personal conditions and contingencies as well as 'trial and error' incrementalism loom large, while comprehensive strategies of organizational reconstruction are still the exception. Again imitation or a blueprint approach do not capture the reality of institutional transformation; rather trial and error incrementalism and adaptive institutionalization appear to have dominated.

Administrative Reforms and the New Public Management

Before addressing the question whether and, if so, to what extent, the New Public Management (NPM) debate has influenced administrative transformation in the new Länder, some remarks on the situation in the West German Länder and local authorities might be useful. It should be pointed out, at the outset, that in West Germany interest in NPM only dates back to the beginning of the 1990s (see Reichard, 1994; Wollmann, 1996a; 1996c) and has, at least initially, focused almost exclusively on local authorities as the main 'workhorses' in the German administrative system when it comes to implementing Federal and Land legislation, policies and programmes.

A number of factors and actors have combined in giving NPM a rapidly rising profile on the western local agenda. The single most important contribution has probably been made by the *Kommunale Gemeinschaftsstelle für Verwaltungsvereinfachung* and its director, Gerhard Banner, who has been instrumental in calling for an all-out modernization drive in local administration, under the programmatic heading of a 'new guidance model' (*neues Steuerungsmodell*). Drawing on the international NPM debate and choosing the Dutch city of Tilburg as its guiding model, the *Gemeinschaftsstelle* has been diffusing and propagating a modernization message that centres on performance-oriented budgeting, decentralized resource management, controlling, contracting out, organizational development and personnel development (Banner, 1993). This initiative has coincided with a number of efforts aimed at pushing forward the debate on the modernization of the public sector:

- A significant reform push came from the Public Services, Transport and Traffic Union (ÖTV) which, under its then chairwoman, Monika Wulf-Mathies, played a crucial role in launching a campaign on 'Future through Public Services' in 1988 and has funded local projects in order to test and demonstrate the feasibility of proactive reform measures (*Gestaltungsprojekte*) (Wulf-Mathies, 1991).
- In 1992, at the School for Public Administration in Speyer, the decision was taken to organize a competition among 'innovative' county and municipal authorities (Hill and Klages, 1993).
- Similarly, in late 1992/early 1993, the Bertelsmann Foundation organized an international competition in a worldwide search for the cities that were most innovative in their administrative practice (Bertelsmann Stiftung, 1993). A US city (Phoenix, Arizona) and a New Zealand town (Churchtown) were the front-runners, while German cities lagged behind. This result was seen by many as an indication of the lack of international competitiveness of Germany's public administration. Furthermore, the Bertelsmann Foundation has been funding pilot projects on public administration reform in a number of cities, including Potsdam and Dessau in East Germany.

In the West German Länder, in the meantime, dozens of municipal authorities and a number of county administrations have embarked on reform concepts related to NPM ideas (Reichard, 1994: 67). While, in most cases, such reform initiatives are still fairly fragmented and tackle politically soft targets, such as municipal zoos or municipal cultural facilities, several municipalities and counties have adopted ambitious and comprehensive reform strategies which affect key areas of local politics and administration (Reichard, 1994: 67ff).

Reform pressure in the west has strengthened demands that in the east the historical opportunity to create new administrative structures should be exploited, before the inertia of existing institutions takes over. These demands are mainly put forward by West Germans (see Hill, 1992a; 1992b;

1993; 1994), while in the East German counties and municipalities, NPM concepts appear to have met with limited active interest. It seems that most of the organizational energy of local actors has been absorbed by the efforts to put in place a traditional administration in line with the western model and to cope with the unprecedented problem load. As a consequence, little time and attention have been left for realizing modernization projects.

However, pressure to take a closer look at NPM precepts is mounting. First, the eastern counties and municipalities find themselves in a permanent budgetary crisis, and thus are confronted with the need to cut expenditure and make their administrations more efficient. Second, local government faces major challenges in personnel policy. On the one hand, many authorities are in urgent need of qualified personnel and are severely understaffed in administrative key functions such as building inspection or physical planning. On the other, they are evidently overstaffed in others sectors, notably social service provision, as many of the public service-oriented organizations that were formerly subordinated to state agencies or were integrated into state enterprises have been transferred to local authority responsibility (Bundesvereinigung der kommunalen Spitzenverbände, 1994: 82f). Accordingly, local staffing levels in the east tend to be much higher than in comparable western local authorities. The pressure on the counties and municipalities to reduce their staff is increased by the Länder governments which, for instance in Brandenburg,[14] have put forward quotas to regulate the maximum number of employees the county and municipal authorities should employ.

In the face of organizational, personnel and financial burdens, notably arising from the transfer of social service institutions after 1990, current reform concepts tend to emphasize privatization and contracting out, and the traditional analytical approach of critical task review (*Aufgabenkritik*) is brought to bear. As the county and municipal authorities have been exposed to pressure from Land governments to reduce the number of deputy mayors, the reduction in the number of administrative divisions may well go hand in hand with a shift towards a more decentralized local resource management.

An instructive example of a predominantly privatization-oriented reform strategy can be observed in the city of Gotha in Thuringia (see Reichard, 1994: 79). In order to reduce its personnel, the local authority has been eager to transfer municipal tasks to legally independent organizations which remain under city ownership (*Eigenbetriebe*) and has also shifted tasks to private organizations and firms. Only the latter constitutes privatization in a substantive sense. Within two years, the municipality reduced its staff by almost 45 per cent, though most of this decrease was accounted for by the transfer of personnel to *Eigenbetriebe*. Of course, in the case of such *Eigenbetriebe*, the city remains at least indirectly financially liable. At the same time, the organizational form of an *Eigenbetrieb* may serve as a door-opener to more economic efficiency. Another example can be found in the city of Potsdam, the capital of Brandenburg. In a difficult budgetary situation which is marked by exceptional overstaffing,[15] the city council decided on 2 January 1995 to introduce a 'new guidance model' in order to achieve a 'citizen-oriented, efficient and lean administration' (*Der Tagesspiegel*, 6 January 1995: 12). To act as an administrative change agent, the new position of an administrative director was created and an experienced administrator was recruited to this post.

Despite such initiatives and the encouragement which the Brandenburg government has given to local authorities to pursue comprehensive organizational reforms (see Ziel, 1994), East German local authorities have, on the whole, been quite hesitant to take up the NPM debate. There are a number of reasons for this. First, it could well be, as some argue, that key NPM precepts can only be made to work after traditional formal organizational structures have been put in place. Following this line of argument, decentralized resource management, for example, can only be successfully implemented if viable central budgetary structures existed in the first place. In this sense, East German actors are right to build up traditional organizational structures before trying to venture into the world of NPM. The prevalent hesitancy may also be connected to the above-mentioned inclination and trained ability of the administrative newcomers to improvise and practise ad hoc problem solving, instead of thinking and acting strategically and in organizational terms. It is primarily endogenous reasons which, so far, have made East German local actors stick to adaptive institution building and shy away from innovative institutionalization.

Conclusion

The institutionalization of local government in East Germany has followed two distinct dynamics. Decisions regarding the creation of the legal and territorial setting and the contextual framework for the operation of local authorities have mainly been taken at the level of Länder politics and government. By contrast, the local arena played a crucial role in decisions on the organizational design of local administrations. In both cases, the extraordinary West German presence in East Germany's transformation process has had a marked influence as an exogenous change agent (Wollmann, 1995; 1996b). However, contrary to what is often suggested, endogenous factors have also played a conspicuous role in many key dimensions of administrative institutionalization. While the transfer and transplantation of West Germany's institutions have established the parameters within which the institutionalization process in East Germany has developed, these parameters have allowed for significant variation in institutional choice. Institutionalization has differed, not just in its outcomes, but also in its processes. This becomes clear when one looks at the often intense conflicts accompanying crucial institutional choices in Länder governments and parliaments and also major organizational decisions within local authorities.

At the Länder level, the comprehensive approach towards interlocking a sequence of local authority-related institutional reforms (local government charters, territorial county and municipal reforms, functional reforms) and the rigorous pace can be attributed to reform coalitions of the East German political leaders, including Minister–Presidents, ministers and parliamentarians, on the one hand, and West German aides in top administrative positions, notably in the ministries of the interior, on the other. In this process, top-level western administrative aides, some of whom have decided to stay in East Germany permanently, have exhibited an increasing readiness and ability to accept endogenous conditions and concerns. The sequence of reforms has been pursued by Länder governments and parliaments in a top-down, almost centralist manner, but has been politically moderated by local-level involvement, particularly by leaving the small municipalities unimpaired as political units (except in Saxony).[16] By and large, institution building processes at this level have been promoted by endogenous factors. If one tries to locate institutionalization on our scale ranging from imposed, through imitative and adaptive to innovative, it seems to have predominantly followed an adaptive pattern, often with innovative elements, rather than pure imitation.

At the local level, the institutionalization process in terms of organizational restructuring and rebuilding has been influenced by actor constellations which differed distinctly from the Länder level. Here, reform coalitions of politically ambitious local councillors and reform-minded administrative leaders have been rare. The local authorities' new administrative leaders, most whom have been newcomers to the world of politics and public administration, have been struggling with unprecedented problems. In organizational matters, they have tended to resort to improvisation, short-term crisis management and ad hoc problem solving, and they have concentrated on local contingencies and endogenous needs rather than the design of comprehensive and long-term organizational schemes. Although local institution building has, accordingly, tended to lack an innovative dimension, it shows, again, many features of adaptive institutional formation rather than a purely imitative blueprint approach.

Notes

1 This chapter draws, in part, on two empirical studies conducted by the author and collaborators with funding from the Research Commission on Social and Political Transformation in the East German Länder (KSPW). For details, see Wollmann and Berg (1994) and Berg and Nagelschmidt (1996).

2 The term 'luggage' has been used to describe the institutional concepts and transfer intentions with which the West German elites arrived at their new East German positions. This contrasts with the institutional and cognitive 'legacies' inherited from the former GDR. See Eisen (1996: 27ff).

3 The five Länder governments formed after the first elections to the new Länder parliaments in October 1990 comprised a total of 47 ministers, of whom 72 per cent were East Germans. The Länder Minister–Presidents were also East Germans, except in Saxony, and, later, Thuringia. See Deutschlandarchiv, 1991, no. 2: 214f.

4 Detailed information on the Federal government's administrative assistance programme to local authorities, which was carried out by the Union of Local Government Associations, can be found in Bundesvereinigung der kommunalen Spitzenverbände (1994). The programme was discontinued at the end of 1994.

5 By June 1993, of approximately 1000 North Rhine–Westphalian officials who had come to Brandenburg, 22 per cent had decided to stay permanently.

6 In the case of the city of Strausberg, for example, with a population of 30 000, six out of 14 former municipal top position holders stayed on in leading administrative positions after October 1990, four of'them beyond October 1992 (see Berg, 1994: 207). This can partly be explained by the exceptionally strong electoral showing of the Party of Democratic Socialism (PDS) in this municipality. In rural areas, too, the chances of old elites holding on to top posts were considerable. See Berg and Nagelschmidt (1996, ch. 3).

7 More than 90 per cent of the newcomers come from state enterprises, some 3 per cent from institutions of higher education, and hardly any from the church. See Wollmann and Berg (1994: 248).

8 Thuringia (enacted 16 August 1993), Saxony–Anhalt (enacted 5 October 1993), Brandenburg (enacted 15 October 1993).

9 That is, in Brandenburg on 5 December 1993 and in the other East German Länder on 12 June 1994.

10 In the case of Brandenburg, the overall territorial and administrative reform strategy was already laid down in the coalition agreement between the Social Democrats, the Greens and the Liberals of late 1990. As early as 29 January 1991, the Brandenburg cabinet requested the Minister of the Interior to start preparing the county territorial reform.

11 For a detailed account of the reforms in Brandenburg and in Saxony, see Eisen (1996: 96ff and 133ff).

12 For details on Brandenburg's territorial reform, see Brandenburg Kommunal, 1992, no. 4: 4.

13 The permanent members of this commission included three high-level government officials, two representatives of local authority associations, one representative of the trade unions and one of the employers' associations. It was chaired by a former Federal minister. See *Bericht der Kommission* (1994: 4); Muth and Zeidler (1994).

14 See Brandenburg Minister of the Interior, circular (*Runderlaß*) of 22 June 1993 on 'Measures for the Consolidation of Municipal Finances'. In Landes- und Kommunalverwaltung, 1993, nos. 5/6: 15f.

15   At that time, Potsdam had more than 30 employees per 1000 inhabitants, compared to
      an average of 27 in other county-free cities in Brandenburg, and a mere 10 in the
      average West German counterpart.
16   See Eisen (1996) who compares the establishment of environmental protection agen-
      cies in Brandenburg and Saxony, focusing on the different constellations of, and
      interactions between, the political–parliamentary arena and the role of West German
      top-level administrative aides.

References

Banner, G. (1993) 'Steuerung kommunalen Handelns', in R. Roth and H. Wollmann
    (eds), *Kommunalpolitik*, Opladen: Leske & Budrich, 350–361.
Berg, F. (1994) 'Transformation der kommunalen Verwaltungsinstitutionen in Stadt
    und Kreis Strausberg', in H. Naßmacher, Niedermayer, O. and H. Wollmann
    (eds), *Politische Strukturen im Umbruch*, Berlin: Akademie-Verlag, 205–30.
Berg, F. and M. Nagelschmidt (1996) *Kommunaler Institutionenwandel*, Opladen:
    Leske & Budrich (forthcoming).
Bericht der Kommission Funktionalreform an die Landesregierung Brandenburg
    (1994), Potsdam.
Bernet, W. (1993a) 'Zu Grundfragen der kommunalen Gemeindeverwaltungs- und
    Kreisgebietsreform', *Landes- und Kommunalverwaltung*, no. 12, 393–7.
Bernet, W. (1993b) 'Gemeinden und Gemeinderecht im Regimewandel', *Aus Politik
    und Zeitgeschichte*, B 36, 27–37.
Bertelsmann Stiftung (ed.) (1993) Carl-Bertelsmann-Preis 1993, *Demokratie und
    Effizienz in der Kommunalverwaltung*, Gütersloh: Bertelsmann.
Bundesvereinigung der kommunalen Spitzenverbände (1994) *Hilfen zum Aufbau
    der kommunalen Selbstverwaltung in den neuen Bundesländern*.
Derlien, H.-U. (1993a) 'Integration der Staatsfunktionäre der DDR im öffentlichen
    Dienst der neuen Bundesländer', in W. Seibel, H. Mäding and A. Benz (eds),
    Verwaltungsreform und Verwaltungspolitik im Prozeß der deutschen Einigung,
    Baden-Baden: Nomos Verlagsgesellschaft, 190–206.
Derlien, H.-U. (1993b) 'German Unification and Bureaucratic Transformation',
    International Political Science Review, **14**, 319–34.
Derlien, H.-U. (1994) 'Kommunalverfassungen zwischen Reform und Revolution',
    in O.W. Gabriel and R. Voigt (eds), *Kommunalwissenschaftliche Analysen*,
    Bochum: Brockmeyer, 47–78.
Derlien, H.-U. and S. Lock (1994) 'Eine neue politische Elite? Rekrutierung und
    Karrieren der Abgeordneten in den fünf neuen Landtagen', *Zeitschrift für
    Parlamentsfragen*, no. 1, 61–93.
Diekelmann, P. (1994) *Verwaltungshilfe und Verwaltungshelfer im Prozeß der
    Deutschen Einigung*, diploma thesis, Free University, Berlin.
Eisen, A. (1996) *Institutionenbildung im Transformationsprozeß*, Baden-Baden:
    Nomos Verlagsgesellschaft.
Goetz, Klaus H. (1993) 'Rebuilding Public Administration in the New German
    Länder: Transfer and Differentiation', *West European Politics*, **16**, 447–69.

Grömig, E. (1994) 'Verwaltungshilfe für ostdeutsche Kommunen', *Das Rathaus*, no. 5, 273–5.

Halstenberg, F. (1993) 'Anmerkungen zum Aufbau der staatlichen Verwaltung in den neuen Bundesländern', *Die Neue Verwaltung*, no. 1, 14–15.

Hanisch, C. (1993) 'Vom Werden und Weg einer Verwaltung – Kreisverwaltung Cottbus-Land 1990 bis 1992', in H. Hill and H. Klages (eds), *Spitzenverwaltungen im Wettbewerb*, Baden-Baden: Nomos Verlagsgesellschaft, 72–90.

Hansch, W. (1993) 'Wanderungen aus den alten Bundesländern in die Region Berlin/Brandenburg', *Deutschland-Archiv*, no. 3.

Hauschild, C. (1991) *Die örtliche Verwaltung im Staats- und Verwaltungssystem der DDR*, Baden-Baden: Nomos Verlagsgesellschaft.

Hill, H. (1992a) 'Effektive Verwaltung in den neuen Bundesländern', in H. Hill (ed.), *Erfolg im Osten I*, Baden-Baden: Nomos Verlagsgesellschaft, 25–38.

Hill, H. (ed.) (1992b) *Erfolg im Osten I*, Baden-Baden: Nomos Verlagsgesellschaft.

Hill, H. (ed.) (1993) *Erfolg im Osten II*, Baden-Baden: Nomos Verlagsgesellschaft.

Hill, H. (ed.) (1994) *Erfolg im Osten III*, Baden-Baden: Nomos Verlagsgesellschaft.

Hill, H. and H. Klages (eds) (1993) *Spitzenverwaltungen im Wettbewerb*, Baden-Baden: Nomos Verlagsgesellschaft.

Keller, B. and F. Henneberger (1993) 'Beschäftigung und Arbeitsbeziehungen im öffentlichen Dienst der neuen Bundesländer', in W. Seibel, H. Mäding and A. Benz (eds), *Verwaltungsreform und Verwaltungspolitik im Prozeß der deutschen Einigung*, Baden-Baden: Nomos Verlagsgesellschaft, 177–89.

Klinger, F. (1994) 'Die unvollendete Integration – Grundprobleme institutioneller Erneuerung in Deutschland', *BISS public*, no. 15, 67–103.

Knemeyer, F.-L. (1992) 'Kommunale Gebietsreform in den neuen Bundesländern', *Landes- und Kommunalverwaltung*, no. 6, 177–82.

Köstering, H. (1994) 'Grundlagen und Probleme einer Funktionalreform im Land Brandenburg', *Die öffentliche Verwaltung*, **47**, 238–49.

Lange, B. (1991) 'Neubau der Verwaltung in Thüringen – Aspekte aus dem Landkreis Rudolstadt', *Landes- und Kommunalverwaltung*, no. 5, 161–2.

Lehmbruch, G. (1990) 'Die improvisierte Vereinigung: Die Dritte deutsche Republik', *Leviathan*, **18**, 462ff.

Lehmbruch, G. (1993) 'Institutionentransfer', in W. Seibel, H. Mäding and A. Benz (eds), *Verwaltungsreform und Verwaltungspolitik im Prozeß der deutschen Einigung*, Baden-Baden: Nomos Verlagsgesellschaft, 42–66.

Lehmbruch, G. (1994) *Institutionen Interessen und sektorale Variationen in der Transformationsdynamik der politischen Ökonomie Deutschlands*, manuscript.

Marz, L. (1992) 'Dispositionskosten des Transformationsprozesses', *Aus Politik und Zeitgeschichte*, B 24, 3ff.

Muth, M. and F. Zeidler (1994) 'Regierungskommission Funktionalreform legte Abschlußbericht vor', *Brandenburg Kommunal*, no. 10/11, 6–8.

Rapsch, E. and C. Simanski (1991) 'Beratung in Kommunen der ehemaligen DDR', *Landes- und Kommunalverwaltung*, no. 6, 196–7.

Reichard, C. (1994) *Umdenken im Rathaus. Neue Steuerungsmodelle in der deutschen Kommunalverwaltung*, Berlin: Edition Sigma.

Reichard, C. and M. Röber (1993) 'Was kommt nach der Einheit? Die öffentliche Verwaltung in der ehemaligen DDR zwischen Blaupause und Reform', in G.-J. Glaeßner (ed.), *Der lange Weg zur Einheit*, Bonn: Dietz, 215–30.

Rose, R. *et al.* (1993) *Germans in Comparative Perspective*, Studies in Public Policy 218, University of Strathclyde.

Scheytt, O. (1993) 'Rechts- und Verwaltungshilfe in den neuen Bundesländern am Beispiel der Kommunalverwaltung', in R. Pitschas (ed.), *Verwaltungsintegration in den neuen Bundesländern*, Berlin: Duncker & Humblot, 70–88.

Schmidt-Eichstaedt, G. (1994) 'Die Kommunalreform in den neuen Bundesländern', *Das Rathaus*, no. 3, 137–44; no. 4, 221–5.

Schubel, C. and W. Schwanengel (1991) 'Funktionelle Probleme beim Aufbau von Landkreisverwaltungen in Thüringen', *Landes- und Kommunalverwaltung*, no. 8, 249–55.

Seibel, W. (1993) 'Zur Situation der öffentlichen Verwaltung in den neuen Bundesländern. Ein vorläufiges Resümee', in W. Seibel, H. Mäding and A. Benz (eds), *Verwaltungsreform und Verwaltungspolitik im Prozeß der deutschen Einigung*, Baden-Baden: Nomos Verlagsgesellschaft, 477–96.

Seibel. W., H. Mäding and A. Benz (eds), *Verwaltungsreform und Verwaltungspolitik im Prozeß der deutschen Einigung*, Baden-Baden: Nomos Verlagsgesellschaft.

Uebler, A. and H. Heinze (1994) 'Grundlagen für eine Neuverteilung von Verwaltungszuständigkeiten im Land Brandenburg', *Brandenburg Kommunal*, nos. 10/11, 9–11.

Veil, T. (1993) 'Kommunalreform in Sachsen-Anhalt', *Kommunal- und Verwaltungsreform*, no. 2, 47–51.

Wollmann, H. (1991) 'Kommunalpolitik und -verwaltung in Ostdeutschland. Institutionen und Handlungsmuster im "paradigmatischen" Umbruch', in B. Blanke (ed.), *Staat und Stadt*, PVS-Sonderheft, Opladen: Westdeutscher Verlag, 237ff.

Wollmann, H. (1995) 'Regelung kommunaler Institutionen in Ostdeutschland zwischen "exogener Pfadabhängigkeit" und endogenen Entscheidungsfaktoren', *Berliner Journal für Soziologie*, **5**, 497–514.

Wollmann, H. (1996a) 'Verwaltungsmodernisierung: Ausgangsbedingungen, Reformanläufe und aktuelle Modernisierungsdiskurse', in Ch. Reichard and H. Wollmann (eds), *Kommunalverwaltung im Modernisierungsschub?*, Basel: Birkhäuser Verlag, 1–49.

Wollmann, H. (1996b) 'Local Administrative Transformation in East Germany Between Institutional Transfer and Legacies', in G. Grabher (ed.), *Legacies, Linkages, and Localities*, Oxford: Oxford University Press (forthcoming).

Wollmann, H. (1996c) 'Modernization of the Public Sector and Public Administration in the Federal Republic of Germany', in M. Muramatsu and F. Naschold (eds), *Policymaking in Japan and Germany*, Berlin: deGruyter (forthcoming).

Wollmann, H. and F. Berg (1994) 'Die ostdeutschen Kommunen: Organisation, Personal, Orientierungs- und Einstellungsmuster im Wandel', in H. Naßmacher *et al.* (eds), *Politische Strukturen im Umbruch*, Berlin: Akademie Verlag, 239–73.

Wulf-Mathies, M. (1991) 'Zukunft durch öffentliche Dienste', in M. Wulf-Mathies (ed.), *Im Wettstreit der Ideen: Reform des Sozialstaats*, Bonn: Bund Verlag, 11–25.

Ziel, A. (1994) 'Reform der staatlichen und kommunalen Verwaltungen – der brandenburgische Weg', *Brandenburg Kommunal*, nos. 10/11, 2–3.

Zöllner, C.W. (1993) 'Notwendigkeit einer Funktionalreform', *Die Neue Verwaltung*, no. 3, 14–15.

8 Beyond the Public–Private Divide: Institutional Reform and Cooperative Policy Making

Arthur Benz

Changing Relationships between the Public and the Private Sectors

Modernization policies in government and public administration, which have been implemented or are currently under way in modern welfare states, deeply affect the relationship between the public and the private sectors. This is particularly evident if we look at privatization, by which functions of the state are passed to the private sector. The same also applies to decentralization, which aims at bringing policy making closer to the citizens. Deregulation intends, *inter alia*, to extend the discretion of private investors, while new forms of providing public goods and services are established in order to empower citizens and to reduce the monopolistic position of public agencies (Naschold, 1993).

In order to comprehend these changes, the simplistic notion of the public versus private discharge of functions is inadequate. The dualist approach of state versus society, hierarchy versus market and more or less privatization, which is often used for political reasons in announcing reform policies, can cause serious misunderstandings about the substance and consequences of public sector change. This danger is especially evident if the public and the private sectors are taken as two systems separated by clearly drawn boundaries. Such a view, which is often inherent in conservative political ideologies and in traditional approaches to state theory, distorts reality and is unhelpful for analyzing modernization in the public sector (see, for example, Brinkinshaw *et al.*, 1990).

Rather than being structured by clear-cut boundaries between the market and the state, policy making in modern societies promotes an increased blurring between both sectors. Government and public administration, while reacting to increasing market failures and greater citizen demands, are forced to apply non-hierarchical coordination and control mechanisms, to share powers with private organizations, to transfer functions to independent institutions and to integrate private actors in public policy making and service delivery. Modern forms of governance and administration combine authoritative regulation, coordination by exchange and negotiation procedures that cut across institutional boundaries. It should be clear, then, 'that in the real world the practice of politics is irredeemably hybrid; that is to say that politics occur through a combination of state officials and machinery, and private "non-state" agencies' (Brinkinshaw *et al.*, 1990: 1).

This line of argument raises the question of how public sector reform policies are influenced by, and affect, cooperation between public and private actors and organizations that links both sectors despite formal boundaries and hierarchical relations. Public authorities and private actors are in several respects mutually dependent; they collaborate in different ways and coordinate policies in negotiations. Studies on British politics and policy making tell us that informal cooperation is the typical style of policy making in Great Britain (Ashford, 1981; Jann, 1983; Feick and Jann, 1988; Vogel, 1986; Windhoff-Héritier *et al.*, 1990). In Germany, some commentators have talked of the rise of the 'cooperative state' (Hesse, 1989; Ritter, 1979), while others have pointed out that policy making increasingly takes place within network-like patterns of governance (Mayntz, 1991). Whether such assessments reflect new developments, or rather provide new concepts for long-established practices, is an open question. Nevertheless, it is fairly uncontentious that relationships between public and private organizations are to a considerable extent of a cooperative nature (Benz, 1994).

Taking this assessment as a starting point, the analysis of modernization policies needs to be based on a broader view of possible changes and effects. Policy making in modern states is not focused on discrete institutional contexts. Rather, it has to be understood as an interorganizational process, which includes public and private as well as central, regional and local organizations. Privatization, deregulation and decentralization do not alter this fact; they merely influence the structural framework of interorganizational processes. The formal rules in this interorganizational framework, which may be affected by reform policies, are only in part responsible for the substance and the outcome of policy making. Of greater importance are the emerging patterns of the organizational networks in a policy area (Mascarenhas, 1993: 326). Public-sector reforms only become effective if they are accompanied by necessary adjustments in informal procedures and interactions in the interorganizational setting, and they consist largely of negotiation and cooperation.

The following sections seek to elaborate some hypotheses on the correlation between modernization policies and cooperation between the public and private sectors. The first part discusses the practice of public–private cooperation. After providing some arguments on the relevance of cooperative policy making, we introduce three typical modes of cooperation between the public and the private sectors. Next we show how privatization, deregulation, decentralization and the New Public Management may affect cooperative forms of policy making and coordination in interorganizational policy networks. The chapter ends with some remarks concerning the tensions between the emergent cooperative forms of policy making and democratic politics, which may trigger unintended consequences for the architecture of the state, and a brief conclusion.

Cooperation as a Significant Policy Style in Germany?

Comparative studies on government and public administration classify Germany as a country with a strong tradition of a state-centred society (Dyson, 1980) and the rule of law (*Rechtsstaat*). Whereas, for example, British government and public administration are seen to be more inclined to informal negotiation between public and private actors (Feick and Jann, 1988: 203), the German policy style is said to be oriented towards formal regulation. Of course, empirical studies could not ignore the various forms of cooperation between government and private organizations, but theories of corporatism, which tend to treat the British case as sectorialized or meso-corporatist, often present Germany as an example of macro-corporatism, characterized by concerted policy making amongst central government and large interest associations.

However, these differences should not be overestimated. To a certain degree, the classification of comparative policy studies is based on an inadequate appreciation of the real world of German politics, government, public administration and policy making. Several empirical studies, including those on the legislative process (Schulze-Fielitz, 1988), implementation of legislation (Mayntz *et al.*, 1978; Rose-Ackerman, 1994) and regional and local policy making (Bachmann, 1993; Heinze and Voelzkow, 1991), have revealed widespread negotiation and cooperation in most policy areas and at all levels of the intergovernmental system (see Benz, 1994: 23–33). In any case, cooperative policy making in Germany is more differentiated than corporatist theories assume. This can be observed not only in central economic policy, but also in the formulation and implementation of other programmes, in particular at the regional and local levels. Gerhard Lehmbruch, the leading proponent of corporatist theory in Germany, accordingly categorizes the German system of interest intermediation as a 'hybrid and rather unwieldy network configuration' (Lehmbruch, 1991: 146) which, in key respects, deviates from corporatist models.

Neither the specific German state tradition, nor the fact that the civil service is dominated by lawyers, prevents government and public administration from using negotiation and cooperation. The paradigm of the state under the rule of the law was never the exclusive guiding model for German state practice, and it has long been modified by the idea of the welfare state. While the latter implied, at least until the late nineteenth century, traits of an authoritarian state, during the twentieth century it developed into a more cooperative model generated by the expansion of social welfare functions (Windhoff-Héritier, 1993). Moreover, one should mention the strong tradition of self-regulation and self-government in quasi-governmental organizations that include representatives from government and societal associations, for example in the fields of social security, health policy or labour market policy. These institutions foster cooperative relationships between public and private organizations.

Although a majority of higher civil servants in German public administrations are trained in the law, they are by no means exclusively preoccupied with the authoritative implementation of formal rules. Training for the civil service ensures a good deal of pragmatism in coping with conflicts between public and private interests. Officials know the law, but they also know its limits and flexibility. This flexibility can be employed when negotiating with the addressees of administrative decisions. Moreover, the German government, like its British counterpart, but for different reasons, possesses only limited powers to intervene in societal processes through authoritative measures (van Waarden, 1993). In Great Britain, the sovereignty of the state is limited by a strong tradition of self-constraint of the state vis-à-vis civil society. This norm is derived from the democratic principle and from a positive estimation of societal self-control and the market economy. In addition, government is faced by strong associations of social interests and private corporations, both of which act as pressure groups against state intervention and as capable partners in cooperative policy making. Although the British government can carry through authoritative decisions if they are supported by a majority in Parliament, it relies heavily on informal bargaining and persuasion. The German state is in a similar way 'semi-sovereign' (Katzenstein, 1987), but for constitutional and institutional reasons. The Basic Law strengthens citizens and private organizations against government and public administration. In addition, in the federal system policy making typically involves compromise between the large political parties.

This gives private interests considerable opportunities to restrain state intervention, if they manage to gain support of one of the large political parties. As a consequence, government tries to implement its policy goals by cooperation rather than risk the 'joint-decision trap' (Scharpf, 1988). Cooperative policy making is further favoured by the decentralization of government and public administration. In Germany, cooperation develops to a considerable degree at the regional and local levels, where the decentralized administrations of the Länder and local government are responsible for implementing legislation and for providing infrastructure and social services. In this context, the density of communication between public administration and addressees of public policies tends to be high.

Non-hierarchical Coordination and Cooperation between Public and Private Actors

Public–private coordination and cooperation take place in a number of ways. They can be distinguished by the potential power of public-sector organizations afforded by the institutional framework. Institutions determine the default condition of cooperative policy making (Ostrom, 1986: 9–12), that is the likelihood that public interests can be pursued even if cooperation with private actors fails. The chances of the realization of the public interest in the case of non-agreement are greatest in the case of negotiated regulation, where formal responsibility remains with government and public administration; they are lower in the case of contracting and exchange, where private organizations fulfil tasks and provide services that state agencies need to purchase or where public administration offers goods and services that the addressees are free to buy or reject. A third form of cooperation, coproduction, occupies an intermediate position between these two poles, and involves the pooling of competences and resources of both sides.

Negotiated Regulation

One of the main topics in discussions about public-sector reform is regulation. Critics have attacked overregulation for impairing efficient markets and for increasing the influence of the implementing bureaucracies. Conversely, empirical studies reveal implementation deficits, which are often regarded as indications of the weakness of the state against powerful addressees (capturing theory) and the inability of public administration to cope with complex tasks. Both views are only partly correct. They suppose a hierarchical relationship between regulating agencies and those subject to rules, while at the same time they fail to take into consideration the changing substance of the law.

The dissolution of the hierarchical relation between the regulating state and the regulated societal actors can be observed both in the formation and in the implementation of the law. 'It is apparently fairly common that in the earlier stages of the legislative process bureaucrats discuss bills and regulations with group representatives. Everywhere we encounter a multitude of advisory committees with the participation of group representatives, and it is not uncommon that similar bodies participate in policy implementation' (Lehmbruch, 1991: 123). In Germany, where close links between public bureaucracies, political parties and interest associations have a long tradition, the practice of negotiated regulation is of particular importance. It is quite usual for regulation to develop in intensive negotiations between government and private interest groups.

Moreover, government, despite its power to regulate, often prefers informal to formal arrangements with private organizations. A recent example is the agreement between the Federal government and private industry on the reduction and treatment of solid waste, which introduces a supplementary private system of waste collection instead of regulating the use of, and levying a charge on, packaging. Although government has the right to regulate, it chooses to foster cooperative forms of problem solving in order to reduce resistance to imposed decisions and to avoid conflict in the policy making process. Kenneth Dyson summarizes the findings of studies in a number of German policy sectors by concluding that 'typical was a style of co-operative regulation, exhibited in a preference for sectoral self-regulation (as in health and in industrial relations) and a tendency for change to be informally negotiated with the main organized interests (as in insurance, environmental pollution and commercial broadcasting)' (Dyson, 1992: 259).

Even if government resorts to legislation, this does not mean that those affected by the law have to conform without being able to exert influence. Cooperative forms of implementation are – to a certain degree – induced by changes in the law itself. Studies on the practice and effects of regulation show that the high complexity of regulated social fields, typical of modern welfare states, has resulted in adjustments in the substance of the law. Instead of immediately constraining the behaviour of citizens and organizations, the state relies more on setting goals, defining standards and providing procedural rules or organizational frameworks. As a consequence, the regulatory effect of the law depends to a great extent on implementation by the responsible administrations, which gain considerable discretionary power. These changes in the law were initially discussed in the context of Anglo-Saxon political and administrative culture (Nonet and Selznick, 1978). More recently, the same development has been described in Germany, despite its legalistic tradition (Habermas, 1992; Teubner and Willke, 1984), in that 'German statutes are not precise statements of policy, but are full of vague and undefined terms that require further interpretation before the acts can be implemented' (Rose-Ackerman, 1994: 1288).

The discretion in administrative decision making, which is granted by the law, has given rise to negotiation processes in implementation. Empirical studies show that such practices occur in different policy fields. Although German public administration seems to be oriented towards formal law, cooperation is not uncommon, as studies on environmental policy (Mayntz *et al.*, 1978), factory health and safety policy (Windhoff-Héritier *et al.*, 1990), town planning and building regulations (Bachmann, 1993) and tax policy (Weingarten, 1993) show. Indeed, some leading civil servants have praised cooperation as a modern form of public administration and recognize it as a common practice (see, for example, Bulling, 1989).

Coproduction

Cooperative regulation is founded, in the last resort, on the authority of the state and its power to create and enforce the law. In contrast to this, coproduction means that public and private actors and organizations voluntarily contribute to producing goods and services, with both sides providing resources and fulfilling specific functions. Examples include the approach towards a cooperative economic policy in several German regions (Heinze and Voelzkow, 1991; Hesse *et al.*, 1991), and the public–private partnerships in the production of infrastructural facilities. In addition, coproduction has gained attention in the local provision of public goods and in service delivery. Here it means that the public producers and the private consumers are directly involved in the joint coordination of relevant activities, in that they combine their productive efforts in order to achieve better results (Parks *et al.*, 1981: 1002).

By assigning the citizen an active role, the practice of coproduction differs from the traditional mode of service delivery. According to Brudney and England, the latter deviates from the cooperative type by the fact that public-service production and consumption are taking place in two separated spheres:

> The first sphere represents regular producers (service agents, bureaucrats) who operate within a service delivery environment defined by supports and demands from the general populace. These service agents employing 'standard operating procedures' (bureaucratic decision rules) allocate goods and services. The second sphere is composed of goods-and-service consuming clients, citizens, interests groups, and neighbourhoods. These consumers may respond (positive

feedback) to the adequacy of service delivery in one of several ways: They may make new demands, support or reject service patterns (e.g., vote for or reject bond issues), or comment through advisory boards, citizens' participation, complaints, and the like. (Brudney and England, 1983: 60)

In the model of coproduction, these two spheres are not separated, but linked. Coproduction 'is based on the assumption of an active, participative populace or consumer producer ... Under such an approach: (1) the feedback is internal to the service delivery process, and (2) part of the consumer sphere overlaps the regular producer sphere and results in co-production' (Brudney and England, 1983: 60). Consumers thus become to a certain degree producers of the goods they demand (Kiser, 1984: 486–8).

The necessity or productivity of coproduction alone does not motivate public agencies or citizens to cooperate. On the contrary, both sides may be able to achieve their goals more easily under the traditional model and, as the outcome of cooperative service delivery is uncertain, they are not necessarily inclined to cooperative behaviour. Studies in regional policy making show that public and private actors are reluctant to engage in cooperation because, in their estimation, short-term costs outweigh long-term benefits (Benz, 1994: 257–62). This problem is aggravated by the attractiveness of 'free-rider' behaviour, and the greater the number of potential producers and consumers, the more likely free-riding is to occur. Whereas in the public sector the number of producers is normally limited owing to the monopolistic position of central, regional or local administrations, circumstances favouring free-rider behaviour may arise because of the multitude of consumers. As Larry Kiser has argued, coproduction requires institutional arrangements that prevent participants from exploiting opportunities to become free-riders (Kiser, 1984: 491–505). Indeed, coproduction is less difficult to achieve in limited groups of users and producers, because individual behaviour is more visible and controllable.

As a consequence, coproduction is more likely at the regional and local levels. It is also made more attractive if it is fostered by central government programmes which provide incentives and motivation for the partners to cooperate. Public–private partnerships in regional development policy, which are currently emerging in Germany, are not only stimulated by pressures of rising competition between regions, but are also encouraged by programmes launched by Länder governments and the European Union. These cases also underline the fact that coproduction has to be induced and promoted by a small group of people who assume the role of 'political entrepreneurs' by initiating and guiding cooperative efforts (Hesse *et al.*, 1991: 144).

Exchange and Contracting: Government as Purchaser and Seller of Goods and Services

Government by contract, that is by purchasing or selling goods and services, marks the clearest deviation from the traditional hierarchical model, but it is debatable whether it should be classified as a cooperative form of policy making. It is characterized by exchange of goods and services between public and private organizations or individuals. Coordination is achieved by the give and take between suppliers and buyers of goods and services. If there is no well-functioning market that determines prices, the value of exchanged goods and services is to be determined in negotiations. Exchange processes include elements of cooperation in so far as the parties have to achieve an agreement on the 'deal'. In contrast to negotiated rule making and implementation, or coproduction, governmental agencies have no right to decide by themselves, should negotiation fail. They have to bargain like private entrepreneurs, who succeed if they meet the demands of their clients. This means that the relationship is primarily guided by the rationality of exchange and not by the public interest or norms of social justice.

That governments buy goods and services from private producers is common practice in infrastructure policies. Roads are not constructed by public organizations, but by private firms commissioned by public administrations. Building construction and specialized technical services for public administration have always been bought from private firms. Further examples for the contract model can be found in regional public transport. In some German regions it is provided by associations of public and private suppliers of transport facilities according to contractual arrangements that are negotiated with an association of regional and local governments responsible for planning and financing. It is also not unusual that public goods and services are sold by public administrations without the consumers being forced to buy them (as is the case with waste disposal services). The supply of public transport, the service of public hospitals, theatres or museums represent further typical cases.

Contracting requires that certain aspects of policy making activities are passed over to, or remain within, the private sector. Thus it implies a separation of power. Activities related to the production and decision making on what is desired and at what cost are taking place in different institutional arenas (Stewart, 1993). Proponents of the contractual approach argue that this organizational differentiation contributes to reducing inefficient political conflicts: 'This contract model separates the political process of determination of objectives and specification of services from their delivery, removing conflict of interest which occurs when those specifying a service are also its deliverers' (Mather, 1989: 233).

However, functional differentiation might also lead to diminishing the influence of government in the production of services. Government cannot independently decide on production and prices, it has to negotiate with private producers and has to take into account the consumers' willingness and capacity to pay. The result of this decision making depends on the relative bargaining or exchange power of the parties (Nash, 1953; Heckathorn, 1980). The position of public organizations as purchasers of goods and services improves when they are faced by many competing producers. As a seller of goods and services, government is often in the position of a powerful monopolist, provided that there are no strong consumer organizations on the demand side. But the exploitation of this advantage is limited by legal or political constraints. In any case, public–private contracting has to be viewed in the framework of the exchange structures that define the bargaining power and the terms of trade. If public agencies have to compete with private suppliers, there may be a reduction in prices, but other public concerns, for example social and environmental considerations, may well be overridden. On the other hand, if public agencies are in a monopolist position without being subject to effective democratic or judicial control, they may disregard specific interests of citizens and fail to produce in an efficient way.

Consequences of Modernization: Changing Patterns of Public–Private Cooperation?

It follows from the above discussion that cooperation can be seen as an essential element of government and public administration in the modern German state. From an empirical point of view, it is then interesting to ask how modernization policies affect the practice of cooperation between public and private actors. Given the current state of research, it is not possible to put forward more than hypotheses; but there are several reasons to suggest that some elements of modernization may strengthen established cooperative networks between the public and the private sectors. At the same time, recent reform projects at the Länder and local levels seem to limit the importance of negotiation and cooperation in favour of market exchange and hierarchical control, though even in these arenas new patterns of informal cooperation may emerge and existing networks persist.

The main thrust of current reform policies in the German public sector cannot simply be read from government programmes and pronouncements. Patterns of modernization policies indicate a path dependency of structural changes and institutional policies. Every reform of structures and routines of policy making is influenced and constrained by these structures and routines, which it intends to change. British reforms, for example, are – as a rule – radical, clearly derived from the ideological position of the majority party, formulated as a consistent programme and implemented 'from above' in a non-cooperative way (Castles, 1990). In Germany, institutional reforms are mostly subject to Federal–Länder bargaining and need to take account of the well-organized interests of public employees. Therefore radical innovations are rare, and institutional changes are implemented in a piecemeal fashion in an incremental process of adaptation to pressing requirements (Hesse and Benz, 1990; Lehmbruch *et al.*, 1988). Very often innovations emerge at the regional or local levels and become gradually diffused within the public sector. Whereas British reform programmes symbolize the need for transforming the status quo, German reform policies tend to be formulated in pragmatic terms in order to avoid conflicts with conservative interests.

There is, accordingly, no single clearly identifiable current approach in Germany to public-sector modernization. In fact, it comprises different elements which do not fit together into a coherent programme. The main reason for this is the federal structure. The Länder governments, which are responsible for the lion's share of administrative functions and the delivery of public services, develop their own modernization policies, pursuing diverse goals, while the Federal government, because of its limited powers, is unable to implement the 'grand design' of an institutional policy. From this follows an incrementalist and partly inconsistent reform policy at the Federal level, which is supplemented by diverse modernization policies pursued by the Länder. Moreover, since unification, modernization policy has been confronted by quite different tasks in East and West Germany (Seibel *et al.*, 1993). Nevertheless, if we leave aside the great variety of partial reforms, public-sector modernization in Germany seems focused on a combination of privatization, functional decentralization and territorial decentralization, each of which implies specific consequences for public–private relationships.

Privatization and Public–Private Partnerships

During the first half of the 1990s, institutional policies in Germany have come to rely increasingly on ideas that have shaped reforms in countries such as Australia, Great Britain and New Zealand (Mascarenhas, 1993). They are based on the conviction that the efficiency of public services can be improved either by transferring them to the private sector or by creating quasi-market arrangements, in which public agencies are required to pursue entrepreneurial strategies. Therefore governments favour the privatization of functions as far as possible. Moreover, in order to promote private investors, and to reduce the role of public bureaucracies, they resort to deregulating private activities.

In Germany, privatization[1] is not guided by a clearly stated policy of 'rolling back the state', but is pursued in a more pragmatic manner. Its main goal is to reduce fiscal stress, to release public corporations from civil service law and to make them more manageable. Unlike the British programme, privatization in Germany does not, first and foremost, aim at exposing public bureaucracies to open competition. As a rule, privatization leads to a sharing of functions between public and private organizations. The reform of the German railways can be cited as an example (see Lehmkuhl, in the present volume). While the former Bundesbahn was transformed into a private corporation, the provision for infrastructure (rail tracks) remained with the Federal government, and the responsibility for regional public transport was passed on to Länder and local governments. Similarly, the provision of infrastructure by private firms, including, for example, motorways or sewage plants, is expected to complement public providers, but not expose them to open competition. Therefore there is a growing concern with contractual relationships in public–private partnerships, with public agencies becoming more businesslike. These forms of cooperation are embedded either in hierarchical control structures or, if there are no adequate competitors, in negotiated regulation. In monopolistic situations, government has to intervene in order to secure public interests and to avoid the exploitation of clients. In contrast to Great Britain, where 'each of the major privatizations of public utilities has been accompanied by the creation of a regulatory agency' (Stewart and Walsh, 1992: 507), the German practice of regulating monopolistic structures is – as a rule – based on negotiation between controlling authorities and private companies.

Similar consequences emerge from policies aimed at deregulation. Rather than shifting responsibility from the public to the private sector, deregulation often results in more dense linkages and cooperation. Indeed, deregulation extends the discretionary power of private investors. Hence it raises control problems which have to be dealt with in negotiations. For example, several Länder governments have decided to abolish the licensing requirement for the construction of one- and two-storey buildings, but this does not mean that private investors are free from all requirements. Instead of a compulsory ex ante approval, there will be an ex post control of compliance with town planning objectives and quality standards. Experience shows that people subject to administrative supervision are inclined to look to the controlling authority for advice in order to avoid intervention after the construction is finished. This early cooperation is attractive for the administrative authority, too, as later sanctions are often difficult to enforce.

Privatization and deregulation thus motivate public administration to cooperate with its clients, because administrators partly lose their power to secure the public interest by taking authoritative decisions. Indeed, this may be one of the goals of deregulation. Modernization of public administration in Germany should change the hierarchical relationship between public administration and citizens while inducing more partnerships (see, as an example, Staatsministerium Baden–Württemberg, 1993: 3). It is interesting to note that even policies which aim at shifting responsibilities to private actors are at the same time accompanied by rising concerns for public–private partnerships. This concern underlines the fact that intensified cooperation is not just a side-effect of current modernization policies, but that, on the contrary, it is a central element of the intended restructuring of the relationships between the public and the private sectors.

Privatization and deregulation may lead to more problem-oriented flexible policy making, in which public administration governs private decisions by persuasion, information and motivation. However, compared to negotiated regulation on the basis of public law and administrative power to implement the law, such policies may reduce the bargaining power of public administration against powerful private investors, while the individual citizen may in turn lose the right to take legal action against controversial activities. Thus, while cooperation is set to increase, the influence of public administration and individual citizens may decrease.

Functional Decentralization, Exchange Relations and Policy Networks

While privatization and deregulation are common elements of a pragmatic restructuring of the public sector at the Federal and Länder levels, recent developments at the local level are mainly influenced by the paradigm of the New Public Management (NPM), in the narrow sense of a new control strategy. Supported by Länder governments, many local governments – and some Länder governments themselves, for example in Baden–Württemberg and Hesse – are experimenting with functional decentralization and new 'models of governance' (Reichard, 1994), where administrative departments are freed from narrow budgetary constraints and detailed political control. As independent agencies, they become responsible for deciding how to meet the demands of consumers of public services in an optimal way. They can dispose of their own budget, which gives them wide discretion on how to allocate resources. The role of politics is reduced to setting targets, standards and resource frameworks and to regulating the relationships between providers of services and consumers as well as the activities of privatized corporations.

Roughly speaking, the new approach to public-sector management currently pursued by several Länder and local governments aims at a two-level style of governance. At the level of service delivery, which may include administrations responsible for implementing the law, independent public agencies contract with consumers or private providers of goods and services according to the rules of the market. Here public and private actors play the roles of producers and consumers which coordinate the supply and demand of public services in exchange processes. The relationships between the independent agencies, which are framed by the allocation of 'global budgets', are to be coordinated by an 'internal market', where they follow the same rationale of exchange. The contractual relationships between agencies and their clients are regulated by performance standards, which are derived from relevant Federal or Länder laws or are set by the authoritative decisions of the elected councils. This is the political level of policy making, which should be separated from that of service delivery.

According to the theory of an 'entrepreneurial city administration', the elected councils are to take on a supervisory role on the basis of hierarchical superiority (strategic controlling). It is an open question whether this new form of political control of local administration will operate in practice. It is probable that elected politicians, who generally are more interested in the day-to-day work of local governments, will lose influence, and that control of administration will be sought through the appointment of agency managers according to political criteria. In any case, reforms of local administration will change the separation of power between politics and administration and will alter relationships between citizens and local governments.

Although the theory of NPM provides plausible arguments to suggest that local government may work in a more efficient way and be able to cut expenditure in times of decreasing revenues, its implementation and operation will depend on the way relationships between public administration, politicians, interest groups and citizens will adjust to the new formal structures. Given limited experience in Germany (see Reichard, 1994), we can only speculate about future developments, but two scenarios seem likely. First, exchange relationships may emerge where coproduction existed. This means that the idea of a community government, according to which local governments should provide services for the citizens and with the citizens (Stewart, 1989: 240–45), is effectively losing ground. Instead, local policy making is transformed into a series of contracts (Mather, 1989: 232–3), with local governments becoming divided into function-specific exchange networks. However, this can mean that autonomous agencies get involved in more intensive cooperative relationships with their clients, which are founded on the provision and receiving of services, resources, information and advice. Such a development may be in accordance with intended goals, if it leads to a more consumer-oriented administration. But it can also easily turn into a clientelistic relationship, with public administration becoming an advocate of certain special interests. As a consequence, the influence of elected politicians will diminish because clientelistic relationships are almost impossible to control. At the same time, public administration will become more fragmented into separated and increasingly uncoordinated spheres (Reichard, 1994: 84–5).

Second, it is likely that elected politicians will not refrain from dealing with specific affairs of local administration. Democratic processes at the local level give them incentives to act in this way. Members of local councils gain support from their electorate if they engage in solving individual problems rather than by proposing policy programmes or formulating general objectives. Therefore they have a genuine interest in being immediately involved in the day-to-day work of administrative agencies. This is more often the case since, as in a functionally decentralized administration, close cooperative relations between agencies and their clients emerge. The involvement of elected politicians may change these relationships, not in the sense of breaking them up, but by transforming them into a series of policy-specific 'iron triangles'. Presumably, this scenario is more realistic for big cities than for small communities. It is, however, based on empirical evidence of the reality of democratic politics in local government, which is marked by relatively close personal linkages between politicians and citizens. Moreover, implementation research suggests (Goggin *et al.*, 1990) that the top-down approach of strategic controlling is likely to be supplemented by a bottom-up approach of coordination between politics and service delivery. Hence we can expect the emergence of cooperative relationships between members of the controlling political bodies and managers of the agencies, who modify hierarchical relationships by informal negotiations. These relationships can cut across the boundaries of the public sector where certain functions of service delivery are contracted out.

According to both scenarios, functional decentralization seems to imply not only that the influence of the consumers will force public administration to work more effectively and efficiently, but also that it will strengthen networks of 'administrative interest intermediation' (Lehmbruch, 1991) that already exist in different policy domains. It is the interplay between these tendencies that will shape the outcome of current public-sector reforms at the local level.

Territorial Decentralization and Emerging Regional Cooperation

Territorial decentralization has always been a guiding norm of modernization policies in Germany at both the Federal and the Länder levels. In recent years, it has been possible to distinguish two approaches towards decentralization. The first has to do with the structure of the federal system and has been part of a revision of the Federal Constitution. The second concerns the regional structure of the Länder and relies more on emergent cooperation in regional networks.

The reform of the Federal Constitution was put on the agenda in connection with German unification, but included objectives that had been discussed in West Germany since the 1970s. One of the central themes in the debates was the proposal to give the Länder additional legislative competences and discretionary powers in fiscal matters. Moreover, a territorial reorganization should strengthen the administrative and economic capacities of the small Länder. However, as far as decentralization efforts were concerned, the result of the constitutional reform was disappointing (Benz, 1995). The Länder parliaments failed to gain any further competences; instead, the Länder executives succeed in extending their participatory rights in EU-related policy making. Overall, the effects of constitutional reform on the intergovernmental system were minimal.

Of greater importance is the clear trend in several Länder towards the regionalization of policy making (Heinze and Voelzkow, 1991; Hesse *et al.*, 1991; Krafft and Ulrich, 1993). Some Länder governments, including North Rhine–Westphalia and Lower Saxony, encourage regionalization and important impulses can be traced back to the regional policy of the European Union. However, for the most part, effective structural change is the result of cooperation between public and private organizations. This 'regionalization from below' is part of the reform approach of the Länder governments. The former North Rhine–Westphalian economics minister, who was responsible for regionalization policy, outlined this approach in the following way:

> It is based on the perception that a strong regional economy and a future oriented policy of structural adjustment can only develop effectively if they are supported by the resources of the whole region, that is if the 'endogenous potential for development' is activated. Such a policy of structural adjustment and renewal cannot just be decreed from above, nor is it enough just to make the necessary funds available. Success in this field is dependent much more on the mobilization of creativity as well as the will, in the individual regions, to co-operate and succeed in shaping a distinctive locational profile capable of contributing to regional wealth generation. (Jochimsen, 1992: 91)

This implies that Länder governments do not intervene in creating regional structures, but are involved as reform promoters and moderators of decentralized cooperation.

Cooperation in the form of coproduction of regional development projects, planning concepts and infrastructure (technology parks and institutions for vocational training) does not emerge automatically. It has to be guided by 'political entrepreneurs', who in most regions come from public administration or chambers of industry and commerce. They form a core group of closely cooperating actors, while the larger regional conferences meet only sporadically. Regional cooperation develops more in informal processes and emergent networks linking an elite of public and private actors than in institutional structures that are shaped by reform policies.

Regionalization of structural policy, then, shows that the German public sector is not only affected by the policies of institutional reform, which trigger adjustments of public–private cooperation and coordination; instead, new patterns of cooperation by themselves contribute to changing routines and structures of policy making in the public sector. In this context, territorial decentralization in Germany is more the outcome of a de facto transfer of power and responsibilities to lower levels of the political system than the result of reform policies 'from above' (Hesse and Benz, 1990). Therefore networks of cooperation, rather than being brought about by reforms of the institutional setting, can themselves induce institutional adjustments in the public sector. From this point of view, they have to be taken as an element of modernization processes in the public sector (Mayntz, 1991).

Networks of Exchange and Cooperation and Democratic Politics

Developments in the German public sector imply a new division of responsibilities between public and private organizations; make public administration more independent of elected councils and parliaments; transform public policy making into processes of exchange and negotiation; and result in new cooperative networks that tend to exclude opportunities for extensive participation. These findings raise the question of how policy making in the new structures and networks is legitimized.

Proponents of current modernization strategies argue for the need to rethink the basis of legitimizing policy making. They present new concepts of democratic politics which take account of their ideas of a modern public sector. Two different lines of reasoning are offered. The first, inherent in the philosophy of NPM, is derived from public choice theories, which criticize decision making based on the majority principle as leading to inefficient results (Buchanan and Tullock, 1962). One of the central tenets is to protect government from the immediate pressure of interest groups and political parties. Contracting, competition and evaluation procedures are to replace the direct interference of party politicians and reduce participation of citizens in administrative decision making. As consumers, citizens should be given the opportunity to 'punish' agencies that do not meet performance standards, by choosing another service provider in the market. This is thought to lead to a depoliticization of public services. Consumer influence is believed to provide an optimal quality of services. It is assumed that, for this reason, outputs will be accepted by citizens. Thus there is, at first glance, no need for further democratic legitimation of policy making. It is the quality of public policy that justifies decisions.

This line of reasoning leaves two problems unresolved. It overestimates the feasibility of a competitive market in the field of public policy and the influence of individuals as consumers; at the same time, such a concept of legitimizing policy making deviates from the traditional understanding of democratic politics, which has its institutional core in elected assemblies. Democracy requires that political decisions be grounded in deliberative processes, which are organized in parliaments or local councils. Moreover, citizens under a democratic government should have the right to participate in processes of administrative decision making. The alternative theory implies that the influence of democratic politics is reduced – at best – to the setting of quality standards, targets and financial frameworks. However, it is doubtful whether elected politicians are either able or willing to assume such an altered role. It is to be feared that, according to the first scenario outlined above, elected politicians will lose influence against independent agencies. 'Government by contract carried too far sets boundaries to the political process, limiting it to defined points in time and to defined terms. That is to limit the process of learning, of responding to change and of changing that is at the heart of governing' (Stewart, 1993: 12). The other scenario would have the consequence that the separation of powers, which privatization and functional decentralization are aiming at, will be avoided by politicians looking for informal influence.

The second argument in defence of public-sector change has evolved from discussions on regional cooperation and negotiated regulation. It implies that cooperative policy making can be legitimized if it ends in a consensus among all relevant interests. Cooperation is connected to the concept of a 'discursive democracy' (Dryzek, 1990), which is set against the much-criticized reality of an 'adversary democracy' in established parliaments and in party politics. Consensus claims to be a decision principle which is more in accordance with the democratic norm of including all societal interests, compared to the majority principle. Moreover, cooperation is said to create better decisions because conflicts are dealt with in a productive way, that is by changing positions towards solutions all can support, and because discussions can increase the accuracy of perceptions, stimulate processes of mutual learning and produce alternatives, which do not enter the agenda in the procedures typical of a majoritarian democracy (Mansbridge, 1980: 271–3).

However, this theory of legitimation is not compatible with the norms of democratic politics that are grounded in existing political institutions. Cooperative networks at the regional level include in most cases leaders of regional and local governments, quasi-governmental organizations, such as chambers of industry and commerce, associations (notably trade unions and employer associations), non-profit organizations and private firms. They deal with affairs which often touch responsibilities of Länder parliaments and local councils. Tensions between cooperative and democratic institutions arise because the latter feel deprived of their power and find it difficult to control effectively processes of cooperation. The same holds true with regard to negotiated law making, if legislation by parliament is circumvented. In addition, cooperative policy making is only effective if it takes place in small groups. Therefore it has a tendency towards elitist politics with an exclusive circle of participants (Hesse *et al.*, 1991).

It seems likely that tensions between cooperative politics and democratic politics will grow in the future, as it is almost impossible to draw clearly the boundaries of the institutionalized democratic processes and to find a stable division of functions between politics and public administration. Therefore, the outcome of modernization policies and adaptive processes in the public sector will depend not only on the persistence or change of network structures and modes of cooperation, but also on the way the problem of legitimation can be addressed. Policies of public-sector modernization have to be accompanied by the search for a new balance between public–private policy networks and democratic politics (Scharpf, 1993).

Conclusion

As organization theory tells us, reform policies aimed at modernizing the complex structures of government and public administration can control only part of the organizational reality directly. Each reform process is to be considered as an interplay between 'prescribed orientation' and 'emergent detachment' of policy networks (Hinings and Greenwood, 1988: 21). We have, therefore, to be aware 'that a successful organizational transformation is less likely to follow an imposed alteration of prescribed frameworks than the development of systems of operation which become part of day-to-day activity and are then consolidated and furthered by revisions of authoritative (prescribed) arrangements' (Hinings and Greenwood, 1988: 112). In modern governments, a multitude of emergent cooperative networks between actors and organizations exists both inside the public sector and between the public and the private sectors. The persistence and dynamics of these networks are of considerable relevance to the outcome of reform policies as well as for the 'emergent detachment' of ineffective structures.

It is difficult to draw an unambiguous picture of the connection between current modernization policies and the development of cooperation. Given the current state of research, assessments of the outcome of contemporary modernization necessarily remain speculative. The previous sections tried to sketch some plausible tendencies. It was argued that, although the consequences of public-sector modernization are often discussed in terms of more or less state, their essential features are changing modes of coordination and cooperation which link both sectors.

This conclusion applies even in the case of privatization and deregulation. The practice of negotiation between public authorities and private producers of goods and services is likely to persist. Privatization of public policies may even increase the need for negotiated coordination and cooperation in order to manage interdependence between functions which are transferred to the private sector and those which remain in the public sector. Territorial decentralization and deregulation may foster the development of regional and local policy networks which are, for their part, responsible for a considerable degree of de facto regionalization and decentralization in the intergovernmental system. More far-reaching consequences may be caused by functional decentralization, which can be observed, above all, in local government. These reforms will be accompanied by adjustments to cooperative practices and it is an open question whether cooperation will help or hinder the intentions of reform programmes. In sum, modernization policies do not abolish negotiation procedures or established policy networks linking the public and the private sectors. On the contrary, their real effects depend on the dynamics of network patterns, which can either stabilize or destabilize processes of modernization in the public sector.

What is of paramount importance in this context is the rising tension between cooperative forms of public–private policy making and the institutions of democratic politics, with elected representative bodies at the central, regional and local levels. Even if we follow arguments put forward to justify the legitimacy of public–private cooperation and government by contract and exchange, the incompatibility between the norms embedded in existing institutions and the theories guiding the new model of the public sector remains a practical problem. The most challenging task of political and administrative science is to find convincing and feasible solutions to lessen this tension.

Note

1 I do not consider privatization in the Eastern Länder as it represents a special case of transforming a formerly socialist economy (see Czada, in the present volume).

References

Ashford, D. (1981) *Policy and Politics in Britain: The Limits of Consensus*, Oxford: Oxford University Press.

Bachmann, B. (1993) *Verhandlungen (mit) der Bauverwaltung*, Opladen: Westdeutscher Verlag.

Benz, A. (1994) *Kooperative Verwaltung. Funktionen, Voraussetzungen und Folgen*, Baden-Baden: Nomos Verlagsgesellschaft.

Benz, A. (1995) 'Verfassungspolitik im kooperativen Bundesstaat', in K.-H. Bentele *et al.* (eds), *Reformfähigkeit von Industriegesellschaften*, Frankfurt/ New York: Campus, 145–64.

Brinkinshaw, P., I. Harden and N. Lewis (1990) *Government by Moonlight*, London: Unwin Hyman.

Brudney, J.L. and R.E. England (1983) 'Toward a Definition of the Coproduction Concept', *Public Administration Review*, **43**, 59–65.

Buchanan, J.M. and G. Tullock (1962) *The Calculus of Consent*, Ann Arbor: University of Michigan Press.

Bulling, M. (1989) 'Kooperatives Verwaltungshandeln (Vorverhandlungen, Arrangements, Agreements und Verträge) in der Verwaltungspraxis', *Die Öffentliche Verwaltung*, **42**, 277–89.

Castles, F.G. (1990) 'The Dynamics of Policy Change', *European Journal of Political Research*, **18**, 491–513.

Dryzek, J.S. (1990) *Discursive Democracy. Politics, Policy, and Political Science*, Cambridge: Cambridge University Press.

Dyson, K. (1980) *The State Tradition in Western Europe*, Oxford: Martin Robertson.

Dyson, K. (1992) 'Regulatory Culture and Regulatory Change: Some Conclusions', in K. Dyson (ed.), *The Politics of German Regulation*, Aldershot: Dartmouth, 257–71.

Feick, J. and W. Jann (1988) '"Nations matter" – Vom Eklektizismus zur Integration in der vergleichenden Policy-Forschung?', in M.G. Schmidt (ed.), *Staatstätigkeit. International und historisch vergleichende Analysen*, Opladen: Westdeutscher Verlag, 196–220.

Goetz, K.H. (1993) 'Public Sector Change in Germany and the UK: Differences, Commonalities, Explanations', paper presented at the Workshop, 'German Public Sector Reform in the Light of the British Experience', London School of Economics and Political Science, 17–18 September.

Goggin, M.L., A.O'M. Bowman, J.P. Lester and L.J. O'Toole (1990) *Policy Implementation: Towards a Third Generation*, Glenview, Ill.: Scott Foresman/Little, Brown.

Habermas, J. (1992) *Faktizität und Geltung*, Frankfurt/M.: Suhrkamp.

Heckathorn, D. (1980) 'A Unified Model for Bargaining and Conflict', *Behavioral Science*, **25**, 261–84.

Heinze, R.G. and H. Voelzkow (1991) 'Regionalisierung der Strukturpolitik in Nordrhein-Westfalen', in B. Blanke (ed.), *Staat und Stadt. Systematische, vergleichende und problemorientierte Analysen 'dezentraler' Politik*, Opladen: Westdeutscher Verlag, 461–76.

Hesse, J.J. (1989) 'The Purpose of a Contemporary Staatslehre', *Yearbook on Government and Public Administration*, Baden-Baden: Nomos Verlagsgesellschaft, 55–80.

Hesse, J.J. and A. Benz (1990) *Die Modernisierung der Staatsorganisation*, Baden-Baden: Nomos Verlagsgesellschaft.

Hesse, J.J., Ang. Benz, A. Benz and H. Backhaus-Maul (1991) *Regionalisierte Wirtschaftspolitik*, Baden-Baden: Nomos Verlagsgesellschaft.

Hinings, C.R. and R. Greenwood (1988) *The Dynamics of Strategic Change*, Oxford: Blackwell.

Jann, W. (1983) *Staatliche Programme und 'Verwaltungskultur'*, Opladen: Westdeutscher Verlag.

Jochimsen, R. (1992) 'The Regionalisation of Structural Policy: North Rhine–Westphalia in the Europe of the Regions', *German Politics*, 1, 82–101.

Katzenstein, P. (1987) *Policy and Politics in West Germany. The Growth of the Semi-Sovereign State*, Philadelphia: Temple University Press.

Kiser, L.L. (1984) 'Toward an Institutional Theory of Citizen Coproduction', *Urban Affairs Quarterly*, 19, 485–510.

Krafft, A. and G. Ulrich (1993) *Chancen und Risiken regionaler Selbstorganisation*, Opladen: Leske und Budrich.

Lehmbruch, G. (1991) 'The Organization of Society, Administrative Strategies, and Policy Networks', in R.M. Czada and A. Windhoff-Héritier (eds), *Political Choice*, Frankfurt/New York: Campus, 121–58.

Lehmbruch, G., O. Singer, E. Grande and H. Döhler (1988) 'Institutionelle Bedingungen ordnungspolitischer Strategiewechsel im internationalen Vergleich', in M.G. Schmidt (ed.), *Staatstätigkeit, International und historisch vergleichende Analysen*, Opladen: Westdeutscher Verlag, 251–83.

Mansbridge, J.J. (1980) *Beyond Adversary Democracy*, New York: Basic Books.

Mascarenhas, R.C. (1993) 'Building an Enterprise Culture in the Public Sector: Reform of the Public Sector in Australia, Britain and New Zealand', *Public Administration Review*, 53, 319–28.

Mather, G. (1989) 'Thatcherism and Local Government: An Evaluation', in J. Stewart and G. Stoker (eds), *The Future of Local Government*, London: Macmillan, 212–35.

Mayntz, R. (1991) *Modernization and the Logic of Interorganizational Networks* (MPIFG discussion paper 91/8), Cologne: Max-Planck-Institut für Gesellschaftsforschung.

Mayntz, R., E. Bohne, H.-U. Derlien, B. Hesse, J. Hucke and A. Müller (1978) *Vollzugsprobleme der Umweltpolitik*, Stuttgart: Kohlhammer.

Naschold, F. (1993) *Modernisierung des Staates. Zur Ordnungs- und Innovationspolitik des öffentlichen Sektors*, Berlin: Ed. Sigma.

Nash, J.F. (1953) 'Two Person Cooperative Games', *Econometrica*, 21, 128–40.

Nonet, P. and P. Selznick (1978) *Law and Society in Transition: Toward Responsive Law*, New York: Harper.

Ostrom, E. (1986) 'An Agenda for the Study of Institutions', *Public Choice*, **48**, 3–25.

Parks, R.B., P.C. Baker, L.L. Kiser, R. Oakerson, E. Ostrom, V. Ostrom, S.L. Percy, M.B. Vandivort, G.P. Whitaker and R. Wilson (1981) 'Consumer and Co-Producers of Public Services: Some Economic and Institutional Considerations', *Policy Studies Journal*, **9**, 1001–11.

Reichard, C. (1994) *Umdenken im Rathaus. Neue Steuerungsmodelle in der deutschen Kommunalverwaltung*, Berlin: Ed. Sigma.

Ritter, E.-H. (1979) 'Der kooperative Staat. Bemerkungen zum Verhältnis von Staat und Wirtschaft', *Archiv des öffentlichen Rechts*, **104**, 389–413.

Rose-Ackerman, S. (1994) 'American Administrative Law Under Siege: Is Germany a Model?', *Harvard Law Review*, **107**, 1279–1302.

Scharpf, F.W. (1988) 'The Joint-Decision Trap: Lessons from German Federalism and European Integration', *Public Administration*, **66**, 239–78.

Scharpf, F.W. (1993) 'Versuch über Demokratie im verhandelnden Staat', in R. Czada and M.G. Schmidt (eds), *Verhandlungsdemokratie, Interessenvermittlung, Regierbarkeit*, Opladen: Westdeutscher Verlag, 25–50.

Schulze-Fielitz, H. (1988) *Theorie und Praxis parlamentarischer Gesetzgebung, besonders des 9. Deutschen Bundestages (1980–1983)*, Berlin: Duncker & Humblot.

Seibel, W., A. Benz and H. Mäding (eds) (1993) *Verwaltungsreform und Verwaltungspolitik im Prozeß der deutschen Einigung*, Baden-Baden: Nomos Verlagsgesellschaft.

Staatsministerium Baden–Württemberg (ed.) (1993) *Verwaltungsreform Baden-Württemberg. Erster Bericht der Regierungskommission Verwaltungsreform*, Stuttgart: Staatsministerium BW.

Stewart, J. (1989) 'A Future for Local Authorities as Community Government', in J. Stewart and G. Stoker (eds), *The Future of Local Government*, London: Macmillan, 236–54.

Stewart, J. (1993) 'The Limits of Government by Contract', *Public Money and Management*, **13**, 7–12.

Stewart, J. and K. Walsh (1992) 'Change in the Management of Public Services', *Public Administration*, **70**, 499–518.

Teubner, G. and H. Willke (1984) 'Kontext und Autonomie: Gesellschaftliche Steuerung durch reflexives Recht', *Zeitschrift für Rechtssoziologie*, **6**, 4–35.

van Waarden, F. (1993) 'Über die Beständigkeit nationaler Politikstile und Politiknetzwerke', in R. Czada and M.G. Schmidt (eds), *Verhandlungsdemokratie, Interessenvermittlung, Regierbarkeit*, Opladen: Westdeutscher Verlag, 191–212.

Vogel, D. (1986) *National Styles of Regulation. Environmental Policy in Great Britain and the United States*, Ithaka: Cornell University Press.

Weingarten, J. (1993) *Finanzverwaltung und Gesetzesvollzug*, Opladen: Westdeutscher Verlag.

Windhoff-Héritier, A. (1993) 'Wohlfahrtsstaatliche Intervention im internationalen Vergleich Deutschland – Großbritannien', *Leviathan*, **21**, 103–26.

Windhoff-Héritier, A., S. Gäbe and C. Ullrich (1990) *Verwaltungen im Widerstreit von Klientelinteressen*, Wiesbaden: Deutscher Universitäts-Verlag.

Index

N.B. (1) Page references to tables are in italics.

N.B. (2) Page references to notes are suffixed with 'n'.

Böhret, C., and Hugger, W. (1979) 35
Böhret, C., and Junkers, M.-T. (1976) 33
Börnsen, A. (1992) 57
Bötsch, Wolfgang 57, 60–1
Brandt, Chancellor Willy 31, 34
Braunthal, G. (1990) 34
Breuel, Birgit 95, 114n
Breuel–Schommer agreement 99, 114n
Brinkinshaw, P., Harden, I., and Lewis,
        N. (1990) 165, 166
Britain 166, 168, 175, 176
British Telecom 54–5
Brohm, W. (1988) 5
Bross, P. (1992) 50, 59
Brudney, J.L., and England, R.E.
        (1983) 172
BT-Drucksache
        12/6269 83
        12/6717 61
        12/6718 61
        12/8060 62
        12/8101 62
Buchanan, J.M., and Tullock, G. (1962)
        181
Budäus, D. (1994) 12
budgetary reform 30
Bulling, M. (1989) 171
Bulling Commission 33
Bulmer, S. (1986) 8
Bulmer, S., and Paterson, W. (1987) 8
Bundesbahn/Reichsbahn *see* DB/DR
Bundesminister für Verkehr (1992) 74,
        85
Bundespost *see* DBP
Bundesratsdrucksache 131/93 82
Bundestagsdrucksache 12/5015 82, 83
Bundesvereinigung der kommunalen
        Spitzenverbände (1993) 82
Bundesvereinigung der kommunalen
        Spitzenverbände (1994) 153,
        156, 159n
bureaucracy state in decline 20–2
Burmeister, J. (1993) 21

Castles, F.G. (1990) 175, 185

CDU/CSU–FDP (Christian Demo-
        cratic–Liberal) coalition 48,
        57
civil service
        East Germany 37
        and railways 75
        reform 32–4
        and telecommunications 63–4
        training 33, 168
Clasen, R., *et al.* (1995) 13
communalization of tasks
        (*Kommunalisierung*) 151
consensus 182
contracting and exchange, government
        as dealer in goods and
        services 173–4
contracting out 39
coproduction 171–2, 180
corporations, with Federal/Länder
        interest 39
Council of Ministers (1993) 54
counties, defined 119
'county-free' cities (*kreisfreie Städte*)
        119, 120, 151, 152
CSU *see* CDU/CSU–FDP
CWI (1993a) 53
CWI (1993b) 58
Czada, R. (1988) 48
Czada, R. (1994) 10, 19
Czada, R. (in present volume) 13, 19,
        40, 93, 184n
Czada, R., and Schmidt, M.G. (eds)
        (1993) 113

data protection 34
DB AG (Deutsche Bahn
        Aktiengesellschaft 75, 85–6,
        87
        debt relief 84
DB/DR (Deutsche Bundesbahn/
        Reichsbahn) 72, 77
        'AG' effects 86
        deregulation pressures 72–3
        dual character 71
        government commission 73–4